PHENOMENOLOGY AND EMBODIMENT

Northwestern University
Studies in Phenomenology
and
Existential Philosophy

Founding Editor †James M. Edie

General Editor Anthony J. Steinbock

Associate Editor John McCumber

PHENOMENOLOGY AND EMBODIMENT

Husserl and the Constitution of Subjectivity

Joona Taipale

Northwestern University Press
Evanston, Illinois

Northwestern University Press
www.nupress.northwestern.edu

Copyright © 2014 by Northwestern University Press. Published 2014. All rights reserved.

Printed in the United States of America

10 9 8 7 6 5 4 3 2 1

Library of Congress Cataloging-in-Publication Data

Taipale, Joona, 1978– author.
   Phenomenology and embodiment : Husserl and the constitution of subjectivity / Joona Taipale.
      pages cm. — (Northwestern University studies in phenomenology and existential philosophy)
      Revised version of the author's thesis (doctoral)—University of Helsinki, 2009.
      ISBN 978-0-8101-2949-8 (cloth : alk. paper) — ISBN 978-0-8101-2950-4 (pbk. : alk. paper)
      1. Phenomenology. 2. Subjectivity. 3. Husserl, Edmund, 1859–1938. I. Title. II. Series: Northwestern University studies in phenomenology & existential philosophy.
   B829.5.T265 2014
   142'.7—dc23

                                                2013032439

♾ The paper used in this publication meets the minimum requirements of the American National Standard for Information Sciences—Permanence of Paper for Printed Library Materials, ANSI Z39.48-1992.

Contents

	Acknowledgments	ix
	Introduction	3
	Part 1. Selfhood and the Lived-Body	
1	Self-Awareness and Sensibility	21
2	The Environment and the Lived-Body	33
3	The Bodily Self	56
	Part 2. Intersubjectivity	
4	A Priori Intersubjectivity	69
5	Reciprocity and Sociality	87
6	Historicity and Generativity	99
	Part 3. Normality and Objective Reality	
7	Primordial and Intersubjective Normality	121
8	Transcendental Consequences	147
9	Paradox of Subjectivity Revisited	156
	Concluding Remarks	169
	Notes	175
	Bibliography	221
	Index	239

Acknowledgments

This work was written mainly in 2006–9 in Helsinki and Copenhagen, and an earlier version of it was accepted as a doctoral dissertation at the University of Helsinki in 2009. In many ways, the process of writing was positively influenced by the dialogue with several colleagues and friends, and I am thankful for all the collegiality, critique, and encouragement that I came to experience.

I want to express my gratitude first and foremost to Sara Heinämaa, who generously commented on and discussed the book in various phases. I am very much indebted also to Rudolf Bernet, David Carr, Steven Crowell, Anthony Steinbock, and Dan Zahavi for their thoughtful comments on earlier versions of the book. I am further grateful to Anthony Steinbock for initiating the publication process, and I thank the anonymous reviewers for their insightful comments, as well as Jane Bunker, Liz Hamilton, and Nathan MacBrien for carrying the project forward at Northwestern University Press. I am much obliged to Dieter Lohmar for the access to Husserl's unpublished manuscripts at the Husserl-Archives in Cologne. Yet another thanks is directed to the executive committee of the Nordic Society for Phenomenology, the activities of which I became strongly involved with while writing the book. I also want to thank the Academy of Finland, the Emil Aaltonen Foundation, the University of Helsinki, and the Center for Subjectivity Research at the University of Copenhagen for providing the material conditions for writing this book.

I am grateful to the director of the Husserl-Archives in Leuven, Ullrich Melle, for permission to quote from Husserl's unpublished manuscripts, and I also thank Springer Science+Business Media for permission to reuse some material that previously appeared in my article "Twofold Normality: Husserl and the Normative Relevance of Primordial Constitution," *Husserl Studies* 28, no. 1 [2012]: 49–60.

A very special thanks goes to my closest colleagues in Helsinki, Jussi Backman, Timo Miettinen, Simo Pulkkinen, and Mirja Hartimo, without whom I hardly would have ever written this book, and to the whole staff of my current academic base camp, the Center for Subjectivity Research.

ACKNOWLEDGMENTS

Last but not least, I want to thank my wife, Eveliina, and my daughters Pihla and Veera: your loving presence repeatedly restores my perspective on life, and I thus dedicate this book to you.

Copenhagen, June 2013

PHENOMENOLOGY AND EMBODIMENT

Introduction

In the dawn of the modern era, philosophy was reinterpreted as the study of consciousness, and along with this move the body was cast into the side of the object, and hence pushed into the margins of philosophy. Descartes famously argued that the body is something completely different from mind, a particular thing standing over against the latter, and something that the mind could also well do without.[1] Whereas the Cartesian tradition followed suit, the empiricist tradition proceeded in the opposite direction, and interpreted the subject of consciousness as a mundane being. As a consequence, rationalism ultimately developed into an absolute idealism and spiritualism, reducing the body to consciousness of the body, whereas empiricism eventually culminated in a type of naturalism that, on the contrary, reduced consciousness to the body as a material, worldly thing. However, it is rather symptomatic that, regardless of their remarkably different developmental directions, as to the notion of the body rationalism and empiricism did not end up offering an alternative to one another: despite the disagreement concerning the metaphysical and epistemological status of consciousness and reason, both lines of thought equally conceived the body as a thing of the objective world.[2]

Kantian philosophy, too, was seduced by this objectifying way of thinking. By investigating the general "conditions of possibility" of world-experience, Kant thematized the ultimate a priori structures of consciousness and reoriented philosophy according to "transcendental" cognition. Yet, even though some of Kant's early writings indicated wider possibilities,[3] he never ended up constructing a general and concise argument about the constitutive, transcendental significance of embodiment or bodilyness. Instead, in his *Critiques* he explicitly treated the body in terms of an external thing, and admitted, in a strikingly Cartesian manner, that "I distinguish my own existence, that of a thinking being, from other things outside me (to which also my body belongs)."[4] The power of objectifying thought can hardly be exaggerated. Modern philosophy and science are strongly labeled by the peculiarity that the body is generally introduced as an empirical thing.

The tendency to reify and objectify the body is rather curious, considering that it is only in exceptional cases that our body is actually *experienced* as a mere empirical thing or an object of consciousness. In our normal everyday life we of course may once in a while become more or less explicitly aware of our own physical appearance. For example, when we are speaking in front of a large audience or addressing persons that we admire, our visual or auditory outlook may become thematic to ourselves. Similarly, when we are in pain, when we feel the "call of nature," or when we see ourselves in the mirror, our conscious attention may turn toward a certain part of our body. In addition to these common experiences, there are pathological cases of schizophrenia and depression, for instance, in which a patient may experience her[5] own body as a mere thing devoid of vitality and feeling. Yet, it is rather indisputable that this is not the way we usually experience ourselves. If, while walking, for instance, we become aware of our body as an objective thing, our experience of walking changes remarkably; our movements at once lose their naturalness, so that we become incapable of walking properly. From the fact that the aforementioned types of bodily experience are possible, one should not infer that all bodily experiences are generally or fundamentally characterized by self-objectification.

In the light of experience, therefore, the tendency to discuss the body mainly in terms of an object for consciousness is indeed curious. To be sure, our body undoubtedly has empirical and objective dimensions to it, and theories that study the body in this manner are undeniably important and crucial in many regards. However, all theories that conceive the body merely, or fundamentally, as an empirical thing or an object of consciousness fail to account for how we normally, and most of the time, experience our own body, and all such theories are hence bound to remain *philosophically* insufficient and unsatisfactory. As far as experience is consulted, our body is not normally a mere object, which literally means something standing over against us. We never experience ourselves as disembodied minds who are in contact with things and other people only in a mediated manner, through a body. Accordingly, besides a theory of *consciousness directed at the body* (a theory already well covered in the tradition) what is needed in order to satisfy experience is a theory of *bodily consciousness*. In other words, what is required is a philosophical explication of how the body experientially presents itself before it is objectified in reflection.

The Phenomenological Approach

One of the most influential approaches that has risen to this important challenge is Husserlian phenomenology. With his successors Husserl relocates the body in the midst of the transcendental field, and he offers a conceptually rich and methodologically elaborated framework, as well as vast and detailed analyses, that oblige us to reconsider the philosophical significance of embodiment.

The starting point of Husserl's philosophy is what he calls the phenomenological reduction (*phänomenologischen Reduktion*).[6] The reduction is a move in which the philosopher takes a critical distance to her assumptions concerning the validity and manner of the being of the world in order to describe and analyze the essence of consciousness in which these assumptions are constituted. In the natural attitude (*natürliche Einstellung*), consciousness is directed at worldly things, events, and their various interrelations, and the existence of these is taken for granted.[7] Thereby the *manner* in which these have the sense of something existing remains unthematic.[8] In Husserl's conception, philosophy is supposed to strive for ultimate self-responsibility—responsibility for all its fundamental premises and assumptions—and thus it cannot remain within the natural attitude where something is taken for granted. According to Husserl, the ultimate task of philosophy is to clarify the manner in which the world *comes to* exist for us, how it *comes to* be taken for granted—and in such clarification one cannot assume the givenness of the world. Phenomenologists stress that if the existence-sense of the world is presupposed, it cannot be studied: if one assumes in the manner of naive realism or "common sense" that we are conscious of the world *because* it exists, the ultimate consciousness in which the world gains its sense for us as something existing cannot be disclosed. In this case, consciousness would be considered as something secondary, something "merely subjective," and hence the natural attitude is unable to study consciousness as the dimension of sense-constitution.[9] The phenomenological reduction is needed precisely because, in the natural attitude, absolute consciousness cannot be made thematic: any attempt to examine absolute consciousness within the natural attitude would be as successful as an attempt to lift oneself from one's shoelaces.[10]

The realm of consciousness can be disclosed only by radically distancing oneself from the natural attitude. This critical distance is established in the phenomenological reduction, where the existence-sense of the world and things, which was taken for granted in the natural attitude, is now interpreted as an "establishment" of consciousness, and in this sense the world is "bracketed" or "put into parentheses." The *phenomenological epoché*—the initiating moment of the phenomenological reduction—is a movement that "brackets" the positing of the world as such.[11] The positive aspect of this "bracketing" is that world-consciousness, the sense-bestowing activity in which the world gains its existence-sense in the first place, can now be subjected to philosophical analysis.

However, it is important to emphasize that everything that was experienced before the reduction is still experienced. Phenomenology does not get rid of the world, but only aims at disclosing its pre-philosophical sense, "the sense that this world had for all of us before any philosophizing," and this is why "also the philosopher within the epoché must 'naturally live through' the natural life"—otherwise there would be nothing to describe.[12] As Husserl repeatedly stresses, in the reduction nothing is actually *lost*.[13] What has changed, instead, is that the *constitution* of things and the world now comes to light, and this constitution can therefore be analyzed in a rigorous philosophical manner. It would be a gross misunderstanding to maintain that, in phenomenology, the world is considered "merely" as to its *sense*, whereas ontology allegedly investigates the *being* of the world, and existentialism our factual being-in-the-world. By investigating the *constitution* of the world, phenomenology is investigating all of these aspects.[14] That is to say, the *sense* of the world is not an abstract layer of the concrete world, but the experienced world in its full concreteness.

It is worth highlighting that Husserl is criticizing neither the natural attitude as such, nor the special sciences that all operate within it.[15] The natural attitude—whereby the constitutional origin of things and world remains unthematic—is the normal attitude of life: while riding a bicycle, while walking, talking with someone, or building a complex mathematical proof, we normally have a constant reliance and confidence about the being and validity of the world and the things that we experience. In this sense, the natural attitude is the fate of the phenomenologist as well—after all, "I as a . . . transcendental philosopher have not ceased to be a human being."[16] Instead, as Husserl emphasizes, the "countersense only arises when one philosophizes": it is only when philosophy is grounded in the natural attitude that one actually treats the world as absolute reality, thereby failing to notice that "the world itself has its whole being as a certain 'sense' which presupposes absolute consciousness as the field where sense is bestowed."[17] The sense of a "world beyond all possible consciousness" proves self-contradictory or countersensical. Reality gains its sense *as reality* from the experiencing consciousness, and therefore an idea of an "*absolute reality is just as valid as [an idea of] a round square*."[18] Another way of putting this is to say that a world beyond all possible consciousness could not actually *mean* anything to anyone—it could not *make sense*. As Husserl also puts it, "if transcendental subjectivity is the universe of possible sense, then an outside is precisely—nonsense."[19] To interpret consciousness as something secondary or "merely subjective" is for Husserl a reductio ad absurdum. The world is a horizon that we experience all the time, and no such theory that allows for the possibility of denying our immediate contact with the world can be satisfactory. In the words of Maurice Merleau-Ponty: "We must not, therefore, wonder whether we really perceive a world, we must instead say: the world is what we perceive."[20]

Accordingly, what is inhibited in the phenomenological inspection is not the world as it appears, but the philosophical and everyday *absolutizing* of the world. By abstaining from positing the world as an absolute dimension and by instead considering the world as something constituted, the phenomenological reduction takes "nothing away from the fully valid being of the world as the all of realities, just as nothing is taken away from the fully valid geometrical being of the square by denying that it is round."[21] Nevertheless, the reduction has important philosophical consequences. In the reduction, the naive assumption of the natural attitude that things can appear *because* they somehow already exist is turned upside down: everything that has the sense of something "existing" is now grasped as receiving its experiential characterization (its "sense") in and through our conscious experiencing. In this sense, *appearing* is discovered as being constitutively more fundamental than objective existence which is posited in the process of appearing. In this sense, consciousness has a *constitutive* primacy over the world. Yet, we are not led to a private realm or an "inner world," and the reduction is not a solipsistic or a subjectivistic move.[22] Another, related, misunderstanding is that in Husserlian phenomenology the world is only a projection of consciousness, or something that is included in the latter. Phenomenology is a method of transcendental sense-clarification, not a particular ontological view or "metaphysical construction." Phenomenology is "ontologically neutral," and, in this sense, it is *beyond* realism and idealism.[23]

Constitution and Facticity

As a reversal from the "ready-made world" (*die fertige Welt*) of the natural attitude to the constitution of the world, to "the advent of being to consciousness" (*l'apparation de l'être à la conscience*), the phenomenological reduction unravels the relation between the world and the experiencing subjectivity as an *intentional correlation*.[24] Husserl's entire life work, as he himself proclaims, was an attempt to clarify this correlation; the correlation as such is the field of transcendental phenomenology.[25]

The phenomenological notion of "constitution" can be outlined in terms of this correlation. In listening to a melody, for instance, the flow of sound-impressions is *lived through* immediately, and yet we do not experience a disorganized flow or a collection of particular sounds.[26]

Instead, the flow of our auditory experiencing is "intentionally directed" to a temporally arranged complex, to a unitary melody. In this sense, the melody is intentionally *constituted* in the flow of appearing. The present sound-impression internally connects to the expected continuation of the flow and also "retains" the impression of the preceding ones, and this synthesis of consciousness designates a *constituting event* where the melody is constituted as the correlate of the flow of our experiencing. Although the temporal or event character of constitution is perhaps best manifest in auditory experiences, appearances of other sense spheres are likewise "adumbrated" in the temporal flow of consciousness: the immediately lived visual appearances, for instance, are synthesized and thus a unitary visual intention occurs. And in this manner, more generally, we have intentional experiences *of* unitary things—whether acoustic, visual, tactile, or intersensory. The thing—as well as the world as "the horizon of all horizons" (*l'horizon de tous les horizons*)[27]—*transcends* our *consciousness* of it.

To say that the constituting consciousness is "intentionally directed" to what is constituted in it is another way of saying that *subjectivity* is intentionally "related" to the world. However, as David Carr aptly emphasizes, "intentionality is not a 'relation' in the strict sense of the term."[28] Namely, the constituted and the constituting are necessary parts of the whole of experience, and the "relation" between them is not an occasional and contingent one. Subjectivity is not related to the world accidentally or "once in a while," but subjectivity and the world belong together a priori:[29] one is not graspable without the other.

Following Kant, Husserl names this new kind of experience a *transcendental* one.[30] However, the range of the phenomenological notion of "transcendental" deviates remarkably from the Kantian notion. It is important to stress the disparity between Husserl's transcendental phenomenology and Kantian transcendental philosophy, since, as Merleau-Ponty emphasizes, "Husserl's transcendental is not Kant's transcendental."[31] According to Husserl, Kant was seeking "to go back to the subjective conditions of possibility of an objectively experienciable and knowable world" but got involved in "mythical talk, whose literal meaning points to something subjective, but a mode of the subjective that we are in principle unable to make intuitive to ourselves."[32] Due to his lack of a phenomenological method, Kant took factical subjectivity as a theme for psychology, whereby his transcendental philosophy, investigating the a priori structures of consciousness, remained aloof from what is given in intuition.[33] That is to say, Kant's notion of "inner perception" remained bound to the psychology of his day, whereby he conceived the transcendental dimension as inaccessible in terms of intuition.[34] In this regard, Husserl restores *intuitivity* to transcendental philosophy. With the phenomenological method of categorical and eidetic intuition, the pure categories of experience that Kant had to "deduce" are now discovered *in* the experiencing subjectivity, and as such they can be viewed intuitively.

Therefore, whereas Kant, lacking a proper method, conceived the factical life of subjectivity as a matter of *a posteriori knowledge*, as something *empirical,* Husserlian phenomenology discovers *transcendental subjectivity* "in its individual facticity," as a "Heracleitan flux" or temporal becoming.[35] What in phenomenology counts as "transcendental" is defined purely in terms of what is discovered in the reduction, that is to say, in the procedure of reducing the objective world to its manner of givenness.[36] What is transcendental is, accordingly, the constituting flow of lived experiences, the dimension of sense formation (*Sinnbildung*):[37] subjectivity in its factical givenness to itself.

The notion "transcendental" retains its Kantian core, however, as it refers to the realm of "conditions of possibility."[38] It is just that the factical constituting subjectivity in its essential structures is interpreted as the "condition of possibility" for the empirical world. This is also the manner in which Husserl justifies his decision to employ the term "transcendental":

> Only idealism ... attempts to lay hold of subjectivity as subjectivity. ... But idealism was always too quick with its theories and for the most part it could not free itself from hidden objectivistic presuppositions; or else, as speculative idealism, it leaped over the task of interrogating, concretely and analytically, actual subjectivity, i.e. subjectivity as having the actual phenomenal world in intuitive validity—which, properly understood, is nothing other than carrying out the phenomenological reduction and putting transcendental phenomenology into action. This explains, by the way, why I call the phenomenology I have developed "transcendental" and why I speak in it of "transcendental subjectivity." For when Kant gives the old word a new meaning through his *critique of reason*, one can easily convince oneself that the quite different idealism of Berkeley and Hume, indeed any idealism, looked at more closely, has the same thematic field and poses questions within this field which are only differently formulated.[39]

In other words, Husserl conceives transcendental phenomenology as the "necessary style of a philosophy"[40]—thus provocatively claiming that philosophy is not properly aware of itself until it assumes the form of a rigorous study of the constituting subjectivity. Whereas Descartes, according to Husserl, discovered subjectivity, but let it slip away, Kant realized the transcendentality of subjectivity, but lacking a proper method was not able to bring subjectivity into its givenness.[41] In this sense, *Husserl revises the philosophy of consciousness by combining, with the phenomenological method, transcendentality and intuitivity.*

Moreover, the transcendental reduction is always also an *eidetic* one: phenomenology investigates the general or essential features of the full concrete facticity of transcendental subjectivity.[42] These features are not deduced by reason but rather found in the factical stream of lived-experiencing, and in this sense the eidetic method "bases the possible on the real" (*fonde le possible sur le réel*).[43] In Husserl's words, "Possibilities of imagination as variations of essence do not float freely in the air, but are constitutively related to me in my facticity, [to me] with my living present that I factically live through."[44] Therefore, "transcendental philosophy is necessarily related to me, and from me, to . . . humanity."[45]

The Husserlian union of transcendentality and intuitivity opens new possibilities for philosophy. First and foremost, the phenomenological method enables one to speak about transcendental individuation and thus also of transcendental intersubjectivity—of problems that lie beyond the scope of Kantian philosophy. Merleau-Ponty argues:

> This is why the problem of knowledge of other people is never posed in Kantian philosophy: the transcendental ego which it discusses is just as much other people's as mine, analysis is from the start located outside me, and has nothing to do but to determine the general conditions of possibility which make possible a world for an ego—myself or others equally—and so it never comes up against the question: *who is thinking?*[46]

In Husserlian phenomenology, instead, the transcendental ego is not a formal, general, and common subjectivity, but *factical* and *unique*:[47] "this pure I—which plainly Kant had in mind, as he spoke of the I of transcendental apperception—is not a dead pole of identity."[48] Transcendental subjectivity has individual habitualities and peculiarities, and Husserl even speaks of "transcendental person" and "transcendental 'personality'" (*transzendentaler Person, transzendentalen 'Personalität'*).[49] Transcendental subjectivity is temporal, intersubjective, and—as I will argue in detail—embodied.

In this connection, one should distinguish between *static, genetic,* and *generative* analyses of constitution. A "static phenomenology" studies the intentional correlation by brushing aside the internal temporality (or "event" character) of constitution, and the scope of static phenomenology is an experience isolated from its temporal background. Husserl initially began with such analyses, and in his earliest works he interpreted the genesis of meaning, like Kant, as a mere psychological issue.[50] On the other hand, even when combining the analyses of internal time-consciousness with the analyses of intentionality, thus entering from static to "genetic phenomenology," Husserl did not abandon static analyses, but thought that static analyses facilitate the entrance to phenomenology.[51] In this pedagogical sense, static analyses maintain their primacy. A genetic phenomenology examines the temporal *becoming* of meaning in the constituting subjectivity, and the scope of genetic phenomenology is accordingly the experiential life of an individual ego.[52] "Generative phenomenology" again broadens the scope: it investigates the intersubjective-historical aspects of temporal sense-constitution that are tacitly operative in our individual experiences.[53]

Accordingly, the phenomenologist could analyze, for instance, an object-perception in a *static* manner by elaborating the essential features of the thing–horizon structure of perception. On the other hand, the phenomenologist could also examine, in a *genetic* manner, how this perception is motivated by kinesthetic self-awareness, how it internally refers to preceding perceptions which are sedimented in consciousness, how one can "learn" to perceive unitary things in the first place. Thirdly, the phenomenologist could investigate the manner in which the concrete intersubjective-historical meaning of the thing is appropriated from others, how cultural meanings are carried over generations, and how they are internally connected in intersubjective temporalization. Accordingly, whereas static analysis presupposes an abstraction from *intra*subjective and *inter*subjective temporality, genetic analysis approaches the correlation from the point of view of individual subjectivity (thus explaining how *inter*subjective temporality is primordially revealed), and generative phenomenology analyzes constitution from the point of view of an intersubjective subjectivity (thus explicating how subjective temporality is revealed in intersubjective experiencing). In a concise phenomenological analysis, these lines of research often interpenetrate and complement each other.[54]

Throughout this work, I will the employ the terms "transcendental" and "constitution" in the phenomenological sense briefly outlined above. That is to say, to inquire into how something is constituted is to describe the essential features of the lived experiencing in and through which this something comes into being for consciousness.

Tracing the Constitutive Significance of Embodiment

What about the body? In the light of this preliminary clarification of the transcendental, *constituting* subjectivity, it might first seem that the body is still first and foremost something *constituted* and empirical, a particular object for consciousness. It might first seem, namely, that Husserlian phenomenology is merely subscribing to the received, traditional view according to which the body is not a subject matter for philosophy but rather for special sciences—such as physiology, biology, and neurology. A closer look proves that this is actually not the case.

To be sure, even as an external thing our own body distinguishes itself from all other things and bodies by certain unique features. Our own body is, first of all, a thing that is always *near*, and our external perceptions of it are bound to remain limited and somewhat fixed: unlike in the case of any other object, from our own body we cannot spatially distance ourselves—we cannot move around it, in order to take another angle to it. Moreover, whereas all other things can be moved only by moving one's own body, and thus only in a mediated manner, our own body we can move immediately. To express it differently, we have to move our own body if we want to move other things, whereas our own bodily movements are not effected by first moving something else. Moreover, our own body is also peculiar insofar as it is a thing that we can immediately sense. Not only can we externally perceive our body and externally witness its contact with the environment and things, but we can also immediately feel our bodily movements and sense the contact, and we can also empirically pinpoint the locus of a sensation on the surface of our body. Nevertheless, even if we granted that our own body has such peculiarities, as a peculiar thing our body still pertains to the *constituted* realm, and not to the *constituting*, transcendental realm: the body is still interpreted as something over and against consciousness, as a thing in the empirical environment.

If we take a closer look at the aforementioned features of our own body, however, taking them as "leading clues" for an analysis of their constitution, we will get an idea of the body in its constituting or transcendental significance.

First, our body is always in our immediate proximity, whereas other things are oriented around us: they are "right," "left," "near," "far," and so on. This points to the fact that our spatial experience of the environment is oriented according to a central "here." However, as a spatial thing, the body is located *in* the oriented space, and it would be circular to argue that a particular empirical thing *in* the oriented environment would serve as the orientational center of the environment—this would *presuppose* spatial orientation rather than serving as a *description* of its constitution. Instead, the constitution of an oriented environment (as well as our perceived body in it) points back to a perceiving and space-orienting consciousness, and hence to a kind of consciousness that must be spatial in some sense, but not in the same sense as the things that it perceives.

INTRODUCTION

Second, our body is constituted as a thing that we can move immediately. Yet, we would contradict ourselves if we maintained that our body is first and foremost, or fundamentally, experienced as an immediately movable thing *in* the horizon of possible movement, since the constitution of the horizon of possible movement already presupposes another kind of bodily self-awareness: the horizon of possible movement can appear as such only to an embodied consciousness. That is to say, the constitution of the environment as the horizon of possible movement, as well as the constitution of one's own body as an immediately movable thing *in* it, points back to a constituting consciousness that must somehow already be embodied, but not in the same sense as movable spatial objects.

Third, our body is constituted as a thing in and on which sensations are localized. Yet, it would obviously be misguiding to say that sensing amounts to nothing more than an intentional experience of a sensation located on a particular thing. Take pain, for instance. We may be able to more or less accurately pinpoint the spot "where" it hurts, and yet we do not experience pain as being located five centimeters above the ground, inside our shoe, and so on. This is another way of saying that sensations, like pain, are not originally discovered as events *in* the empirical environment. To be sure, sensations can be objectified as a state of the empirical body, and their locus can be pinpointed to others, but this presupposes that they are already experienced in another manner—before becoming *conscious of* pain (an intentional object), we must already *be in* pain. More generally, sensing does not amount to a kind of disembodied awareness of sensations on, or in, the empirical body; instead, it refers to a mode of immediate bodily self-awareness.

In this manner, the peculiar characteristics of our own body as an object in the environment refer back to an embodied subjectivity to which these characteristics are experientially given. That is to say, our own body can be constituted as a constantly proximal, sensing, and immediately movable thing only insofar as our constituting consciousness is itself somehow embodied. In this way, we are led to realize that our own body *cannot* be experienced as a mere physical thing: insofar as we experience our body in such an objectifying manner, we must already be bodily self-aware in another, more fundamental sense. To put it in Husserlian terms, insofar as we *have* a worldly body (*Körper*), we must already *be* a lived-body (*Leib*).[55]

As this brief elaboration suffices to show, by investigating consciousness precisely in its subjectivity—that is to say, in respect to the manner in which it reveals itself from within—phenomenology opens up the possibility to reconsider *embodiment in its constitutive significance*.

INTRODUCTION

The main task of this book is to systematically outline and explicate this significance, and to develop some of its most crucial and interesting consequences.

I will pursue this task by analyzing the role of embodiment in the three basic constitutive relations of consciousness, all captured in the phenomenological concept of "subjectivity": (1) consciousness in relation to itself (self-constitution), (2) consciousness in relation to other subjectivities (intersubjectivity), and (3) consciousness in relation to objective reality (world-constitution). I will elaborate and analyze these dimensions of subjectivity one by one, investigate the role of embodiment separately in each of them, and thus deliver a systematic phenomenological explication of the constitutive significance of embodiment in the basic dimensions of subjectivity. It should be noted already at this point that the chosen order of exposure is not meant to imply any claims concerning ontological or epistemic primacy—accordingly, although intersubjectivity, for instance, is not properly introduced until the second part of the book, this by no means suggests that others have no significant role in bodily self-constitution which is discussed in the first part. My decision to scrutinize the basic dimensions of subjectivity one by one serves the purposes of presentation, and the various and complex ways in which they intersect and overlap will be explained in the progression of the book.

The phenomenological tradition will provide my investigation with both a method and a context. I will throughout employ Husserl's phenomenological method briefly outlined above, and my investigations will be supported and illustrated mainly by the rich descriptions and analyses provided by phenomenologists—most importantly, Husserl, Merleau-Ponty, Sartre, and Henry. However, I will not try to build an argument concerning the development or historical interconnections of their ideas, and likewise I will keep the discussions with the commentators to the endnotes. This is another way of saying that my treatise is motivated, outlined, and oriented thematically and systematically, and textual exegesis will serve as a means for a phenomenological investigation of the embodied subjectivity. Accordingly, instead of splitting the work of Husserl or Merleau-Ponty into phases, and clarifying what they do (or do not) say about embodiment in certain works or phases of their careers, I will assume the phenomenological attitude and investigate subjectivity in relation to itself, to others, and to objective reality. I will illustrate why these essential structures of experience can be properly understood only by recognizing their bodily foundations, and in this manner I will disclose the fundamental constitutive significance of embodiment in all conscious life.

INTRODUCTION

In line with the division into three basic constitutive relations, my treatise will be divided into three parts. In part 1, I will explicate the bodily foundations of self-awareness. This involves studies of kinesthesia, sensing, localization, body schema, perception, spatiality, and motility. By investigating these elements of self-awareness, I will argue that selfhood must be fundamentally embodied. After elaborating different modes of selfhood and investigating the purely subjective features of embodiment, I will investigate the intersubjective significance of embodiment. In part 2, I will describe and analyze our experience of others, both its structure and its genesis. By studying perspectuality, horizonality, anonymity, empathy, sociality, personality, historicity, generativity, natality, and mortality, I will show how intersubjectivity genetically emerges from bodily experience, and argue that all further types of intersubjectivity presuppose and refer back to this fundamental level. I will distinguish between "a priori intersubjectivity," "social intersubjectivity," and "generative intersubjectivity," and argue that there is a constitutive hierarchy between them which is maintained in all experiences and which unfolds as an irreducible tension between genetic and generative phenomenology. This topic is further analyzed and developed in part 3, which focuses on the role of embodiment in the constitution of objective reality. Here I will investigate the internal relation between subjectivity and intersubjectivity, and explicate the complex constitutive significance of normality. I will illustrate the normative structures of experience by examining our experience of non-human animals, and eventually reinterpret the "paradox of subjectivity" in terms of a tension between primordial and intersubjective self-constitution. This argument will echo my previous elaboration of the different types of intersubjectivity. My main aim in this part is to show that the constitution of the objective world has two irreducible constitutive sources: world-constitution is bound to the embodied abilities of the individual members of the intersubjective community, on the one hand, and to a generatively inherited normality, on the other. The internal relationship between these two sources—that is, between primordiality and intersubjectivity—can be introduced in terms of what I call a "normative tension." This analysis will enable me to argue, finally, that the "paradox of subjectivity" is eventually rooted in the complex structures of embodiment. By doing so, my intention is not to suggest a solution to the paradox, but rather to clarify its constitutional origins.

The primary literature of my investigation consists in Husserl's published works and research manuscripts, as well as the writings of Merleau-Ponty, Sartre, and Henry. That is to say, my focus is not on Husserl exclusively, and this is also the reason why I choose to speak of "Husserlian phenomenology" rather than of "Husserl's phenomenology."

The fact that, of the aforementioned phenomenologists, Husserl is chosen as the main source, is because his work in this thematic area is the most resourceful, both in depth and in coverage.

What Husserl wrote on embodiment is scattered around his work, and hence a brief interpretative note is required. Husserl's view was modified and revised many times during his lifetime, and there is no doubt that his thought never reached perfect clarity concerning the issue. Whereas Husserl's published texts only hint at or touch upon the theme of embodiment, and might even give the impression that Husserl merely treats the body as an intentional object, the posthumously published works, lectures, and other manuscripts (in all making up approximately three-quarters of Husserl's total oeuvre)[56] reveal embodiment as a central problem that underlies and founds active intentionality and explicit consciousness that have a focal status in Husserl's publications. Due to the vast labor of many scholars, it is generally recognized today that Husserl's thought should not be estimated only in the light of his publications; the research manuscripts not only offer the published works a broader context, but they also establish many remarkable expansions of the themes examined in the published works.[57] Even though not explicated in them, embodiment lies at the bottom of the analyses of the published works, and is presupposed in them, so that, eventually, it turns out that in phenomenology, the lived-body plays a "comprehensive role" (*umfassende Rolle*).[58]

In my interpretation of Husserl, I will consult his work on the whole, and I will likewise favor commentators who are able to situate the particular claims of the published works in their appropriate context. Unfortunately, in many commentaries of Merleau-Ponty the strong Husserlian background of Merleau-Ponty's work is downplayed, and so, as interesting as these commentaries may be in regard to Merleau-Ponty's thought per se, they are neither reliable documentations of Husserl's view, given that they completely neglect Husserl's ideas of the passive foundations of active intentionality, nor reliable sources in evaluating the intellectual relationship between Husserl and Merleau-Ponty.[59] Although one should be careful not to naively identify the two thinkers with one another, one should bear in mind that Husserl's phenomenology, especially his analyses of the lived-body, served as the explicit starting point of Merleau-Ponty's *Phenomenology of Perception*.[60]

In the past decades, the Husserlian account of embodiment has attracted a relatively large amount of interest in the commentary literature. Yet, even when Husserl is interpreted in a favorable light, the comprehensive constitutive significance of embodiment has not been emphasized. Previous studies that, one way or the other, touch upon the matter can be roughly divided into four categories. (1) In general introductions to Husserlian phenomenology, embodiment is discussed as one particular theme among others; introductory works either only briefly touch upon the topic or, at most, dedicate a chapter or subchapter to it, and thus end up presenting embodiment as a special problem without underlining its fundamental transcendental role.[61] (2) On the other hand, there is a wide range of studies that directly or indirectly apply the Husserlian descriptions and insights to interdisciplinary and philosophical research. Such studies range from contemporary philosophy of mind and cognitive science to sociology, psychopathology, and gender research.[62] (3) Besides these, there are several thematic phenomenological studies, drawing on the work of Husserl, Merleau-Ponty, or both, that touch upon particular constitutive aspects of embodiment—these include, for instance, explications of the constitution of space, analyses of the relationship between the lived-body and the physical body, and examinations of bodily self-affectivity and bodily selfhood.[63] (4) In addition, there are phenomenological contributions that *exegetically* analyze Husserl's notion of the lived-body: how this notion develops in Husserl's production, how it is related to certain preceding conceptions of the body, how it relates to and differs from Merleau-Ponty's view—and so on.[64]

In contrast, my aim here lies neither in clarifying Husserl's notion of the lived-body per se, in comparing the Husserlian account of embodiment with certain other accounts, nor in focusing on certain consequences of the constitutive significance of embodiment. My aim is rather to execute a comprehensive and systematic phenomenological investigation into the role of embodiment in the constitution of self-awareness, intersubjectivity, and objective reality, and therewith contribute a detailed clarification of the fundamental constitutive role of embodiment in the basic relations of subjectivity. In short, my task is to disclose the significance of embodiment in the constitution of subjectivity.

Part 1

Selfhood and the Lived-Body

1

Self-Awareness and Sensibility

The first task here is to investigate the role of embodiment in the constitution of self-awareness. I will explicate the temporal and affective structure of self-awareness, examine how self-awareness is localized, discuss the role of bodily self-awareness in the constitution of the perceptual environment, and investigate the transcendental and empirical aspects of selfhood. I argue that self-awareness is fundamentally bodily self-awareness, and this argument will serve as a basic clarification upon which the two latter parts of my treatise will be built.

Self-Awareness and Awareness of Self

How is self-awareness constituted, and how is it related to intentionality? These questions can be approached by first investigating the relation between self-awareness and reflection.

The phenomenological reduction discloses experiences as intentional, as experiences *of* something. This "something"—that is, the intentional object—is foreign to, something else than, the act of experiencing. When we perceive something yellow, sharp, or hot, our act of perceiving is not something yellow, sharp, or hot; there is a difference between our experiencing and the objects of our experiencing. Moreover, intentional experiences are not mere formal relations between a mind and an object, but *conscious* experiences—"unconscious consciousness" is a contradiction in terms.[1] Namely, all experiences share the common feature that they *reveal* themselves to the subject that lives through them. Feeling sad, suffering pain, submerging into a novel, falling in love, calling a cab, discussing with friends, solving mathematical problems, and even dreaming—these are not processes to which the subject has an external relation, but something that the subject immediately *undergoes*. Experiences (*Erfahrungen*) are essentially something that one lives through, and this is what gives all experiences the feature of being *lived experiences* (*Erlebnisse*).[2]

Husserl claims that experiences are "conscious" in two senses. First, experiences are intentional: they intend something and are aware of this something as intended. On the other hand, experiences are also aware of themselves. Husserl writes: "Every experience is conscious of something, but there is also consciousness of every act,"[3] an "inner awareness" (*inneres Bewusstsein*) of experiencing, or "internal experience" (*innere Erfahrung*).[4] For instance, as we perceive something, we are "conscious" not merely in the sense that our streaming perception presents us with a unitary object; we are also "conscious" in the sense that the streaming perception immanently manifests itself to us as a flow of appearing.[5] That is, while perceiving the unitary object, we are at once aware of the stream of the subjective appearing. This self-awareness is not an additional relation that could be taken away without altering the intentional experience itself.[6] For example, when walking around a building, to be aware of the identical building is precisely to be aware of a unity *in the continuing flow of appearances*. Without this inner awareness, we could not experience the synthesis of the appearances, and thus we would not experience any unitary objects either. Thus, as Sartre puts it, "every positional consciousness of an object is at the same time a non-positional consciousness of itself."[7] Sartre also specifies that "this self-consciousness we ought to consider not as a new consciousness, but as *the only mode of existence which is possible for a consciousness of something*. Just as an extended object is compelled to exist according to three dimensions, so an intention, a pleasure, a grief can exist only as immediate self-consciousness."[8] In other words, intentionality is *essentially* accompanied by self-awareness.

One should avoid confounding this primal self-awareness with a type of *reflection*. Husserl stresses that we must distinguish between "the pre-phenomenal being of experiences, [i.e.,] their being before we have turned towards them in reflection, and their being as [reflected] phenomena."[9] Indeed, if we maintain that the self-awareness of object-awareness is always reflective, and thereby presents experiences as inner objects, we would fall into an infinite regress: as a type of object-awareness, reflection itself would also have to be aware of itself in a reflectively objectifying manner, and so on ad infinitum.[10] Therefore, all self-awareness cannot be *fundamentally* an objectifying kind of awareness.

Upon this matter, phenomenologists agree. As Husserl puts it, "being-lived is not being-objectified"; Sartre argues that "consciousness of self is not dual: if we wish to avoid an infinite regress, there must be an immediate, non-cognitive relation of the self to itself"; Levinas similarly suggests that "to live is a sort of transitive verb"; and Merleau-Ponty speaks of "a life present to itself, an openness upon oneself."[11] Experiences are lived *before* they are reflected upon, and to live one's life is not the same as to observe one's life. In this sense, all experiences, regardless of whether they are reflected or not, are self-aware.[12] As Sartre exemplifies, "pleasure cannot exist 'before' consciousness of pleasure":[13] "There is no more first a consciousness that receives *subsequently* the affect 'pleasure' like water which one stains, than there is first a pleasure (unconscious or psychological) which receives subsequently the quality of 'conscious.'... There is an indivisible, indissoluble being."[14]

We are not self-aware only when we reflect. And, again, when we do reflect, the act of reflection is itself lived and not reflected upon. Reflection modifies self-awareness that was already operative, and reflection is possible only because we are already self-aware in this manner. As Sartre puts it, "it is the non-reflective consciousness which renders the reflection possible: there is a pre-reflective cogito which is the condition of the Cartesian cogito."[15] Reflection never captures the lived experience *as beginning* but rather *as having already begun*, Husserl likewise argues:[16] it does not *create* its object (the experience) but discovers and objectifies something that we already lived through in a non-reflective and non-objectifying manner.

It is precisely in the sense of this constant pre-reflective, non-objectifying self-awareness that consciousness is endowed with a primordial sense of selfhood or "ipseity."[17] Experiences are *mine*, they have a fundamental "mineness," insofar as they are not only externally viewed but lived through by me. Yet, this does not mean that experiences are fundamentally lived as belonging to *a self* separate from these experiences. We must distinguish between self-awareness and awareness *of* oneself. Namely, the self is not the *object* of inner awareness, not an immanent object. Rather, selfhood *is* this immanence: the pre-reflective mineness of experiencing serves as the minimal form of selfhood.[18] This primordial ipseity is something that cannot be questioned. Even schizophrenic patients who suspect that someone else is thinking *their* thoughts or controlling *their* body question only the authorship and not ownership: the person in question remains the subject of the thought that feels alien.[19]

No reflection is accordingly needed for self-awareness. As Husserl puts it, the "life of consciousness... is at once... consciously a being-for-itself, constituted as subjective."[20] Because of the incessant self-manifestation, consciousness is essentially subjective: experiences are something that happen to a "me"; they are "mine," they are characterized by fundamental mineness. That is to say, precisely insofar as they are "conscious," experiences are originally labeled by first-person givenness. Accordingly, with Husserl, we can define *subjectivity* as self-aware consciousness, while *selfhood* refers to the dimension of self-awareness of consciousness.

Self-Awareness as Temporal Self-Affectivity

Self-awareness is not awareness within an isolated "now." For instance, when being stung by a mosquito, the instantaneous pain emerges against a background horizon with no pain—it *begins* at some point of time, and *fades* away—and it is only against this temporally unified self-awareness that the pain appears as something instantaneous. To give another example, when we see a bird flying by, the impression of the bird on the left is replaced by an impression of the bird on the right, but the preceding impression does not thereby vanish without a trace. The preceding impression is still consciously *retained* as the immediate background of the present one, and this, again, motivates an anticipation of the continuation of movement, a *protention*, so that, in the moment when the bird is in front of us, it does not appear like in a snapshot: instead we *see it moving*.

To be sure, as Husserl notes, it is not until reflection that appearances become "differentiated" and "singled out."[21] Originally, before reflection occurs, appearances are "fused" into the stream of consciousness, and their temporal interrelations remain quite implicit. In other words, the retentional, impressional, and protentional moments are unified into a "living present" (*lebendige Gegenwart*) of experiencing. Nevertheless, the bird does not appear on the left and on the right *at the same time*, but we are aware of a *succession*—we see the bird coming from the left and heading to the right. In other words, as we are internally aware of our experiencing, we are at once aware of a continuum. Already in a pre-reflective manner, we are aware of the inner *temporality* of our experiencing—phenomena are temporally organized.[22] This inner awareness of the temporal form of consciousness is what Husserl calls "inner time-consciousness" (*inneren Zeitbewusstsein*).[23]

Inner time-consciousness, moreover, is not a mere formal awareness. Husserl stresses that "consciousness is nothing without an impression" and that "the actually present now-point . . . is constantly filled in some way."[24] This is not a description of a mere contingent fact, but is based on an essential insight: we cannot be aware of a mere temporal frame "now," "before," or "after" without any "content": insofar as we are aware of temporality, we are aware of *something happening* now, a while ago, or soon.[25] Husserl emphasizes accordingly that, in the literal sense, the term "time-consciousness" is an abstract notion: "Time-constitution only establishes the universal forms of order—succession and coexistence—in regard to all immanent data. But form is nothing without content. Enduring immanent givenness is [something] enduring only as to the givenness of its content."[26] An awareness of temporal succession without awareness of *something* succeeding *something* is unthinkable: should the elementary "temporal content" (*Zeitfülle*)[27] be taken away, no internal awareness would remain whatsoever, and hence no time-consciousness either.[28] Husserl writes: "the moment of the original temporal position is . . . nothing by itself; the [temporal] individuation is nothing in addition to what has individuation"; the temporal continuum is not a continuum as to its form, but "a concrete continuum of content" (*ein konkretes, inhaltliches Kontinuum*).[29] In other words, time-consciousness cannot be actualized without a feeling of going through, or, if you will, a feeling of existing.

How, then, should we characterize inner time-consciousness without neglecting this elementary material? In what sense are we aware of the procession of our experiencing? If the form (impression–retention–protention) is nothing without content, then what constitutes the *necessary material* of temporal self-awareness of experiences?

In this regard, Husserl often uses the concepts of "primal impression" and "primal *sensation*" interchangeably, and explains that "sensation" and "impression" signify the same thing.[30] He argues, accordingly, that "the word 'impression' is appropriate only to original sensations," and that therefore "the now-point itself must . . . be defined through original sensation."[31] Accordingly, "every experience is sensed,"[32] and inner time-consciousness is fundamentally the form of this "sensible" self-awareness of consciousness.

However, it should be emphasized that the notion of "sensible" self-awareness does not refer to a *dyad* relation in which a subject, for instance, sees or touches herself. It has been claimed, by Henry and others, that to describe self-awareness in terms of "sensing" is inadequate and misleading, since it gives the impression of a duality between the sensing and the sensed—whereas self-awareness, as already argued, is supposed to be something immediate.[33] In line with Henry and others, I will mainly employ the more general term "self-affectivity" while referring to this immediate material self-awareness. In other words, "self-affectivity" is here taken as another name for the *livedness* of experiences, that is, a name for that which makes experiences *lived experiences*.[34]

Conscious life "not only *is*, but *is lived*";[35] there is "something it is like" to be conscious. These are alternative ways of saying that self-affectivity is an essential feature of all consciousness, a condition of possibility for experiencing. Should the impressional phase of consciousness not be affectively present—that is, *lived*—we could not be internally aware of the temporal succession of appearances, and thus experiencing would not be possible at all.[36] The experiential difference between present and past phases of consciousness is an affective difference. To be sure, when thinking about a mathematical problem, for instance, the *sensuous intensity* of our experiencing is remarkably different from when tasting a lemon, for instance, but the fact that mathematical thinking is not accompanied with an explicit sensuous feeling does not mean that it lacks affective self-awareness. Sensation is "the primal content" (*primären Inhalt*) of time-consciousness, and therefore self-affection pertains to all levels of constitution.[37]

The Husserlian notion of sensation is broad in the sense that it not only covers the proper "sensuous experiences" (touching something cold, hearing a piece of music, and so on). As the primal content of self-awareness, sensation pertains to all kinds of presenting acts (that is, to every act that is not mere fantasy)—and hence also to "acts of higher order" even though these are no longer directly and properly localized.[38] In this vein, Husserl argues that "every experience is 'sensed,'" and "sensation is here nothing other than the internal consciousness of the content of sensation."[39] Therefore, as Husserl writes elsewhere, "sensations are the indispensable material for all basic sorts of noeses."[40] With the "internality" of self-sensing Husserl wants to emphasize that the affective self-relation of experiencing is immediate and that we do not live our life from afar: according to Husserl, impression or sensation "must be taken as a primary consciousness that has no further consciousness behind it in which it would be intended."[41] In order to be sensuously self-aware, we do not need to touch or see ourselves—as already argued above, self-awareness is not the same as an awareness *of* oneself. In themselves, sensations are not yet acts, and self-affectivity is accordingly not yet an active self-relation. In short, intentional experiencing is lived through in a non-intentional manner.[42]

Without this affective self-awareness intentional experiences would not be possible, and in this sense, *self-affectivity* or *self-sensing* is a necessary condition of possibility for all experiences.[43] It is worth emphasizing that what is thereby presupposed is not only an abstract *form* of self-awareness, but a concrete self-awareness—form is not self-sufficient, it is "nothing without a content," as we already saw Husserl arguing. The elementary content, which necessarily accompanies all intentional experiences, is sensation.[44] Therefore, as Zahavi puts it, taken concretely time-consciousness "is a pervasive sensibility, the very sensing of sensations."[45] In this manner, self-affectivity is necessary even in mathematical thinking. Mathematical proof cannot be constituted without the inner temporality of mathematical consciousness, and "a judging consciousness of a mathematical state of affairs is an impression, [even if] the mathematical state . . . is not something temporal."[46] Mathematical thinking is a self-aware temporal construction of supra-temporal theorems, proofs, lemmas, and so on—and, as such, mathematical consciousness must be affectively present to itself. The constitution of every kind of identity (be it a geometrical theorem, a spatial object, or a symphony) presupposes the temporality of experiencing, and therefore it presupposes an immediate sensible self-presence of consciousness—even if this self-affectivity may remain implicit and tacit, which is the case in mathematic thinking, for instance.

To sum up, sensings are the primal content of all experiencing, and self-affectivity designates the elementary and non-intentional self-awareness that accompanies all intentional experiences: *all* experiences—and not only the primarily sensuous ones—are sensed. Accordingly, whereas "time-consciousness" refers to a formal structure of pre-reflective self-awareness, "self-affectivity" refers to self-awareness in its essential *materiality*. This is what Husserl means when he explicitly considers "sensing as the original consciousness of time."[47]

It is due to this essential entanglement and equiprimordiality of sensing and time-consciousness, that awareness of time is inseparable from awareness of space. This idea becomes clearer after we have elaborated and discussed different kinds of sensing.

Kinesthetic and Hyletic Sensing

There is a certain ambiguity at work in this phenomenological analysis of sensing. Namely, Husserl distinguishes between "two kinds of sensations, with totally different constitutive functions."[48]

On the one hand, there are *hyletic sensations*. Hyletic sensations make present something beyond them: "I do not see color-sensations but colored things, I do not hear tone-sensations but the singer's song."[49] Our attention does not normally dwell in our sensuous undergoing, but in the realm of the sensed. Hyletic sensing is a "presenting time-consciousness" (*gegenwärtigenden Zeitbewusstsein*).[50] Hyletic sensing constitutes the basis of our awareness of sensuous exteriority: hyletic sensations involve a difference between the sensing and the sensed, they present something other than the sensing itself, and this is why they can be called "external sensations."[51] For instance, we sense colors, and insofar as our sensing is not colored, we accordingly sense something "other." What our hyletic sensing presents, transcends our self-awareness—and thus it also transcends our primal sense of selfhood. This is why Husserl considers "the hyletic sphere as the ultimate non-egoic sphere."[52]

The exteriority constituted in hyletic sensing is not limited by the surface of a sense organ (skin, eye, tongue, etc.). Instead, also sensations felt *inside* our body—such as headache, heartbeat, "turning" of the stomach, the feeling of a lump in the throat, fullness, nausea, and so on—count as hyletic experiences in the sense that they *present* something.[53] For instance, an immediately sensed pain refers beyond itself, say, to our leg—the sensation presents our leg. In other words, not only *external* receptivity, or *exteroception*,[54] but also *interoception* or "somaesthesis" involves a difference between sensing and the sensed, and therefore qualifies for a type of a presenting, hyletic experience. In the sense of referring beyond themselves, hyletic sensations are "proto-intentional":[55] they serve as the primordial basis of intentional object-constitution and world-constitution.[56]

On the other hand, there are kinesthetic sensations. Things appear as being spread "around us," "near," "far," "in front of our eyes," "on the left," "under our feet," within or out of reach, and so on. The experience of orientation implies a point of reference, and this "absolute here" (*absolute Hier*) or "zero-point of orientation" (*Nullpunkt der Orientierung*), as Husserl puts it,[57] requires *kinesthetic sensing:* an immediate bodily self-affectivity that includes a passive proprioceptive awareness (postural schema) as well as an active awareness of movement.

It should be emphasized from the beginning that kinestheses do not, *by themselves,* constitute the body as a thing in the midst of the spatial environment—this constitution requires hyletic sensing as well. Husserl stresses that by talking of kinestheses or "movement sensations," "we do not want to suggest that we sense the movement of a thing or even that the movement of a thing is presented in these sensations."[58] Instead, kinesthetic sensations should be distinguished from all forms of presentational (*darstellende*) sensations: they "make possible a presentation without being presentational themselves."[59] Husserl writes:

> Sensations of movement . . . play an important role in the apprehension of every external thing, but they are not themselves apprehended in such a way that they make representable either a proper or an improper matter; they do not belong to the "projection" of the thing. Nothing qualitative corresponds to them in the thing, nor do they adumbrate bodies or present them by way of projection. And yet without their cooperation there is no body there, no thing.[60]

That is to say, unlike vision and touch, for instance, kinesthesia does not constitute a particular sense-field (there is no sensuous quality that could be present only to kinestheses), and, for this reason, kinesthesia does not qualify as a particular sense among others.[61] Kinesthetic awareness is not an objectifying awareness of one's own body—not even a receptive and marginal one—and it should be distinguished from interoception. To be sure, without constantly bearing this in mind, any talk of "movement sensations" is obviously misleading.

Whereas in the case of hyletic sensing one can distinguish between the sensed and the sensing, in the case of kinesthetic sensations no such difference prevails: the kinesthetically *sensed* is nothing other than the kinesthetic *sensing* itself.[62] Nevertheless, it is important to emphasize that hyletic sensations are lived through just as intimately and originally as kinesthetic sensations are, and in this sense hyletic sensations, too, are *mine* and constituents of *selfhood*—even if they *present* something that is neither mine nor part of myself. That is to say, even if the blue sky is something other than our sensing, our *sensations* or "*sensings*" of the blue sky are not lived through in any lesser manner.[63] Presenting sensations, too, can have their existence only as *lived* experiences. Or, as Henry puts it, the manner of being of hetero-affection is self-affection.[64]

The fact that both hyletic and kinesthetic sensing are lived through in an immediate manner has important consequences to our main concerns. Namely, as self-affectivity is originally twofold in this sense, this means that selfhood originally involves a difference. This might initially seem to suggest *split* self-awareness—upon closer scrutiny, however, this is not the case. Indeed, kinesthetic sensations form "continuous multidimensional systems," and they can acquire this continuous unity only "by filling a span of time."[65] However, kinestheses and the flow of appearing are *not two parallel continuums,* but rather two aspects of one continuum:[66] "The appearance in its temporal extension has two essentially different components, the [presenting] component and the K[inesthetic] component. The former supplies the 'intention toward,' the latter the motivation of this intention."[67] Husserl also specifies that kinestheses do not *precede* hyletic sensings: "every change whatsoever in *K*[inestheses] conditions univocally a change in [appearances] in such a way that the *same span of time* that is filled with the one change is also filled with the other."[68] It is not that we are first aware of our movements and then of the environment—and neither do we first experience a chaotic environment which is subsequently oriented in relation to our kinestheses. Between the motivating kinestheses and the motivated sensuous appearances there is an *associative* relation—"a natural correlation" (*corrélation naturelle*), as Merleau-Ponty puts it—that involves no temporal distance.[69] Husserl writes: "Kinesthetic courses . . . [are connected] with the appearances of things in accordance with associative motivations. . . . By motivation we mean that certain data and their protentional horizons are demanded as co-emerging along with the emergence of other data in our lived-experiences."[70] For instance, when we turn our head from left to right, we do not first see the environment sliding from right to left and realize its immobility only subsequently. Rather, our hyletic experience of the environment is originally organized in relation to our kinesthetic awareness—that is, we do not experience the environment moving because hyletic sensing "consults" the kinesthetic sensing, so to speak. For instance, if we fix our eyes on a flying bird, so that the bird is all the time straight in front of our eyes, we still experience the bird moving—even if the background of the perceptual field is completely homogeneous, a perfectly blue sky.

Accordingly, we do not have two lines of sensations, but one continuous and unitary experience that has two moments with different constitutive functions: "The temporal series on both sides are identical, and, in their filling, they correspond reciprocally and univocally. The associative connection joins together the corresponding phases through co-existence and joins the pairs, in their continuous sequence, through succession."[71] In other words, our external sensing "streams on in temporal coincidence and in fusion with a continuity of kinesthetic circumstances."[72] Kinesthetic sensing functions as a motivation in hyletic experiences, and we are not dealing with two parallel continuums of sensing, but two equiprimordial and necessary moments of a unitary experience.

Kinestheses provide the perceptual "circumstances" (*Umstände*) in reference to which the environment is hyletically sensed.[73] In themselves, however, kinestheses are unable to constitute a world: they are "not bearers of intention that penetrate them"; rather, they function as the circumstances so that a "determinate change in the circumstances results in a determinate change in the appearances."[74] If we move our head, the visual appearances change thus-and-so. However, Husserl stresses that appearances are dependent on kinestheses in a *functional* manner.[75] External appearances indeed necessitate kinestheses, but this dependency is functional in the sense that any appearance is not tied to any particular kinesthesis.[76] Husserl writes:

> The manifold of places is something absolutely invariable, something always given. And this manifold is never given without a k[inesthesis], and neither is a k[inesthesis] given without the total manifold of places which is merely fulfilled in a changing manner. To that extent we have a fixed association, one that is never to be disturbed, yet it is not between *one* k[inesthesis] and *one* place, but between the entire extension of places and "k[inesthesis] in general," though, once again, to be sure, this is not a definite k[inesthesis].[77]

Kinesthetic sensations constitute functional systems. Namely, certain kinestheses can also serve vicariously for other kinestheses without compromising the identity of the appearance. For example, we can see the same bird regardless of whether, in following its movement, we turn our head, our eyes, or both—and likewise, we can perceive one and the same object by touch, by sight, or by hearing. "The kinesthetic sensations form continuous multidimensional systems,"[78] where the same appearance and object can be constituted through different kinestheses. The appearance is constituted as identical in relation to different series of kinestheses because "there is a phenomenological kinship between the kinesthetic sensations of the eye and the kinesthetic sensations of the head and thus in general among the kinesthetic sensations of the various systems."[79] In this functional manner, kinestheses and hyletic sensations operate together and stand in a reciprocal dependency.[80]

However, given their different roles in the functional unity of consciousness, kinestheses cannot serve vicariously for hyletic sensations or vice versa: kinesthetic sensations "have indeed their determinate proper type over and against all visual and tactile sensations and are specifically bound together with these sensations and, if you will, are interwoven with them, but they still cannot blend with them in the sense of exchanging functions with them."[81] That is, kinestheses and external sensations have their irreplaceable functions in one unitary consciousness, and "sensibility" is a general name for their cooperation. Kinesthetic and hyletic sensations are intimately united into one awareness, so that "in every perceptual process we see a constitutive duet being played."[82] Consequently, self-constitution does not precede the constitution of the non-self, nor vice versa, but these are equiprimordial.[83] Merleau-Ponty states this concisely: "The consciousness of the world is not *based* on self-consciousness: they are strictly contemporary. There is a world for me because I am not unaware of myself; and I am not concealed from myself because I have a world."[84] It is not the case, for instance, that we are on the one hand hyletically aware of the environment and on the other hand kinesthetically self-aware; it is not the case that self-awareness is initially closed off from what it is not, and would have to first establish a relation to this exteriority.[85] Rather, self-awareness and awareness of exteriority belong originally together. Before explicating this further, let me offer a brief summary.

Until now, I have elaborated the sense in which consciousness is inseparable from a primal self-awareness. Self-awareness was introduced as the necessary experiential dimension of consciousness: it amounts to the "livedness" of lived experiences, to the "gone-throughness" essentially pertaining to experiences no matter what kind, and as such it makes up the *subjectivity* of consciousness. Secondly, I explicated that, according to Husserl, self-awareness has a temporal structure, and I then argued that inner time-consciousness necessarily involves a material dimension: to be self-aware is necessarily to *sense* oneself. Selfhood, accordingly, is not a mere formal feature of consciousness, but a dimension of *self-sensing* or *self-affection*. Thirdly, I distinguished two kinds of sensibility—kinesthetic and hyletic—arguing that both are lived through immediately, and that both therefore pertain to self-awareness.

In this light, subjectivity can be now defined as the meeting point of the immediately lived (kinesthetic-hyletic) interiority and the experiential exteriority that is presented in hyletic sensing—in short, *subjectivity is a lived relation to what is other to it*.[86] In the words of Husserl: "The ego is not conceivable without the non-ego, to which it is intentionally related."[87] As we saw above, this view is generally accepted among other phenomenologists as well: "the For-Itself is a relation to the world"; "internal transcendental experience is also a transcendent experience."[88] Accordingly, subjectivity is not shut into immanence, but is always already affected by what is other to it; to be aware of oneself is to be aware of oneself in relation to what is not part of oneself. And this, as I argued, is another way of saying that self-awareness is inseparable from a preliminary form of intentionality. That is to say, whereas I argued in the beginning that intentionality is inseparable from self-awareness, I have now ended up arguing that this also holds vice versa.

The intimate relation between interiority and exteriority becomes clearer after I have investigated the *localization* of affective consciousness. This will enable me to clarify, later on, the sense in which the constituting subjectivity is embodied.

2

The Environment and the Lived-Body

The constitution of our sensuous environment goes hand in hand with our bodily self-constitution. We can be conscious of the environment only insofar as we are bodily self-aware, and our bodily self-awareness correlates with, and thus also *outlines*, our awareness of the environment. I argued above, in more general terms, that self-awareness and intentionality are equiprimordial and intimately related: we are originally aware of ourselves in being aware of what is other to us. Moreover, the relation between the perceiving self and the perceived environment is not a relation between two distant poles: it is not normally the case that the environment appears "out there," whereas we ourselves are "in here." The perceived environment spreads *around* us—as the German words *Umwelt* and *Umgebung* suggest—which implies that *we* cannot be located outside the environment. That is to say, the self is not merely *related* to the environment, but is in *immediate contact* with it. This can also be captured in existential terminology by saying that the self is "situated." Bodily situatedness is not something that is added to the self later on, so to speak. Instead, as will be argued, bodily situatedness is a fundamental structure of subjectivity.

To be sure, bodily self-awareness is intimately linked to several phenomenological topics that will not yet be introduced in this part of the book. One should bear in mind that this is only for the purposes of presentation; although intersubjectivity, for instance, is properly discussed only later on, namely in part 2, this by no means suggests that others are not relevant for bodily self-constitution. The intersubjective dimensions of embodiment are throughly discussed later on. Let me now focus on the affective contact with the environment and clarify how the self is embodied in and through this contact.

Constitution of Sense-Fields and the Localization of Sensings

Our primordial contact with the environment is established by many different types of hyletic sensing, and yet we perceive only one environment.[1] Why is there only one environment and not many of them, corresponding to our different senses? In order to clarify this issue, we need to investigate hyletic affection in more detail, and clarify how sense-fields are constituted.

Particular sensed elements gain affective prominence by *standing out* from a background. Affection, in other words, necessarily involves a *contrast*—we could even say that affection *is* this contrast.[2] Affection is a necessary condition for object-constitution:[3] an object (a perceptual as well as an imaginary object) can be constituted only by standing out within a field (whether perceptual or imaginary), and insofar as no such contrast occurs, no object appears. Husserl argues that sense-fields themselves "have no actual standing out in relation to each other. Standing out, difference, distance, [and] contrast are possible only *within* a field."[4] The "background" and the prominent "foreground" are relative concepts: what stands out stands out against its background, and the background must therefore be part of the same homogeneous field. A visual feature, for instance, cannot be sensuously contrasted with an olfactory feature: the red color of a rose cannot stand out *against* the scent of the rose. Instead, insofar as a color gains an affective prominence and stands out as a primal "object" for itself, it does so against a colorful background: it stands out within a visual field.[5] Similarly, spatial shapes emerge against a spatial background, and so on.

Furthermore, the foreground and the background must not only be homogeneous, but also *temporally simultaneous*. A brown wallet can be contrasted against a white table only if both appear within the same living present. That is, the experience of homogeneity is necessarily an experience of temporal coexistence. Husserl thus defines the "sense-fields" as *fields of coexisting homogeneous content*.[6] The constitution of a sense-field *precedes* contrast and affection: it is *within* a homogeneous field that the object stands out in the first place. Contrast between the less prominent background and the more prominent foreground can, in other words, be constituted only *within* a certain homogeneity: the gradual scheme of foreground/background is established within a homogeneous field that was there already. In this manner, sense-fields are constituted passively, and as such they are *pre-given* in our experience of objects (which necessarily involves activity).[7]

The constitution of sense-fields apparently signifies the primordial constitution of a unitary, homogeneous environment. However, returning to my question, as there are several sense-fields, why are there not as many environments? We cannot see sounds or hear colors, and yet we normally experience them as belonging to the same environment, instead of two isolated realms. In relation to one another, sense-fields are heterogeneous: "Every sense-field is a unitary field for itself: Everything visual is connected through visual homogeneity, everything tactile through tactile homogeneity, everything acoustic through acoustic homogeneity, etc."[8] And yet, instead of a manifold of sense-fields, we normally experience one multisensory but still unitary world-horizon.[9] For instance, when we see a black dog barking, the barking that stands out in the acoustic field, and the black figure that stands out in the visual field, normally appear as moments of one and the same phenomenon.

Particular sense-fields somehow "communicate" in our perceptions.[10] But what is it that unifies our perception? One unifying feature is temporal coexistence. Husserl writes:

> Sense-fields are not chaotically connected to one another, or this does not have to be the case. If each one constitutes objects for itself, it is indeed constituted as enduring in the shape of time. Since the fillings of uniform, i.e., parallel duration are not homogeneous, they cannot contrast with one another, they cannot conflict with one another, and this is precisely due to the fact that the duration is completely fused with the parallel duration—every simultaneous element is the simultaneous element of one fused simultaneity, a simultaneity that only diverges according to different, heterogeneous filling.[11]

In other words, the parallel durations of the data of different sense-fields "each derive from a single primordially impressional present" and therefore we have "affective nexuses of heterogeneous elements through the homogeneous shape of time."[12]

Indeed, this sensuous coincidence breaks apart if the simultaneity is disturbed. This happens when, for example, we look though binoculars across a lake and see a dog barking while hearing the barking in a "delayed" manner. In this case we *know* that the barking that we hear and the shape that we see belong together, and this is why we experience the barking *as delayed*. However, sometimes even simultaneity is not enough to establish an intersensory unity. Some schizophrenic patients report that although they quite well *know* that the twittering they hear belongs to the bird they see in front of them, they nevertheless have two separate simultaneous perceptions: "I can hear the bird and I know that it is twittering, but that it is a bird and that it is twittering, these two things seem to be so remote from one another. There is a gap between . . . , as if the bird and the twittering had nothing to do with one another."[13] In this case the sensations are simultaneous but disconnected and without communication, and thus there is an experience of dissociation. This example implies that the perceptual unity of sense-fields cannot depend on temporal simultaneity alone. Intersensory objects are more than a bundle of simultaneous sensuous characteristics without unifying interrelation. Simultaneity, in other words, is a *necessary* but not a *sufficient* condition for the unity of sense-fields.

Indeed, taken literally "time-consciousness" is a formal and abstract notion, as already explained; a mere "shape of time" can establish, Husserl argues, no more than a "formal unicity" (*formalen Einheitlichkeit*) of the sense-fields.[14] An intersensory environment is constituted when the sense-fields coincide not only temporally but also *spatially*—the auditory and visual features appear as features of the same thing insofar as they are sensed in a particular direction and at a particular distance. That is to say, what unifies our sense-fields (and thus constitutes a unitary perceptual environment) is that which constitutes the spatiality of our experiencing. How, then, is spatiality constituted: what kind of affectivity is required for it? Apparently, it would be circular to make an appeal to a certain further *hyletic* experience—this would beg the question because the relation of the further hyletic field to the other fields would impose itself as a new problem. Instead, what all the hyletic sensations have in common is that they are related to kinesthetic self-affection.[15]

However, by themselves, as already said, kinestheses present nothing, they are not presenting sensations, and *alone* they are unable to constitute spatiality. It is rather in the "constitutive duet" of hyletic and kinesthetic sensing that a unitary perception is established and a unitary environment constituted. Should one be deprived of kinesthesia, one could not experience any stable identity, and hence no environment either; and nor could one experience the environment when deprived of hyletic sensibility. Both kinesthetic and hyletic sensing are necessary conditions for world-constitution—although, in themselves, they are insufficient conditions.

In order to describe how the unity of the intersensory environment is constituted, let me now explicate how our sensings are *localized*, that is, how our sensings *gain a certain spatiality*. This will also enable me to clarify the manner in which the self is fundamentally embodied.

When we are stung by a mosquito, for instance, we have an immediate experience of the locus of the painful sting on our skin and not a non-localized pain that is somehow connected with our awareness of the objective locus of the insect. When the mosquito stings us, our hand, without any deliberation on our part, lashes *to the locus of the mosquito*. One perhaps tends to reply that this is just a matter of "blind instinctual movement" that involves no awareness of the spatial location of the pain. This, however, is not plausible: if we would claim that such movements would be "blind" and deprived of all teleological directedness to a particular spatial locus, we would have to maintain that when we do hit the mosquito, this is only by accident. Instead of considering it as a matter of a frequently successful accident, we should maintain that our movements involve an initial, functional or *"operational" intentionality* that Husserl and Merleau-Ponty have discussed in detail.[16] Pain never occurs without spatial localization. The sting is perhaps felt in the upper body, in the arm, or under the elbow: localization is a gradual process, but not a process that starts from a pure pain without any localization. From the start, the pain is spatially localized.

On the other hand, if we treat localization as a type of objectification—if we claim that pain is originally experienced as located in objective space—then we would have to conclude that we are primarily *aware of pain*, instead of *being in pain*. This, too, conflicts with our normal experience. Pain originally has a spatial localization, but it is not experienced as an object.[17] The localized sensation is neither closed to immanence nor something pertaining to the transcendent world. Instead of simply falling on either side of the dichotomy of immanence and transcendence, hyletic sensing underlies this dichotomy.

The *immediacy* of our contact with the world should be emphasized. We are affected by the environment and by worldly things. For example, when we touch something hot, we tend to quickly pull our hand away, and when we suddenly see a bright light, we tend to close our eyes. That is, our kinesthetic movements are not only motivated freely by ourselves, but also by the environment as we experience it. In other words, our self-consciousness is affected and motivated by our consciousness of the environment, and vice versa. This is possible only insofar as we have something *in common* with the world. If consciousness and its environment did not share any "common ground," "meeting-point," or "common middle term,"[18] if they had no locus of coiling, enveloping, or folding (*Umschlagspunkt, Umschlagstelle*),[19] they would remain disconnected dimensions: there would be a gap between the environment and our experiencing. This clearly conflicts with experience. We can do justice to experience neither by considering the self as an extra-worldly entity, nor can we say that the self is simply included in the world. Instead, we must hold that sensible self-experiences are "localized," but at the same time we must refrain from considering this primordial "embodiment" as self-objectification.

The notion of localization should be clarified in detail—this clarification will help us to understand the intimate relation between the self and the world, and it will have an important role in my argument concerning embodied subjectivity.

When we touch a table, for instance, its *cool surface* is something *alien* to our sensing. Only the *sensation of* the cool surface is lived through immediately: that is, the sensing is a really inherent part of our life, whereas the sensed is not. However, it is not the case that we experience "on the one side" a non-localized sensing, and "on the other side" the locus of coldness without any interrelation. There is an intimate relation between the sensing and the sensed, interiority and exteriority: the sensation of coolness is localized *on* (and *in*) our hand. Our hand senses, but it is also something sensed, and while palpating the cool surface of the table, my hand is not a mere sensible object, but something that connects *me*—the self-affective dimension—to the sensuous environment. Localization serves as the meeting point and common ground for the sensing and the sensed, consciousness and the environment.

To avoid misunderstandings, let me emphasize that it is not the case that we are first conscious of our body and that sensings are subsequently localized in its surface. Rather, it is the localization of sensing that constitutes our primal experience of spatial exteriority in the first place. In other words, localization is the primal form of embodiment. Husserl characterizes sensings as "specifically lived-bodily occurrences" (*spezifische Leibesvorkommnisse*), but stresses that they are not occurrences in nature.[20] Even though the localized sensing "extends" *on* (or *in*) a certain area of the body, this "extension" must be distinguished from the extension of real properties of things and objects.[21] Like "joy and sorrow are not in the heart in the manner that blood is in the heart, tactile sensations are not in the skin like bits of the latter's organic tissue": the localized "sensing is not a *state* of the material thing [called] hand, but it is precisely the *hand itself*."[22] In short, "it is not the physical body that senses, but I sense."[23]

As the sphere of localization, the lived-body is not the objective body. If a mosquito stings us while our hand rests on the table, we do feel the sting on or in our hand, but it would be absurd to say that we feel the sting five centimeters above the table, for instance. To give another example, it is quite different to *feel chilly* in the autumn breeze, on the one hand, and to experience one's own body as a *cold object*, on the other— the latter experience would undoubtedly count as a pathological one.[24] These examples show that localization neither *presupposes* nor *entails* an experience of oneself in the objective space.

However, the localized body also has a certain spatiality, and in a certain sense localization counts as "spatialization." The movement of our hand lashing or swiping away the mosquito is not an aimless and random movement but a teleological one: it *aims at the spot* where the sting-sensation is localized, and in this functional or operational sense the swaying movement is *intentional*. Yet, *the space where the pain is originally lived is not the objective space, but a bodily space (Leibesraum)*:[25] a lived space constituted by our abilities of sensation and movement. Accordingly, we must distinguish between the spatiality pertaining to the "localized body" and the spatiality of the "objective body."[26]

This means that localization of pain, for instance, is not objectification of pain: in the case of objectification pain is reflected as a state of the objective body, and as such it may well have an exact locus. In contrast, localization is essentially inexact and more or less vague. However, this does not suggest that pain is not initially lived precisely as *head*ache or as *stomach*ache, and so on. As Sartre argues, already prior to reflection, "pain contains information about itself; it is impossible to confuse pain in the eyes with pain in the finger or the stomach."[27] Even if the localization of the ache is non-thematic and even unclear, we are never in doubt whether we have a headache, a stomachache, or no ache at all. Likewise, the sting of a mosquito is not localized in an *exact* manner: we manage to spontaneously strike at the spot where the insect is only because we do not need to consider our body as an objective thing in order to do this, and because no "exact precision" is thus required—and, if asked, we will indeed find it hard to pinpoint the exact area on our skin that was stung without "testing" by touching our hand.[28]

Similarly, the localization of kinestheses is essentially vague. When we reach for a glass of water, for example, our kinesthetic sensation is what we live through, and not something that is presented to us as an object. Husserl writes: "this [experience of] *I move myself* does 'not yet' signify [the experience of] the phenomenal, corporeal movement of my lived-body. The lived-body is 'not yet' constituted here."[29] That is, in self-movement the body is not present as an object. As Henry puts it: "No phenomenological distance intervenes between movement and us; movement is nothing transcendent."[30] However, even though kinestheses are originally non-presentational, they are not closed off from the world. Instead, kinestheses are *drawn to the world* by the properly localized hyletic sensations.[31] For example, when we lift our hand off the cold surface of a table and then move it back again, we experience the following conditionality: *if* we carry out such and such kinestheses, *then* we sense coldness, and *if* we carry out certain other kinestheses, *then* the hyletic sensation of coldness fades away. By experiencing this conditionality, the executed kinestheses are associated with the dimension of localized sensations and, in this mediated manner, kinestheses are localized. Although this localization may be "rather indeterminate," the kinesthetic self-movement is thus nevertheless apprehended as spatial movement.[32]

Moreover, we must be aware of our spatiality in order to be *motivated* in performing kinesthetic self-movement. For example, when spontaneously dodging a rapidly approaching snowball, our evasive movements are motivated only because we are somehow aware of the fact that the snowball is approaching *us* and that a kinesthetic effort might prevent it hitting us: that is, we must be aware of the fact that the perceived ball and the *kinesthetic standpoint* from which we perceive the ball belong to the same realm. This is why Husserl states that the constitution of the body as the "center of spatial orientation" and as the "organ of free movement" *rests upon localization*.[33] Worldly objects can appear as oriented and the environment can appear as our horizon of movement only if we are tacitly aware of the fact that the point of view from which we perceive the environment somehow *participates* in the same reality as the objects we perceive. Should we not be aware of our bodily situatedness in this way, our perception would have no experienced point of reference: things could not appear as far, near, left, and so on. In other words, *we can perceive the environment only insofar as we are embodied.*[34]

However, as I have repeatedly stressed, we do not have to *objectify* our body in order to experience our spatial posture or the spatiality of our kinesthetically sensed movements—and, to be sure, we would probably never succeed in dodging snowballs if we first had to reflectively pinpoint ourselves in the objective space.[35] Bodily spatiality is not originally the spatiality of a thing *in* the world, but the spatiality pertaining to our *experiencing* of the world. The lived-body is spatial not only in the sense that it is extended, but also—and more fundamentally—in the sense that it is *space-constituting*.

Embodiment and the Lived Environment

Bodily localization is the condition of possibility for bodily self-objectification, and the body is given in pre-objective manner prior to reflection. Husserl identifies localization with "mundanization" (*Verweltlichung*):[36] as a sensing being, the self is originally absorbed in the perceptual environment. Moreover, our embodied condition is originally revealed to us through our awareness of the environment, in the sense that our perception of the environment *indicates* our lived-body. Let me elaborate this "indicating" in detail by modifying an example given by Sartre.

Sartre describes a situation where, while reading a book, we start to get a headache.[37] Apparently, the experience of headache does not originally manifest itself as an experience *of* pain in a particular area of our objective body—our body is not initially in our focus, but our "point of view and a point of departure,"[38] whereas our focus is rather in the story that we are absorbed in. The localization of the ache is not a matter of either/or, but a temporal process that involves degrees. Initially, before being localized in our head, the ache reveals itself in and through certain alterations in our experiencing: for instance, the lines and paragraphs of the book may appear to quiver and demand our attention, the whole perceptual field is permeated by an unpleasant swarming, so that the story of the book becomes difficult to read, and our reading of the story is eventually interrupted. The ache permeates our perceptual field, but the localization of the ache is still quite vague: the aching seems to *surround* us rather than being limited at a particular locus (head).[39] Yet, the orientation of the altered perceptual field indicates a center. The altered appearances point back to altered self-affectivity as their motivating source, and in this manner, the motivated alterations of the visual field reveal their origin. The ache is eventually associated, for example, with the movement of the eyes, of the neck, and is thus *localized* in the head. In this manner, we come to apprehend the ache "through the world" (*par le monde*).[40] However, the unpleasant swarming that vaguely permeates the visual field not only *refers to* or *announces* the headache, it already *is* an experience of headache.

Drew Leder argues that whereas pain eventually turns our attention to ourselves, motivates a self-objectification, and hence tends to isolate us from the extra-bodily world, pleasure instead opens us to the world.[41] For instance, in tasting something delicious, we are not focused on the fact that the sensations are localized on the surface of our tongue, but we focus on what we taste. By contrast, while tasting something spoiled, the taste is explicitly localized *on* our tongue—in this case our nausea is at least partly motivated by the sudden awareness of our contamination. Similarly, in regard to the olfactory, visual, and auditory: affectively pleasant sensations motivate a turning toward, they motivate us to open and give ourselves to the sensed (whereas our body remains relatively implicit), whereas affectively unpleasant sensations motivate us to turn away, to shut ourselves from the sensed (thereby forcing a sort of self-objectification). To be sure, in their habituality, most of the hyletic and kinesthetic sensations that we live through remain neutral in the sense that they are affectively no more pleasant than unpleasant. They are normally localized without attention. In walking, for instance, we constantly tacitly sense our moving feet, and the ground beneath our feet, but this is not where our attention is normally focused as we walk (unlike the case if we have a painful blister on our foot or if our knee starts to hurt).

Moreover, the environment correlates with our lived-body on the whole—not only with some of its sensing organs. This can be illuminated by giving an example of tiredness. Like pain, tiredness is not originally present to us as an intentional object: we are not only conscious *of* tiredness, but we *are* tired. That is to say, rather than being a *correlate* of object-awareness, tiredness, too, is a type of pre-reflective self-awareness: a modification of self-affectivity—of "livedness." As already argued more generally, we can become intentionally conscious *of* our tiredness only insofar as we already *are* tired, and so too we can become conscious *of* our body, only insofar as we already *are* our body. In this light, a distinction between the *lived-body* and the *lived experience* (e.g., tiredness, pain, pleasure) proves to be problematic. Namely, "being tired" and "being embodied" are not two separate experiences, and it cannot be said that the lived-body *has* an experience of tiredness. Rather, when we are tired, our whole experience of the environment is modified, and this experience is a bodily experience. That is to say, it is originally our *bodily* experience that is modified when we are tired. For instance, if we are exhausted after an intense sports exercise, walking home demands a much greater effort, and hence the way home might exceed the subjective limits of a "walking distance"—home seems to be further away. But the apparent growth of distance is not just a consequence of our tiredness: it *is* an experience of tiredness.[42] After all, it is not the case that the experience of distance is primarily lived through in a neutral and non-affective manner, and that tiredness is projected upon it as a secondary "feeling," and neither is it the case that first we are tired in a disembodied manner, and that it is only afterward that tiredness manifests itself in the alterations of our lived environment[43]—as if experiences would first arise as disembodied and received localization only subsequently. In this manner, our embodied condition is originally revealed to us through our awareness of the environment. By experiencing the apparent growth of distance it is our lived-bodily (dis)ability that we experience; and, vice versa, should our bodily experience not go through even a slightest alteration, we would not *be* tired. In this sense, more generally, lived experiencing is fundamentally embodied. However, in all this, the lived-body normally remains non-thematic. Characteristics such as "center of spatial orientation" and "organ of free movement" do not refer to the lived-body as an *object* in the midst of space.[44] To experience the environment in a bodily manner does not presuppose that we at the same time *have* our body as an intentional correlate or "noema." Instead, in the pre-reflective and pre-objective level of self-awareness, the body remains—in a special, non-literal sense—*transparent*.[45] Normally, when we are not suffering from a bodily malfunction, and when we are not faced with too difficult a motor assignment, our functioning bodily organs remain experientially "transparent" in the sense that they are not quite given as palpable and visible things like the things that we touch and see with our body. For instance, when seeing a bottle of water and reaching for it, the moving hand that enters our visual field is not normally present as a thing approaching another thing next to it: the hand is something visible, but not thematic like the bottle of water that we are grasping. This kind of "transparency" is a prerequisite for normal bodily functioning. On the other hand, it should be emphasized that the experiential transparency of our body cannot be complete. Like the reification of the body, a complete experiential transparency of the body, too, would result in pathology. As already argued, if our body did not tacitly appear as somehow belonging to the sphere of reality, the bottle of water could not appear as being *within reach*, and we could not be motivated to grasp it.

When we experience the environment as oriented, we already tacitly constitute ourselves as the center of orientation—we could not experience the oriented environment without being tacitly aware of our actual bodily posture and movement. Moreover, we are not only aware of the environment as it is *oriented at the moment*, but we are also pre-reflectively aware of the environment as a horizon of *possible movement* (as we shall see later on, this fact has a major significance for the constitution of others). The lived-body is, Husserl argues, originally given as a "practical kinesthetic horizon."[46] In other words, we are aware of the fact that we *can* move, and this "faculty is not an empty ability but a positive potentiality," or, as Husserl also puts it, a "lived 'I can.'"[47] For example, our ability to run is not isolated from our perception of a bus that is slowing down at a bus stop 50 meters away: the perceived environment immediately appears differently depending on the perceiver's faculties, as the field of "positive potentialities," and so the faculty is constitutive of the intention as a whole. In negative terms, for a person who *cannot* run, the bus immediately appears as being too far away to catch. All this precedes active deliberation; we at once perceive the bus *as reachable* or *as unreachable*. Our awareness of the spatial environment as a horizon of movement refers to our implicit awareness of our bodily actualities and potentialities, and we are originally aware of our body by being aware of the environment as an oriented horizon of possible movement.[48]

This analysis enables me to address the question of the unity of sense-fields. According to what has already been said, when we see a cup of coffee on the table, we not only see the cup actually in front of us, but see it at once as something to which we *can* assume different positions: the cup appears as something that can be viewed, not only from the left, from above—but also farther or nearer. Accordingly, "as the process of external perceiving progresses optically, the thing is not only intended optically."[49] More generally, Husserl argues, "For normal persons, things are not constituted as things by building them out from seen things and touched things.... The thing is not split apart by the two groups of appearances."[50] Elsewhere Husserl explains, "Each thing we see is touchable. As such, it points to an immediate relation to the lived-body, but it does not do so in virtue of its visibility."[51] We *see* the cup as an object of possible *touching*, since we *can* move our body. Therefore, the cup does not appear as a sum of sensuous features, but as an *intentional unity* that transcends particular sense-fields. While *seeing*, for example, "the intentions of other senses are continuously co-awakened and must continually accord in the unity of a synthesis with the genuine impressional ones of the optical sphere. They must do so because they are co-constitutive of the objective sense."[52] Merleau-Ponty similarly writes, "What I call an experience of the thing or of reality—not merely of a reality-for-sight or for-touch, but absolute reality—is my full coexistence with the phenomenon, at the moment when... the 'data of different senses' are directed towards this one pole."[53] The intentional object is not only a multi-sensory but an *inter*-sensory object. By shutting our eyes while holding the cup, for instance, the visual characteristics of the object do not disappear, but remain in our anticipatory horizon: *if* we looked, *then* we would see the cup. And if, by opening our eyes, we do not see the cup that we feel in our hands, this does not make us believe that the cup lacks visual properties—instead, it introduces an intersensory conflict (e.g., we do not believe our eyes), which is just a further proof of the intersensory nature of the intentional object.

This is another way of saying that *we primarily perceive with our whole body*—and not with a particular sense. The real object, the cup of coffee, is taken as something that can be seen, touched, smelled, and tasted: taking away one of these features would, instead of mere aesthetic and practical alterations, rather destroy the very objectivity of the cup. A coffee cup that is not tangible or visual is not a *real* cup, and is not experienced as such. To employ my earlier example, the objective sense "barking dog" refers not merely to visual or auditory givenness, but to an intersensory experience: one sense refers to others, they "communicate," as Merleau-Ponty phrases it.[54] Should intersensory references of perception be disturbed or missing, the thing would not be taken to merely lack one contingent feature (e.g., visibility), but the constitution of the thing becomes radically altered. We do not come to experience the real object differently, but the thing instead no longer appears as a *real* thing—the reality of the thing is negated. As Husserl writes, "The moment something does not accord in the tactile sphere, . . . the unity of perception as it accords with all intentions in forming the unity of a whole intention is inhibited."[55] As Merleau-Ponty points out, such a thing would have a status similar to a visual thing that could only be seen with one eye: a thing seen with the left eye does not appear as an actual object if it does not refer to a possibility of being seen with the right eye as well.[56] A thing that is only present to one sense without invoking other sense-spheres does not count as a real thing—it instead appears as a phantom (*fantôme*).[57]

Accordingly, the unity of the perceptual environment is constituted as the correlate of a *schematic functional* bodily awareness,[58] as the correlate of "a universal setting, a schema of all types of perceptual unfolding and of all those inter-sensory correspondences which lie beyond the segment of the world which we are actually perceiving."[59] The "body schema" (*schéma corporel*) is a pre-reflective, functional, and non-objectifying bodily self-awareness, a practical projection of possibilities of movement—and it must be strictly kept apart from "body image," which is a perceptual, conceptual, or emotional representation of one's own body.[60] Our schematic bodily self-awareness—our awareness of our actual and potential posture and movement, which is the condition of possibility for the constitution of a unitary intersensory environment—is not a representation or objectification of the body, but a silent functional awareness of the lived space as the horizon of our bodily possibilities.

Husserl and Merleau-Ponty discuss this schematic bodily awareness under the heading "operative intentionality" (*fungierende Intentionalität*), and Merleau-Ponty sometimes alternatively uses the title "intentional arc."[61] Whereas act-intentionality is the structure of voluntary position-takings (such as judgments, decisions, and deliberate movements), "operative intentionality" pertains to the realm of the *pre-reflective, passive, and involuntary*. Operative intentionality is our bodily way of reacting and adjusting to situations. As such, it is the condition of possibility of active voluntary bodily movements. Getting up from a chair, we intend to establish ourselves in an upright position, and this is achieved by a habitual collaboration of different muscle groups: we use our feet, but we also lean forward, support ourselves with our hands, and the muscles of our back, abdomen, waist, and legs harmoniously support our rising body as well as the movements of our arms. And, if while getting up someone calls us on our right, we perhaps habitually turn our head, direct and focus our eyes," but our standing up does not normally[62] fail because of this sudden turn of attentive regard. This is because our attention was not in our singular bodily movements in the first place.

Moreover, as we turn around facing the person that entered the room, the movement of our eyes is *prepared* and *continued* by the movement of our neck, and this again by other parts of our body—and so on. Our body prepares and supports our activity; it follows our singular movements "like a comet's tail."[63] Like our bodily self-awareness is not an awareness of a mere isolated "now," our deliberate bodily movements are not without a temporal background. Our active movements are rather established against the passive background of preparing and adjustive movements—some of which temporally precede the singular movement and are thus retained as the starting point. Operative intentionality is this manifold and yet unitary intentionality that constantly latently supports our active intentionalities without our attentive regard. Accordingly, our active intentionality is built upon a preceding passive intentionality: as something is given to us, it is given against the background of the pre-given—our perceptions rest upon the "work already done" (*d'un travail déjà fait*) by our body.[64]

At the level of operative intentionality our own body is revealed not as an object but as a functioning subjectivity. There is a magnificent, almost magical synergy between the different areas of our lived-body, and this tacit and non-objectifying bodily self-awareness constitutes our bodily schema. Merleau-Ponty writes, "The thing, and the world, are given to me along with . . . my body . . . in a living connection comparable, or rather identical, with that existing between the parts of my body itself."[65] This is to be taken quite literally. The warmth of the coffee cup is what we feel with our hands, its color is something that we can absorb with our eyes, and its scent is something we breathe into our nostrils and lungs: the unitary intersensory object is the correlate of unitary bodily self-constitution. What is common to all sensuous features is that their appearing is conditioned by schematic bodily self-awareness. *The passive synthesis of the perceptual environment is the correlate of the pre-objective, schematic, synthesis of the lived-body.* As Merleau-Ponty puts it, "operative intentionality . . . produces the natural and pre-predicative unity of the world and of our life."[66]

In this sense, our lived-body is originally given in our experience of a spatiotemporal environment. To sense one's body is to be schematically aware of an organized space, and to experience one's bodily potentialities is to experience the environment as a horizon of movement.[67] And vice versa: to be aware of organized space and of a horizon of movement is inseparable from a tacit bodily self-awareness. It should be emphasized that the environment is not only the correlate of our *explicitly and thematically* felt bodily movements or attended sensations, but of the adjustive and supportive movements and unnoticed sensations as well. As we lift the telephone with our arm, it is not only the sensed movement of our palm, but likewise that of our arm, of our shoulder, the feeling of muscular tension in the back (and so on), that constitutes our experience of spatiality. The horizontal directions ("left," "right," "forward" and "backward") are vague precisely because it is not a certain part of our body, but our body as a whole, that motivates our experience of spatiality.

The intersensory constitution of things presupposes the possibility of perceiving them otherwise (say, from other perspectives), and hence it presupposes the potentiality of movement. *If* we moved thus and so, *then* such and such appearances would unfold. This conditionality is not limited to particular sense-fields: we do not primarily anticipate changes only within a single realm. Rather, by moving closer to an object—say, a coffee cup—then we will not only expect to *see* it differently, but we at once expect that we are able to touch the cup, to smell the coffee, and to taste it. In this manner, the "presumptive," intentional unity of the cup is supported by the lived possibility of kinesthetic motility (by the "*I can*") which essentially belongs to our bodily self-awareness. The intentional object is that which *can* be seen, touched, smelled, tasted, heard, and even if these sensory fields do not overlap as to their sensuous content, they pertain to one and the same thing, because they appear as possibilities of one and the same lived-body. Therefore, as Husserl states, a bond between the sense-fields is established by the system of kinestheses.[68] Accordingly, a schematic bodily awareness—or "body schema"—is a condition for a unitary experience of an intersensory environment. The intersensory environment is essentially the intentional correlate of bodily experiencing.

Bodily Self-Reflexivity and the Primacy of the Tactile

By perceiving the environment as a spatial horizon, we are tacitly aware of our possibilities of movement; and by sensing the environment, we are affected by it and are thus tacitly aware of ourselves, in a non-objectifying manner, as fields of sensing. However, we have seen that the lived-body is not originally present as an object, but as a field, and hence we must ask: on what ground are we justified in talking about the "body" at this pre-objective level? After all, the word "body" is usually taken to refer to things that can be seen and touched, and not to our experience of the spatial environment. To be sure, as Sartre claims, unreflective self-consciousness is something else than "consciousness *of the* body."[69] However, to maintain that the body is not an object, and that it is normally lived in a non-thematic manner, does not imply that it has no spatiality whatsoever. The nature of this original spatiality, which has already been discussed, becomes clear when we take into account how our perceived body is constituted *as our own*. In order to address this problem, I shall investigate the *self-reflexivity* of the lived-body (the self-reflexivity of the field of sensing).

Within the lived space, our perceived body stands out from perceived things as having certain unique features. First of all, this one particular perceived thing is always with us, "near." In order to scratch one's own head, one does not need to move to change one's position. On the other hand, unlike all other perceivable things, this one body is a "remarkably imperfectly constituted thing" (*ein merkwürdig unvollkommen konstituiertes Ding*):[70] by moving, we *can* in principle see each side of all external objects, whereas in the case of this one body we *cannot*. Our own perceived body is not completely included in the spatial realm correlating with the "I can": we cannot take distance to our body in order to see ourselves from without, and we cannot go nearer in order to see our face better. But how does this one particular body appear as *our* body? I argued earlier that the constitution of an intersensory object presupposes a unitary bodily self-awareness. What I have not yet clarified is how one intersensory object comes to appear as our own external body. This will become clear after a further characteristic of the body has been elaborated, namely its ability to generate what Husserl calls *double sensation* (*Doppelempfindung*).[71]

To avoid confusion, let us first consider tactile self-reference without referring to visual sensation of one's own body (i.e., let us imagine that we do not see). In exploring the objects of the tactile realm, one particular thing stands out as a *thing that senses*. When we touch our left hand, we sense the hand as something worldly, external, and alien. The sensing is localized in the right hand, which is thus tacitly constituted as a subjective field of touching. However, as we touch our left hand, we also feel the touch in the touched hand. The framework touching/touched is thus *reversed* when we notice that the left hand also senses: as we turn to explore reflectively our right hand, it is thematized as the touched hand, as something external and alien to our immediate sensing, which is localized in our left hand. In this manner, sensing is "doubled."[72] That is to say, in this experience, the right hand first tacitly reveals itself as the subject of sensing but then comes to appear as something sensed, and now the left hand manifests itself as a subject of sensing.[73]

In the course of such an experience, a peculiar synthesis takes place: the *perceived, transcendent* body and the *perceiving transcendental* body are reversed. The subjective, constitutive field of sensing is discovered *in* the external sense-field, as something constituted, and the constituted thing reveals itself as the constituting subjective field of sensing. The sensing body is no longer completely unthematic and "transparent," and consequently the borderline between the perceiving and the perceived becomes complex. When applauding, for example, neither of the hands is lived fully in a non-objectified manner or merely as something sensed. Rather, both are touching as well as touched, and so the lived-body resists the dichotomy of subject/object. The embodied subjectivity is experientially, as Husserl and Merleau-Ponty both put it, a "subject-object."[74] It is worth adding here that these double sensations do not occur only sporadically, while applauding for instance, as there are many areas in our body where this kind of "self-palpation" is taking place all the time (to give just one example, we constantly sense the mucosa of our mouth, our gums, etc., with our tongue, on the one hand, but we also feel our tongue by our mucosa).

This experiential duality is not without constitutive significance.[75] Whereas in simple tactile experiences, sensings are localized *in the field of sensing*, double sensations are necessary for the constitution of *the field of sensing within our bodily space;* it is eventually owing to double sensations that the subjective field is properly embodied. Localization without the possibility of double sensation could not establish the proper constitution of our lived-bodily exteriority (i.e., the constitution of an empirical body *as ours*). Husserl argues that "*a subject whose only sense was the sense of vision could not have an appearing* [that is, a hyletically experienced] *lived-body,*" because bodily exteriority "can be constituted originally only in tactuality and everything that is localized with the sensations of touch: for example, warmth, coldness, pain, etc." Therefore, "it could not be said," Husserl continues, "that this subject would only *see* his lived-body, for its specific distinctive feature as a lived-body would be lacking him."[76] If we had no tactile sense and no possibility of a double sensation, we could not experience our hand as a field of sensing, as something localized, and we would therefore be unable to discover our empirical body as our own. For such a subject it would seem as if she could immediately and freely move one material *thing* in her visual field—without experiencing it as the body she *is*.[77]

According to Husserl, only tactile sensations are properly, independently localized. This means that the tactile sphere has a constitutive priority.[78] Husserl sharply separates tactile sensations from sensations occurring in other sense-spheres. He argues that the localization of other sensations is dependent on the tactile,[79] and accordingly that *intersensory* double sensations (double sensations across different senses) refer back to *monosensory* double sensations (double sensations within one sense sphere)—this is why, when introducing the theme of double sensation, we first avoided considering the hand touching the other hand as a visually witnessed event. Husserl writes, "I do not see myself, my lived-body, the way I touch myself. What I call the seen body is not something seeing which is seen, the way my lived-body as touched lived-body is something touching which is touched."[80] That is to say, we can touch our touching hand, but we cannot see our seeing eye. This is not an empirical curiosity that could be altered if our eyes were situated differently. Husserl claims that "it cannot be said that I see my [seeing] eye in the mirror, for my eye, that which sees qua seeing, I do not perceive."[81] That is, *by themselves*, visual sensations are not localized in the seeing eye. Husserl argues, "If, ultimately, the eye as organ and, along with it, the visual sensations are in fact attributed to the lived-body, then this happens indirectly by means of the properly localized sensations."[82]

Accordingly, if the seen hand is constituted as an organ of one's own body, it must be experienced as belonging to a subject that also perceives it tactually—and, correlatively, if the touched object and seen object are to be constituted as two aspects of one intersensory object, it is necessary that the visual sensing can be localized in the tactually sensing body. Husserl therefore argues that the localization of visual sensations in one's own body eventually presupposes the possibility of proper double sensations provided by the tactile sphere. All localization refers back to localization within the tactile sphere, and it is in relation to the tactile that other sense-spheres are localized.

In and through localization and double sensation, our immediate kinesthetic self-movement is associated with the external movements of our perceived body.[83] If a wasp suddenly occurs in our field of vision, we flinch, but as we spontaneously try to swat it away, we do not flinch for the second time when we suddenly see our own hand, and this is because the visual experience of the hand in front of our face was something we knew to expect. Moreover, the localization of kinestheses is not restricted to visually perceivable movements. Also, by moving our eyes, we learn that *if* we execute certain kinestheses, the environment *then* visually appears in an altered manner, and in this manner the kinesthetic processes involved in our visual perception are localized in our movable eyes. To give another example, to experience a voice *as one's own*, and hence as pertaining to one's own body, requires that the kinestheses, that are included in vocalization, are localized. This is established in relation to certain interoceptive sensations—such as vibration, trembling, and tension—that are originally localized in the throat. However, as already explained, in contrast to exteroception and interoception, kinesthesis is not a *presenting sense*. By effecting such and such kinestheses, a voice is heard, but without relation to properly localized sensations, the voice could not appear *as uttered*, since it would lack a relation to a localized body. As already argued, mere simultaneity is not enough to bridge the gap between the heard voice and the kinesthetic sensation.[84]

The possibility of "double sensations" is not a mere phenomenological curiosity void of constitutive significance, but a phenomenon that has an important role in the constitution of the lived-body, and hence in the localization of subjectivity. It is originally the reversibility experienced in double sensation (in the tactile sphere) that motivates us to realize that the subjective field of sensing is precisely the lived experiencing *pertaining to a particular body* that can be touched, seen, and so on. In other words, through double sensation we experience the peculiar articulation of internal and external, and understand that the field of sensing and the pre-objective lived-body are one and the same.

This enables me to address the question that was posed in the beginning of this chapter. Namely, what I have just said justifies the use of the word "body" when talking of the spatiality of lived experiencing at the pre-objective level. Even though, while being submerged in experiencing the spatial environment, the experiencing subjectivity does not appear to itself as a mere thing, it is nevertheless precisely an embodied subjectivity.[85] This is what double sensation teaches us, and thus Sartre is mistaken in treating it as something that is not essential for bodily self-awareness.[86]

The Lived-Body as a Multidimensional Being

It should be clear by now that bodily self-awareness has multiple layers or dimensions.[87] From the basis of the Husserlian account, one can distinguish between (1) the body as the immediate dimension of hyletic and kinesthetic self-affectivity, (2) the body as the dimension of localization (something that can be immediately *sensed*), (3) the body as something that can be partially perceived in the external environment, and (4) the body as a mere material thing in a causal framework. The first three make up what Husserl calls the lived-body. Accordingly, the lived-body is an immediate realm of sensing, but it also has an original exteriority, both in the sense of localization and in the sense of being perceivable—but the lived-body is never a mere material thing.

Husserl emphasizes that the layers of the body are not exhausted by the distinction between *Leib* and *Körper*, and argues that the lived-body itself must be recognized as a "two-dimensional unity" (*doppelsichtige Einheit*):[88] "a spatiotemporal experience *of* the lived-body . . . refers back to the lived-body as functioning" and thus "the lived-body presents the difficulty that an experience of it always already presupposes it."[89] Husserl condenses: "My lived-body is conceivable in two senses: [1] immediately in . . . self-manifestation, and [2] in a mediated fashion, in an external manifestation that refers back to self-manifestation."[90]

Elsewhere Husserl names these two manners of givenness of the lived-body as "lived-bodily interiority" (*Innenleiblichkeit*) and "lived-bodily exteriority" (*Aussenleiblichkeit*).[91] This distinction, as we shall see, coincides with the distinction between "being a body" and "having a body," which is later employed by Sartre, Merleau-Ponty, and Henry.[92] What Husserl means by "lived-bodily interiority" is the dimension of immediate kinesthetic-hyletic self-affection: it is not something palpable or visible; it cannot be given as an object,[93] but is what can only be immediately lived. And what he means by "lived-bodily exteriority" is the lived-body in its original exteriority (covering both the localized body and the perceivable body). I will now shed light on the dimensions of the body, as well as their interrelations, and thus explicate the different phenomenological senses of embodiment.

As the center of orientation and as the organ of immediate self-movement, our body seems to be "everywhere and nowhere"; our body is submerged in the environment that it perceives, and it is tacitly revealed in and through the manners in which the environment presents itself, although not originally as a thing in the world:

> My body is everywhere in the world; it is over there in the fact that the lamp-post hides the bush which grows along the path, as well as in the fact that the roof up there is above the windows of the sixth floor or in the fact that a passing car swerves from right to left behind the truck or that the woman that is crossing the street appears smaller than the man who is sitting on the sidewalk in front of the café. My body is coextensive with the world, spread across all things.[94]

Sartre explains that "the body as the center of sensible reference is that *beyond which* I am in so far as I am immediately present to the glass or to the table or to the distant tree which I perceive."[95] As Leder puts it, taking up the formulation of Michael Polanyi, the body is originally the center of orientation *from which* we perceive,[96] and as such it is not simply included among the things that we perceive bodily. In this sense, before consciously *having* a body, we *are* our body; our experiencing is bodily experiencing, and we are embodied already before constituting our own lived-body as such.

This immediate bodily self-manifestation or "lived-bodily interiority" that we are—the dimension of kinesthetic and hyletic self-affectivity—is a constituting dimension, and instead of speaking of "lived-bodily interiority," we could just as well be speaking, with Henry, of the "transcendental body."[97] Yet, as we have seen, to be bodily self-aware *only* in this sense would result in pathology. A person who does not constitute her body in the same realm with the perceived objects could not be motivated in interacting with the environment. We not only *are* our body, but we also *have* a body—in other words, we have a lived-bodily exteriority.

Localization, as I have argued, constitutes our primal experience of lived-bodily exteriority. With localization, the "transparency" of the sensing body is compromised: bodily self-manifestation not only necessarily pertains to our awareness of the environment, but at once it also reveals our immediate relation to the latter. Merleau-Ponty argues that the Sartrean characterization of the lived-body as being "everywhere and nowhere" is apt only in regard to the visual sense, whereas in the tactile sphere the relation between the sensing and the sensed is not governed by distance:

> In visual experience, which pushes [self-]objectification further than does tactile experience, we can, at least at first sight, flatter ourselves that we constitute the world, because it presents us with a spectacle spread out before us at a distance, and gives us the illusion of being immediately present everywhere and nowhere. Tactile experience, on the other hand, adheres to the surface of our body; we cannot unfold it before us, and it never becomes quite an object. Correlatively, as the subject of touch I cannot flatter myself that I am everywhere and nowhere.... It is not I who touch, it is my body.[98]

That is to say, as tactile beings, we are in *immediate* contact with the sensed world, and therefore we are not everywhere and nowhere—but situated *here* and *now*.[99] Touching something, we at once find ourselves *by* it.[100] Therefore, our lived-body serves not only as the pure sensor of the environment, but, as a tactile being, the lived-body is localized, and as such it serves as the "meeting point" between the sensing and the sensed.[101]

In this primal sense, we have a lived-bodily exteriority. As I have argued, this primal exteriority is not an objective or empirical issue; localization is a purely subjective process, and the exteriority constituted in and through it is a *lived* exteriority.

Moreover, lived-bodily exteriority amounts to the exteriority of the lived-body in its self-manifestation. As we saw Husserl arguing, the external manifestation of the body refers back to immediate self-manifestation of the body.[102] Lived-bodily exteriority is what the embodied subjectivity *has*, and not what it *is*. Yet the *givenness* of this exteriority is not itself something external to us but something that we live through immediately. In localization, "lived-bodily interiority" is not replaced by "lived-bodily exteriority." The latter is what we consciously *have*, and this is possible only because *we who have it* are not disembodied minds, but are embodied in a more fundamental sense. As already argued, localization ought to be kept apart from a reflective (objectifying) consciousness directed at a sensation: we are not originally *aware of* pain or *aware of* tiredness, but rather we *are in pain* and we *are tired*. In this sense, the mentioned "transparency" remains a normal feature of the body. But, as said, both complete transparency and complete lack of transparency count as pathological experiences.

Double sensations have an important role in our bodily self-constitution; they provide our lived-body with the characteristic of perceivability (e.g., visibility). When scratching our head, rubbing our eyes, or applauding, for instance, it is not a lifeless thing that we thereby hyletically confront, but our own lived-body in its localized exteriority. Since the touching situation can be reversed, the perceived body appears as our *own*—it appears as the exteriority of our immediate kinesthetic-hyletic self-affectivity, that is, the exteriority of the body that we *are*. As Husserl puts it in a manuscript, "the lived-body in its exteriority carries an apperceived interiority and therein a lived-bodily interiority, an original field of 'I move,' an original bearer of fields of sensation etc., localized sensations."[103] Our perceived bodily exteriority is experientially bound to bodily self-manifestation, and it therefore appears as *lived* exteriority—that is, as being "endowed with an 'interiority'" (*ausgestattet mit einer "Innerlichkeit"*).[104] Our perceived hand appears as *our* external organ of sensing, we *see* it as a member of our self-sensing and self-moving body; and as we see our hand moving over the table and touching its surface we visually perceive the *exteriority of our kinesthetic self-movement* and *the exteriority of our field of sensing*. In other words, we experience our bodily exteriority as that *of* our interiority.

Husserl terms this relation between interiority and exteriority—whereby *exteriority* reveals itself as *lived* exteriority, exteriority *of* interiority (*Äusserlichkeit die Innerlichkeit*)—as "expression" (*Ausdruck*), "enunciation" (*Kundgabe*), or externalization (*Veräusserlichung*).[105] The externally perceived movement of our hand, for instance, appears as an expression of our immediate self-movement, of our immediate self-affectivity. The localized body and the externally perceivable body are elements of the body that we *have*, elements of our lived-bodily exteriority, whereas the dimension of self-manifestation, to which these refer back, amounts to the body that we *are*, that is, lived-bodily interiority. The lived-body, accordingly, is both "perceivable" and "transparent"—on the one hand, it is "everywhere and nowhere," while on the other hand, it is always localized here and now, and can also be perceived in an external manner. In short, we not only *have* a body, but we also *are* a body.[106]

3

The Bodily Self

Thus far, I have argued that the dimension of hyletic-kinesthetic self-affection equals to a primal sense of selfhood, shown how this affective sphere is localized, and clarified the sense in which the self has a perceivable exteriority. What, accordingly, is the relation between the *self* and the *lived-body*? I will answer this question by first specifying phenomenologically the notion of selfhood in relation to activity and passivity. On the basis of Husserl's writings, I will distinguish between *active, passive,* and *active-passive* self-affectivity and discuss the respective modes of selfhood: "agency," "ipseity," and "habituality." I will examine the manner in which these modes of selfhood are embodied, and then investigate how the self may be "expanded" through practical incorporation of tools and equipment. This will enable me to provide a systematic elaboration of the transcendental and empirical features of the embodied self.

Agency, Ipseity, Habituality

Hyletic sensing is not something that we can actively execute or generate, but something that happens to us. Therefore, whether we are talking of activity or passivity in the level of sensibility depends solely on the mode of our *kinesthetic* self-affectivity. When kinestheses are freely executed, we speak of activity. We move ourselves (turn our head, raise our hand, shut our eyes, walk and jump) and in correlation with these free movements, the environment appears differently. Even if we cannot generate or control our hyletic sensations by will, we can shut our eyes, turn our head, move closer, and grasp the object that hyletically affects us. This kind of self-affectivity is an active one, a matter of active selfhood or "agency."

Kinestheses are also often operative without being actively executed, and therefore we should distinguish a mode of selfhood where movements are executed (in the sense that one could also *refrain* from them), but executed *habitually*, without explicit activity. As Husserl puts it, the self not only "exercises itself" (*übt sich*), but also "habituates itself" (*gewöhnt sich*): it "'acquires' capacities, posits goals, and, in attaining these goals acquires practical skills."[1] Indeed, most of our self-movement is *habitual* in this sense. Habitual movements are not "passive" in the sense that they merely *occur* or *happen to us* (like accidents or strokes of luck), but neither are they actively executed. They presuppose activity, but the necessary activity remains non-thematic and implicit. Such movements are "passively active," they pertain to our habitual selfhood.

In contrast to the above-mentioned, passive selfhood equals to a mode of selfhood that completely lacks what Husserl calls "kinesthetic effort" (*kinästhetische Streben*).[2] Here we must distinguish between *kinesthetic effort* and *kinesthetic awareness:* even when we are not kinesthetically active (not even in the sense of habitual activity), we are nevertheless kinesthetically self-aware. Even forced movements are sensed kinesthetically, and even if we lie down and refrain from all active self-movement, we are still kinesthetically self-aware.[3] Our kinesthetic self-awareness does not simply disappear when we cease all our active movement. We are still aware of our bodily posture and the positions of our limbs. Moreover, during our active and habitual self-movements, there are many processes that remain purely passive but are still felt kinesthetically. For instance, the functioning of our eyelids, our heart, and digestion is neither actively nor habitually controlled by us.[4] This passive self-relation accompanies all possible awareness—even dreaming. This passive and minimal form of selfhood is called "ipseity."

Agency, habituality, and ipseity are not mutually exclusive, but different *modes* of our immediate self-relation. Let me illustrate this with an example. When watching a bird fly by, we are not mere passive beholders of the scenery; we not only *see,* but *watch* the bird fly by. We follow the bird by moving ourselves (our head, eyes, upper body, etc.) and in this sense our perception is active—as Alva Noë puts it, "perception is not something that happens to us, or in us. It is something we do."[5] Moreover, as already indicated, a particular movement of the body is at the same time a movement of the whole body. When watching the bird, we *actively* turn our head toward the bird, but this movement is supported by the adjustive movements of our shoulders, of our upper back—and so on. That is to say, our purely active movements are embedded in kinesthetic habituality: there is an "operative intentionality" that surrounds our active-deliberate movements and functions constitutively in the performance of perception. If this adjustive and supporting habituality failed, we would not be able to perceive the bird. In this way, purely active self-movement is based on habitual self-movement, and, accordingly, agency is founded on, and supported by, habituality.[6]

During our activity, we are necessarily also passively self-aware. To continue my example, while following the bird with our gaze, the executed movement of our head, as well as the habitual adjustive movements of our eyes, neck, and our whole upper body—all these are at the same time experienced kinesthetically. But we are not only aware of our kinesthetic *effort* of moving, but also of the *fact* that we move. Active self-movement (whether deliberately or habitually activated) rests on passive self-affectivity: we can engage in activity only insofar as we already passively sense ourselves, and this passive self-relation (which constitutes the "ipseity" or "mineness" of experiences) does not disappear when we actively move ourselves, but prevails as the basis of voluntary and habitual self-movement. When we actively move ourselves, we must at the same time passively feel our self-movement kinesthetically, which means that active selfhood (agency) and habitual selfhood are both founded on passive selfhood. In short, if there is *agency* or *habitual selfhood*, there is also *mineness* or *ipseity*.

In active bodily self-movement, passive and active self-awareness (i.e., mineness and agency) coincide. We actively perform a movement while at the same time affectively experiencing this bodily movement as our own, and there seems to be no gap between the sense of performance and the sense of ownness. In contrast, in the case of habitual movement a certain experiential break occurs between agency and mineness. The habitual movement is given as our own, but not as actively initiated by us. Let me illuminate this phenomenon with an example. When exiting a room or a house, our habitual movement of walking to the door and opening it may well lack all explicit volitional effort. We have learned to walk and open doors, and in the course of time this skill has developed into a habit. We no longer need to pay any attention to our bodily movements while walking, while turning the door handle, or while following the flying bird with our gaze. Nevertheless, the act of opening involves a *mineness*—we feel our bodily self-movement and we are, therefore, able to later on recollect this experience. And yet, we do not actively initiate or control the movements of walking and turning the door handle.

Normally, habituality remains implicit and unproblematic: we are not stunned or perplexed even though while walking our feet find their place in relation to one another, even though our fingers find the right keys on the keyboard, or even though when going out our hand adroitly turns the door handle, as if our body had a will of its own. But when we do become aware of our bodily movement while walking, or while opening the door, habituality loses its force and bodily movements at once become complex, laborious, and strange. The more habitual the movement, the less explicit the effort. As Josef Parnas and Louis Sass have argued, in certain cases of schizophrenia, self-awareness is intensified and heightened.[7] Such cases show that the break between mineness and agency—which is a characteristic of all habituality—may become explicit. In these pathological experiences one's *own* body is experienced as being *controlled* or *moved* by some external instance. Normally, the situation is not completely different: we, who actively reflect upon our walking, are not the performers of our habitual bodily movements. In certain pathological cases, the experiential gap between mineness and agency that normally remains implicit and thus unproblematic may become explicit, and this fundamentally alters the structure of experience.

The distinction between three fundamental modes of selfhood—agency, habituality, and ipseity—makes it possible to develop further the claim that we *are* our body in the sense of lived-bodily interiority. It can be claimed, namely, that the dimension of passive self-manifestation, the dimension of habitually initiated kinesthetic activity, and explicit kinesthetic effort are modes of *lived-bodily interiority*. In this sense, the claim that subjectivity is fundamentally embodied gains further illumination. We are not disembodied subjects that execute and control the movements of a body from afar. Active selfhood refers to a dimension of immediate self-affection, that wills and executes the motion in the manner of kinesthetic effort. In this sense, the active performance of movement is embodied: as we see our moving hand, for instance, we not only see it as a member of *our own* body (i.e., as an expression of the mineness or ipseity of our lived-body) but at once we witness its movement as a *performed* movement—we see not only a *moving* hand but a *moved* hand.[8] In other words, active self-affection is embodied in the perceivable movements of the lived-body, and in this sense, the kinesthetic self ought to be recognized as an embodied dimension—and this indeed is what Husserl means when he discusses the body as the *organ of will* (*Willensorgan*).[9] Moreover, kinesthetic effort is not dependent on whether or not we are thematically and explicitly aware of it, and therefore, what is said about the active self also applies to the habitual self. What we witness is a *performed* movement—regardless of whether this performance is deliberate or habitual.

Incorporation

The claim that the self is embodied must not be understood as a claim that the borderline between self and environment runs on the skin. The lived-body is not spatially confined to the objective locus of the body-thing; there is a certain *disparity* between the lived-body and the objective body. This issue has already been touched upon while discussing localization: in the case of headache, for instance, the pain as experienced is not restricted to the objective boundaries of the head, but it rather surrounds our head like a halo and thus exceeds the limits of our skin. This disparity is a rule rather than an exception. It is not only when we are thematically aware of our body that the difference between the lived-body and the objective body manifests itself. When we walk, sit down, turn our head, touch something, for instance, our kinesthetic self-movement is primarily *constitutive of* the environment and not *constituted in* it. Being aware of the objective location of one's body is not the original manner of being bodily self-aware; as I have explained, the spatiality of our lived-body is different from the spatiality of an objective thing. In other words, there is an experiential gap between lived spatiality and objective spatiality—and correlatively, there is a certain disparity between the bodily space and the objective space.

Husserl's analyses of *practical incorporation* shed light on the disparity between the lived-body and the objective body. Husserl emphasizes that the lived-body itself is not a tool.[10] We are not only unable to throw away our body if it is not working right, but the constitution of tools already *presupposes* immediate bodily activity (*unmittelbare leibliche Wirken*), and to claim that the lived-body is originally a tool would thus lead to an infinite regress. Yet, our lived-body can incorporate tools and practical objectivities.[11]

In bodily experiences—and thereby fundamentally in all experiences—the limit between ourselves and the environment remains somewhat ambiguous. For example, it would be misguiding to state that the shirt that is pressed against our skin is experienced as *surrounding* us, and neither can it be said that we experience others as being located *inside* their clothes. In such descriptions, the borderline between body and environment is drawn on the skin, and the body is objectified as a system defined by this border—as a "bag of skin," as Bernet formulates, paraphrasing Lacan.[12] This is not the manner in which our bodies are originally given to us. Our shirt does not originally appear as something that surrounds us—it is not "out there," whereas we are "in here." Instead, our clothes are "substantially bound" (*fest verbundenen*) with our lived-body,[13] they are incorporated into our lived-body as the center of orientation: "It is no longer my sheer lived-body that is . . . in the zero-orientation . . . , but now it is my lived-body together with the 'conjoined' object."[14]

Moreover, incorporation is not restricted to what we are in immediate tactile contact with. "Each object that is not [the] lived-body can pass, through a certain bodily compartment, into the zero-orientation," whereby the object's manner of appearing changes remarkably: "The lived-body has acquired the object, that previously was there, on the right, left, near, far, in front of, and so on, in such a manner that it [i.e., the object] loses its thereness, suffers the loss of its mode of orientation, and enters into the zero-point of experiencing."[15] While sitting at a table and writing, we do not experience the table as being *under our arms*, just like the stick of a blind person does not originally appear to her as an oriented object, but rather as an extension of her perceiving body.[16] As Husserl puts it, the lived-body can be "expanded or "extended" (*erweitert*); equipments are "things that expand the lived-body" (*den Leib erweiternden Dinges*).[17] When riding a bicycle, for example, our body and the vehicle form a system, and this is not a mere empirical fact. Our body and the bicycle are *united* (*einigt*),[18] so that while riding a bike we can *experience* the imbalances of the whole system, and not merely those of our body. This is why Merleau-Ponty considers the "acquisition of a habit as a rearrangement and renewal of the corporeal schema": "to get used to a hat, a car or a stick is to be transplanted into them, or conversely, to incorporate them into the bulk of our own body."[19]

Husserl argues that even though the incorporated thing cannot provide new kinestheses, the kinestheses of the organ in a way spread into the incorporated thing:

> Herein lies the peculiarity that each joining of an external thing with a bodily member invests the external thing with the characteristic of an extension of the member. This extending does not result in the birth of a new "member," a new organ, insofar as it cannot attain new kinestheses. Instead, the grasping organ, given kinesthetically, expands in a corporeal manner; and so it from now on functions as an expanded organ. In consequence, the extension becomes part of what is experienced as the "organ"—and it is thereby that something like mediate touching (with a stick) and groping, pushing etc. becomes possible.[20]

That is to say, the incorporated object becomes part of our perceiving body; it becomes incorporated into our bodily experience of the environment. Merleau-Ponty follows Husserl and describes the experiential situation of a blind person in the following manner: "once the stick has become a familiar instrument, the world of feelable things recedes and now begins, not at the outer skin of the hand, but at the end of the stick."[21] The blind person primarily senses the street corner *with* the stick, and not the stick with her hand, just as when holding gloves we primarily sense the object with our gloved hands, and not primarily the gloves.

Moreover, while riding a bicycle, the environment as our horizon of movement appears as the correlate of the whole system, and not only of our body—and so, when starting to walk again after a long bike ride, the horizon of movement suddenly appears in a narrowed manner: it is as if a part of *ourselves* was missing. So too the environment appears in an alien manner for the blind person if her incorporated piece of equipment (the stick) is removed: what is missing is not a particular external thing, but something that had a constitutive role in her experience of things. In this sense, it is our bodily *self* that becomes expanded in incorporation, and it is our bodily self that feels incomplete when an incorporated thing is removed.

However, regardless of their intimate unity, there are obvious differences between the givenness of our lived-body and that of the incorporated thing. First of all, we can immediately move our body, whereas the incorporated thing—say, the bicycle or the stick—can be moved only *by* moving our body. Our *kinesthetic awareness* spreads into the incorporated thing, so that we can *sense the movement* of the whole functional system, which means that we experience the incorporated thing as a part of our body, rather than as an external object. Still, we cannot *immediately move* the incorporated thing: we are able to control its movement only mediately, namely by moving our lived-body—and hence the "mediacy" of touching, that we saw Husserl speaking about.[22] Secondly, we can sense the environment *with* a stick and with a bicycle, but only to a certain extent. Apparently, with the stick, the blind person can explore the surface structure and flexibility of external objects, but with the stick she cannot sense whether the object is hot or cold, for instance. Sensations are not properly localized in the incorporated thing. Likewise, while riding a bicycle, we sense the evenness or unevenness of the ground with the bike, but the sense of touch is not properly localized on the tire. And, obviously, if the bicycle breaks down, or if we blow a tire, we do not feel pain.

That is to say, we have no proper immediate kinesthetic sway over the incorporated thing, and neither does it provide us with a proper field of localization. Yet, as already argued, it is not the case that we primarily sense our shirt, gloves, stick, or bicycle, but rather the environment through them. The incorporated has "lost" its status as an oriented external thing, as we saw Husserl writing.[23] That is, we experience the sidewalk *with* the stick, the tennis ball *with* the tennis racket, or the ground and the whole environment *with* the bicycle, but the part of us *with which* we experience these is not an organ proper. Yet, it does not follow from this that the incorporated element is not an extension of ourselves, but a mere additional part of or annex to our objective body. If we argued in this manner, we would also have to accept that our nails are not part of ourselves since they provide no field of localization and since we can move them only by moving our fingers. The incorporated thing apparently pertains to *us*, but precisely as an *extension*, as something *incorporated*. Even if the incorporated "thing" cannot be sensed or moved immediately, it pertains to the manner in which we immediately move ourselves and experience the environment.

This can be further elaborated by connecting it to my previous analysis of the different senses of selfhood. Our kinesthetic and hyletic sensations are quasi-localized into the incorporated thing, and in this sense they are *our* sensations: it is precisely me who senses the shape of the ground with the stick. And, since the stick (no more than the shirt) is not given as an external object that we are touching, the incorporated thing accordingly counts as an extension of our minimal self. Yet, in the sense that we are unable to immediately move the incorporated thing, it cannot be said to be a matter of our purely active self-relation. Instead, the incorporated thing is a habitual extension of our lived-body, an element in our habitual manner of experiencing the environment. Incorporation, accordingly, is a matter of our habitual selfhood. Accordingly, *incorporation designates the extension of the embodied self in the minimal and habitual sense, but not in the active sense*. On the other hand, explicit activity, as already argued, is embedded in habituality, in operative intentionality, and in this sense the active self also becomes expanded through incorporation. Therefore, since the environment is the correlate of the embodied self, everything that is incorporated accordingly receives a *constitutive significance:* different incorporated equipments expand our manner of experiencing the environment.

Transcendental and Empirical Sense of Self

The dimension of hyletic and kinesthetic self-affectivity, or "lived-bodily interiority," is a constituting dimension; it amounts to the transcendental dimension of the lived-body, or the "transcendental body," as Henry would put it.[24] The immediate bodily self-affectivity is a condition of possibility for the constitution of the world, and it cannot therefore be treated as a worldly process. In this sense, the constituting, transcendental subjectivity is fundamentally embodied. However, what double sensation teaches us is precisely that our lived-body also has an exteriority that can be sensed—an exteriority that apparently pertains to the realm of the non-self or non-ego (*Nicht-Ich*).[25] The lived-body, in other words, is not only a constituting dimension but also something constituted.

THE BODILY SELF

In this light, it seems clear that the self and the lived-body cannot simply be identified. As Merleau-Ponty puts it, the body both "is and is not ourselves" (*il est nous et il n'est pas nous*).[26] Husserl likewise emphasizes, on the one hand, that "I am not in space like things are in space, and not in the manner that my lived-body is in space"; "the ego is something that has a spatial 'here' and 'there,' . . . [but is] not itself in space."[27] However, he nevertheless argues, on the other hand, that my lived-body and I myself not only "belong together inseparably" (*unabtrennbar einig*), but that "I am one with my lived-body, I am embodied."[28] That is, even though the lived-body and the self cannot simply be identified, it is nevertheless *not* the case that the self is disembodied—rather, the self is a "bodily swaying ego," an "Ego-body" (*Ichleib*), a "bodily ego" (*leibliche Ichlichkeit*).[29] In short, the self is embodied (*verkörpert, verleiblicht*).[30] This raises the question of whether the transcendentality of subjectivity is thus compromised. In order to reach a closure for the discussion on the embodied self, I will elaborate the transcendental and empirical aspects of selfhood.

Whereas the localization of hyletic sensings constitutes the primal exteriority of the lived-body, argues Husserl, the kinesthetic system originally pertains to the *constituting* self and "makes it a lived-body" (*ihn zum Leib macht*).[31] Since kinestheses pertain to the self, the localization of kinestheses implies the localization of selfhood. As Husserl argues, what is localized is "the kinesthetic system, along with everything subjective . . . , along with everything that pertains to the ownness of the ego."[32] That is to say, the transcendental ego does not contemplate the environment from a distance, but is localized, sensuously situated, in it.[33]

This apparently does not imply that selfhood would or could be reduced to its external appearance. As I have repeatedly emphasized, localization is not self-reification. Localization does not make the self into a mere thing, but instead points to the fact that subjectivity *is* its body— after all, it is only insofar as the body exists in a subjective manner that it can be localized.[34] Localization does not imply that the self becomes something empirical, and, hence, the transcendentality of the self is not compromised: localization does not make the experiential dimension "less transcendental."

However, the lived-body is not merely the transcendental body: it is not only the body that we *are*, but also something that we *have*. The sensed hand, for instance, is experienced as *something that senses* and its movement is perceived as a *performed* movement. Moreover, it is ourselves that we see in our external appearance: we see the hand as our hand and the movement as our movement, and in this sense, our (minimal, habitual and active) selfhood is localized. Our lived-bodily interiority is localized, and in double sensations our body is constituted as an external object. This does not mean that the body is constituted as a *mere* object. Rather, the body can appear as a spatial object only for a space-constituting body. Therefore, in double sensation, the lived-body is constituted, not as a mere object, but as an object-for-itself. Accordingly, the "exteriority" and "interiority" of the lived-body are not mutually exclusive features: the lived-body is both constituting and constituted. This also applies to potentialities of the self. "The lived-body as my lived-body, as the lived-body of my persisting ego, is what it is as embodying, in itself, my *persisting faculties*," so that, accordingly, "to a given egoic consciousness of faculties [i.e., to a given 'I can'] there corresponds a being-constantly-ready-as-an-organ [*das Als-Organ-ständing-bereit-Sein*]."[35]

The *lived*-body can never become a mere object, but, as something constituted, it cannot be simply identified with the constituting subject. In the sense of immediate kinesthetic-hyletic self-manifestation, the self *is* the lived-body, whereas in the sense that lived-bodily interiority is expressed in the movements of a body in the perceptual field, the self *has* a lived-body. In this sense, the embodied self is both transcendental and empirical—but, just as we can consciously *have* a body only insofar as we already *are* a body,[36] we can, more generally, constitute ourselves as empirical beings only insofar as this self-constitution is not a mere empirical process. That is to say, even if the self *has* an empirical "side," the transcendentality of the self is not compromised.

Reversibility does not change this issue. To be sure, in the objective sense, the body is *at the same time* both the touching and the touched—our hand, for instance, can touch our other hand that is touching the table. However, in the subjective sense the situation is different: even if we can touch our hand that is touching the table, we cannot touch our lived experience of touching, our lived-bodily interiority. As Henry puts it: "*As such, affectivity is never sensible.*"[37] Merleau-Ponty writes: "in so far as it sees or touches the world, my body can therefore be neither seen nor touched"; "the two hands are never simultaneously in the relationship of touched and touching to each other."[38] Accordingly, there is an experiential gap between the body *as* the field of sensing and the body that (partly) appears *in* the field of sensing. Yet, the moving hand appears as an organ of touching, and in this sense bodily exteriority appears as an expression of our lived-bodily interiority, of our embodied selfhood.

In the sense of double sensation and reversibility, the transcendental so to speak "descends"[39] into the empirical (i.e., the immediate bodily experiencing, in which the environment is intentionally constituted, is localized). However, the dimension of bodily self-manifestation is preserved (insofar as the body is precisely a *lived*-body), and the transcendental is not thereby *reduced* to the empirical—that is, it does not *become* or *turn into* something empirical. Even if the perceived body is throughout an empirical issue, the perceiving body, to whom the empirical body is given, is not. To treat the empirical as something ontologically self-sufficient contradicts the essential insight that, as something perceived, the empirical is constituted only in and through perceiving: treating the latter as something perceived therefore begs the question and leads to an infinite regress. The lived-body is originally both constituting and constituted—it is a "subject-object."[40] Empirical self-constitution does not exclude, but instead presupposes, transcendental self-constitution. Embodiment does not jeopardize transcendentality.

Having said that, it should be equally emphasized that empirical self-constitution is not a mere contingent annex of subjectivity, something that the latter could just as well do without. If our empirical self-awareness was to fail, we could not experience our kinesthetic self-movement as having anything to do with empirical reality, and thus we could not actively engage with our surroundings—not to mention with other selves. That is to say, both dimensions are essential for the embodied self: as embodied, the self is essentially both *constituting* and *constituted*, both transcendental and empirical. Insofar as we exist, we also experience ourselves in a world—not as mere things, but as manifestations of selfhood.

Summa summarum, the body that we *are* is experienced as the interiority *of* the perceivable body that we *have*, and likewise the body that we *have* is experienced as the exteriority of the body that we *are*. Accordingly, the lived-body serves as an intersection between the transcendental and the empirical, constituting and constituted, and to be aware of one's own lived-body is to be aware of something that is neither merely transcendent nor merely transcendental: the lived-body thus constitutes the primordial connection between experiential interiority and the sensible environment. However, even if the lived-body has an empirical "side" to it, immediate bodily self-awareness (lived-bodily interiority) must nevertheless be recognized as a transcendental issue.

Part 2

Intersubjectivity

4

A Priori Intersubjectivity

Until now, I have been investigating consciousness in relation to itself, and I have argued that self-awareness is fundamentally bodily self-awareness: subjectivity is embodied even before it becomes aware of having a body. What has been said up to now enables an investigation of the constitution of intersubjectivity and intersubjective self-constitution. In order to clarify the complex role that embodiment plays in the constitution of intersubjectivity, it is necessary to distinguish and investigate different types of intersubjectivity and explicate their internal relations. I will here argue that others are originally *implied* already in the horizonal structure of perception in the sense that the perceptual environment is, by principle reasons, always already constituted as being there for *anyone*. By interpreting the "anyone" as "any*body*," I accordingly present the initial form of intersubjectivity in terms of embodied intersubjectivity. I will argue that Husserl's theory of intersubjectivity involves such "a priori intersubjectivity" which is not *founded on* but rather *presupposed in* all our concrete experience of others.[1] This analysis further enables an examination of the constitution of what Husserl calls "social intersubjectivity." I will illustrate the centrality of embodiment in reciprocal intersubjective relations, clarify how a shared environment is constituted in and through empathy and social encounters, and explain how transcendental subjectivity constitutes itself as an individual person among others. Further, through social relations—that is to say, through reciprocal relations between contemporaries—subjectivity constitutes itself as a member of an intersubjective tradition, as a finite member in a historical continuum of life that goes on independently of the individual. In this "generative intersubjectivity" the world is constituted as the historical world.

The three forms of intersubjectivity that I will explicate in the following are, accordingly: a priori intersubjectivity, social intersubjectivity, and generative intersubjectivity. By elaborating the constitution of each of these, I will argue that generative intersubjectivity necessarily has a *genetic* constitution: tradition is something that subjectivity *enters into* in the course of its development. I will also argue that intersubjective self-constitution cannot replace subjective-primordial self-constitution, and nor can generative intersubjectivity replace a priori intersubjectivity.

This enables me to take a new point of view, later on, to what Husserl calls the "paradox of subjectivity."

I will begin by arguing that every perception structurally implies references to possible co-perceivers. This fundamental kind of intersubjectivity does not presuppose concrete experience of others. It will be argued, on the contrary, that concrete experience of others—in Husserlian terms: empathy—is established from the basis of an initial, a priori intersubjectivity.

The Horizonal Other as "Anybody"

Subjectivity is fundamentally open to the alien: it does not first have to find a way out of itself in order to be touched by what is other to it, but instead it is open to alterity from the start. The realization of this openness is the starting point for a phenomenological study of intersubjectivity. While discussing self-awareness in part 1, I explicated how subjectivity originally experiences itself *in* perceiving the environment. Here I will argue that intersubjectivity is revealed in a somewhat similar manner: namely, we are originally related to others already *in* perceiving the environment. Therefore, in order to disclose the a priori intersubjectivity, we need to deepen some of the insights regarding the constitution of the environment in perceptual experience.

As already argued, a sensory appearance that does not co-awaken the intentions of the other sense-spheres—for instance, a seen thing appearing as something that cannot be touched—is experienced as an illusion. Here we find a structural similarity between the intersensory and the intersubjective. Namely, to experience something as being experiencible for oneself exclusively is to experience it as an imaginary or illusory object, and not as a real, actually perceived thing. Moreover, if someone were to originally experience the environment as existing only for her, the possible existence of other perceivers for the same environment would be ruled out in advance. The elucidation of intersubjectivity will necessarily fall short if one sets off with a notion of an isolated subject.[2] In what sense, then, does intersubjectivity initially emerge? How does the environment originally appear? I will answer these phenomenological questions by explicating two essential structures of thing-constitution: temporality and anonymity.

The constitution of unitary things cannot presuppose—simultaneous or antecedent—experience of others. To claim the contrary would lead to a view that begs the question. Namely, in order to experience others, we have to perceive their unitary bodies—and, thus, constitute particular things—and if we assume that the constitution of unitary things already presupposes the experience of others, we would have to maintain that to experience others presupposes that we have already experienced others. Accordingly, the possibility of thing-constitution must precede and be independent of the possibility of the constitution of others—if this was not the case, others could never come to exist for us.

Perceived things are unities of possible appearances, and the horizon of possible appearances can never be perceptually exhausted. Perceived things are not fixed once and for all, their unity remains an anticipatory one.[3] As Husserl even puts it, the "thing itself is actually that which no one experiences as really seen, since it is always in motion."[4] Merleau-Ponty likewise emphasizes that the thing itself remains a "presumptive unity": things necessarily conceal parts of themselves, and perception is a "violent act" in the sense that it assumes more than what is actually given in it.[5] Despite the essential horizonality of perception, we nevertheless experience unitary things: to see a surface, a side, or an aspect, is to see a surface *of* something, a side *of* something, or an aspect *of* something. To put it otherwise, what is intended in a thing-perception is not only the presently visible parts of the thing, but the thing in its ideal multisensory fulfillment. This necessarily involves that the thing, as a unity of possible appearances, is experienced as something that could be perceived from other perspectives and with other senses as well—regardless of the fact that "the ipseity of the thing . . . is, of course, never reached."[6] By turning the thing around, by moving behind it, by moving nearer, farther, and so on, the thing is expected to manifest new aspects of itself. In Husserl's words, "The appearance refers, by virtue of its sense, to possibilities of fulfillment, to a continuous-unitary nexus of appearance, in which the sense would be accomplished in every respect, thus in which the determinations would come to 'complete' givenness."[7] Accordingly, to perceive a thing is to anticipate other possible perceptions of it: it is to "appresent" (*appresentieren*) or "co-present" (*mitpräsentieren, mitgegenwärtigen*) the hidden sides, as Husserl also puts it.[8]

Here we begin to approach the theme of intersubjectivity. Namely, the possible appearances—for example, the back side of a thing—are not experienced as being there only for *subsequent* perceptions: things are instead taken to have their back sides *at the moment*. That is to say, insofar as they are to count as appearances of the same temporally identical thing, the appresented appearances must be constituted as *simultaneous* with the appearance that is given at the moment. This can also be expressed by saying that retention, protention, and primal impression are not successive but simultaneous elements of the living present.

Even though protention amounts to anticipating what is to come, even though it reaches for the future, it does not designate an expectation of subsequent experience, but an element of the living present, and what it anticipates (for example, a hidden aspect of a perceived thing) is taken to exist simultaneously with what is immediately given.[9] Moreover, simultaneous appearances are not fused together inseparably, but there is instead an irreducible multiplicity of potential appearances in every perception. Perception of things therefore not only involves horizons of past and future but also, as Husserl argues, a horizon of simultaneity (*Horizont des "gleichzeitig Gewesen"*).[10] In other words, the thing is taken to *have* all its possible appearances at the same time.[11] The different "sides" of a thing are experienced as the potential appearances of the thing, and they are experienced as "being there" simultaneously—even if our own perceptions are limited to one perspective at a time. To sum up, even though things necessarily *appear* aspectually, we do not experience them as *existing* from one perspective at the time: the appresented appearances are simultaneous with the actually presented ones.

In this sense, perceived things necessarily transcend our experiences of them. There is indeed a certain "truth of solipsism" (*vérité du solipsisme*),[12] as Merleau-Ponty phrases it, in the sense that two subjects cannot perceive a thing from the same place at the same time. Yet, at the same time is should be emphasized that perception is never exhausted by what is immediately given. In the words of Husserl: "While the surface is immediately given, I mean more than it offers."[13] Merleau-Ponty likewise says that "the positing of the object . . . makes us go beyond the limits of our actual experience."[14] Moreover, in a certain sense, the positing of objects exceeds the limits of our *possibilities* as well. Namely, even though we can move around the thing and perceive it from many perspectives, *we ourselves* apparently cannot perceive the object from many locations *at the same time*—and yet the thing appears as something that simultaneously offers other appearances, even if these cannot, at the moment, be actually presented to us. Accordingly, it is as if the thing would appear from all sides simultaneously, as if it would be "seen from everywhere" (*vue de toutes parts*).[15] In the words of Husserl, "One subject cannot simultaneously experience two aspects of orthological multiplicity, but a multiplicity of aspects can exist simultaneously as spread to multiple subjectivities, and it must exist in this manner, insofar as we experience a simultaneously identical thing" (i.e., a thing with a multiplicity of simultaneous aspects).[16] In this sense, due to its horizonal structure, perception essentially involves the co-positing of an open infinity of possible co-perceivers: an "a priori intersubjectivity."[17] Husserl states this by writing the following: "Already each of my perceptions . . . constantly includes [others] . . . as co-subjects, as co-constituting."[18] As Zahavi clarifies, our intentional relation to the environment "a priori implies references to the intentions of others"; or, as Kojima puts it, "my intentionality is a priori mediated and penetrated by the intentionalities of others."[19] Things do not originally appear as being there *for me*, or as being there for me *and* for the other, but they appear as "being there for anyone" (*für jedermann daseinde*).[20]

Having said this, we should note right away that it would of course be wrong to claim that every perception is an experience of others. One should be careful not to confound the horizonal givenness of others with the actual presence of others as others.[21] Apparently, there is an obvious difference between simply perceiving a thing, on the one hand, and being aware of someone else perceiving it, on the other hand— and the latter is not a requisite for the former. The structurally implied, emptily co-posited others are not present as particular persons, they are not present as objects, not even as marginal objects, but as *anonymous co-perceivers*. Husserl stresses that this co-presence of others is original and requires no prior experience of others as such: others originally emerge as "*implicata* of my original intentional life" (*Implikaten meines originalen intentionales Lebens*).[22] In this sense, the horizonal structure of perception essentially implicates the possibility of simultaneous indetermined (*unbestimmt*) and anonymous co-perceivers.[23]

This peculiar sense of otherness should now be clarified. What does it mean to say that the implied co-perceivers remain *indeterminate* and *anonymous*? On the one hand, Husserl argues that no consciousness is thinkable without an ego, and that in the sphere of passivity, too, a primordial selfhood is necessarily constituted.[24] Yet, on the other hand, he sometimes says that passivity is "completely egoless" (*völlig ichlosen*).[25] It is noteworthy that Merleau-Ponty's texts manifest a similar terminological hesitation: at times Merleau-Ponty states that passive consciousness is "subjectless" (*sans sujet*) whereas he at the same time maintains that passive experiences are nevertheless *my* experiences.[26] Both Husserl and Merleau-Ponty clarify their views by arguing that passive subjectivity remains "anonymous" (*anonym, anonyme*).[27] Husserl explains that beneath active self-consciousness there is always a passive self-consciousness, but he emphasizes that the passive "I" is called an "I" only because the word is ambiguous. Husserl clarifies that it is not until reflection that the subject of perception is "named" (*benennt*) as "I," and that reflection is therefore necessarily operative when we use expressions such as "I perceive."[28] Prior to reflection, perception is not yet explicitly constituted as my own: it indeed happens to me and not to someone else, but this "me" ought to be interpreted in a *pre-personal sense*. Merleau-Ponty illustrates that whereas we can rightly say that "I understand the book I have read" or that "I decide to dedicate my life to mathematics," in the same sense of the word "I," we cannot say that "I perceive this apple," and he famously concludes: "if I wanted to render precisely the perceptive experience, I ought to say that *one* perceives in me, and not that I perceive."[29]

Yet all experiencing is characterized by pre-reflective self-awareness, and perception is no exception. In other words, despite anonymity, perception too has a "first-person" mode of givenness.[30] It should be noted here that the term "first-*person*" does not quite merit its name: even if experiences have an ipseity or mineness from the start, this ipseity remains anonymous and pre-personal.[31] Accordingly, when discussing "first-personal givenness," I am not referring to thematic self-presence of subjectivity, but to the pre-reflective mineness of experiencing.

Now, to come back to the theme of a priori intersubjectivity, the tacitly implied co-perceivers remain anonymous: they are not present as particular subjects, that could, say, be counted, enumerated, or named. For example, when hearing a piece of music in a café, other possible co-perceivers are implied in my experience in the sense that I experience the piece of music forthwith as being there for anyone to hear, but this is not the same as to say that the piece of music appears thematically as being heard by me, by my friend opposite to me, and by the seven other persons sitting in other tables in the café, and neither does it mean that I experience the piece of music as being heard by the indeterminate group of people who in fact are presently at the café. Of course, we can *subsequently* reflect upon our experience of the music and thereby also elaborate the subjects to whom the music is or was actually given, but this is not how the music is given prior to reflection. Rather, in a priori intersubjectivity, others remain *horizonal* and *anonymous:* before reflecting upon the issue, the things and the environment appear as something that could be perceived by "*anyone.*"

This is another way of saying that the perceived thing does not originally appear as being there for me exclusively, but rather as something that is simply *perceivable:* music is *audible*, an apple is *visible* and *tangible*. In this sense, as Merleau-Ponty daringly formulates, perceivability seems to dwell in the things themselves.[32] After all, visual experience does not *create* but *discloses* the visibility of the thing; perception does not make the thing into something perceivable, but unveils it as such. This is also the reason why we are never quite surprised when we realize that others see what we see and hear what we hear—instead, we are always surprised at first if the present others seem not to perceive what we do.

Merleau-Ponty further illustrates this matter by claiming that perception takes place in a setting or atmosphere of generality (*un milieu de généralité*).[33] Apparently, he is not thereby arguing for a collective consciousness, or for "subjectivity in general." Instead, the "generality" pertaining to perceptual experience is nothing but the generality of the embodied subjectivity, a "carnal generality" (*généralité charnelle*).[34] In the words of Bernhard Waldenfels, "the ego, appearing in the accusative or the dative, precedes the ego in the nominative. From the very beginning I am involved, but not under the title of a responsible author or agent."[35] For instance, while I am absorbed in marveling at a perfectly blue sky, the perception of the blue sky is not something I execute, but rather something that happens *to me* or *in me*. I may have deliberately turned my gaze toward the sky, but "the power of my will or consciousness stops there": like sleep in the night, sense perception emerges without my initiative.[36] My body, which is sensitive to colors, is "indicated" by the perceived environment, as we saw Sartre arguing, but what is thus indicated is not a unique and personal perceiver, but rather a *pre-personal* subject—a subject that is, in this sense, "like anyone." To be sure, the current sensuous experience is mine in the sense that it is lived through by me alone, and yet the sensuous capacities of my body are not mine alone. Correlatively, the *visibility* of the blue sky, as well as the *audibility* of music are something "generally" available, instead of being reserved for my own perceptions exclusively. Accordingly, even though perception is characterized by a first-person givenness, it is equally true that each perception takes place within an "atmosphere of generality."

Likewise, the otherness that is implicitly appresented in each of our perceptions is not the otherness of a particular personal subject, but the emptily intended alterity of other simultaneously possible perceptions of the perceived thing. In this sense, as Husserl puts it, the other is initially found in the "horizon."[37] The thing itself is the thing as if perceived from everywhere, and it is this infinity of appresented simultaneous other points of view that constitutes the open infinity of implied co-perceivers. Obviously, we do not experience the focal thing as being actually observed by its surroundings, which is another way of saying that, in a priori intersubjectivity, the appresented co-perceivers are not actual perceivers, but the merely *implied* and *emptily intended* other perceivers, projected originally by the generality of the embodied perceiver.

We ought to stress here, however, that even if not particularized or personified, the implied co-perceivers are nevertheless *specified* in a certain sense. Namely, perception structurally implies co-*perceivers*, which is another way of saying that the "anyone" in question must at least be "a subject of a lived-body."[38] Therefore, when discussing a priori intersubjectivity, instead of "any*one*," we should rather be talking of "any*body*." For instance, as visible and tangible, the perceived thing is a correlate of *organs of sight and grasping*, but as the thing does not originally appear as being there for oneself exclusively, this means that it does not appear as the correlate of *one's own hands and eyes* alone: it rather appears as being perceivable to anybody. Moreover, this anticipation is not limited to one sense sphere, but it reaches also to intersensory association—for instance, what I see is constituted as being not only visible but also tangible to anybody. Likewise, when seeing and touching my own hand, for instance, my body is constituted as perceivable—not only to me myself but to anybody. More generally, the environment originally appears as a general field of perception, and in this sense, as Husserl puts it, "nature is thus, always already, *nature for anyone.*"[39]

What accordingly is appresented in thing-perception is an open infinity of co-*perceivers:* the implied "anyone" is characterized by the capability of perception, and thus anyone is to be understood as embodied. In other words, things originally appear as being there for *anybody*, and therefore a priori intersubjectivity amounts to a "lived-bodily intersubjectivity" (*Intersubjektivität des Leibes*),[40] or "intercorporeity" (*intercorporéité*).[41] The perceived environment originally appears as being palpable, touchable, visible, audible, olfactory—not to *our* body exclusively, but to *anybody*. The reference to "horizontal others" is not a contingent and secondary reference, but one without which we could not constitute unitary things, just like the reference of a visually given object to its possible tactile givenness is not something contingent and secondary, but necessary for the constitution of the real thing as such. Intercorporeity refers to this fundamental entanglement (*Ineinander*) of the own and the alien in a unitary bodily experience: it refers to the manner in which the own and the alien are interwoven in a "functional community of one perception."[42]

As I hope to have shown by now, a thing that does not implicate the possibility of other simultaneous appearances—that is, a thing that does not appear in the mode of being there for anybody—is not constituted as a real, actually perceived thing. The reference to possible co-perceivers is needed for the constitution of perceived things as such, and a priori intersubjectivity is therefore a necessary structural feature of perception. This implies, moreover, that a priori intersubjectivity must also be operative in our concrete experiences of others. I will investigate this in the following.

The Bodily Foundations of Empathy

As a "structure of constitution" (*Struktur der Konstitution*), a priori intersubjectivity serves as the basis for further types of intersubjectivity.[43] The perceived environment originally appears as being there for anybody, and therefore it is not problematic for us to experience other perceivers *in concreto*. At the level of perception, to quote Merleau-Ponty, there is "no problem of the *alter ego* because it is not [explicitly] *I* who sees, not *he* who sees, because an anonymous visibility inhabits both of us."[44] An actual empathic experience *of* others cannot be made intelligible if the possibility of givenness to anybody is not given from the start. But how, exactly, does an empathic experience of others emerge?

The emergence of the self–other relation has a complex temporal structure that must be elaborated. I will argue in the following that the concrete other—the other as experienced in empathy—is necessarily constituted as a particular *example* of the potential "anybody." It should be noted already at this point that this claim by no means challenges the uniqueness of the other—as I see it, these are not two mutually exclusive alternatives. As I will argue, empathy does not amount to a "creating" but to a "disclosing accomplishment" (*enthüllendes Leisten*) in the sense that it reveals the underlying a priori intersubjectivity—which, as I argued above, thus serves as its condition of possibility.[45] Accordingly, my claim is that the concrete experience of others can be understood—although not exhausted—in terms of a *fulfillment* of a priori intersubjectivity.

However, I will start my exposition of the genesis of empathy with a brief diversion to certain developmental theories.[46] In his lecture course "The Child's Relations with Others" ("Les relations avec autrui chez l'enfant," 1950–51), Merleau-Ponty investigates the classical psychoanalytic view, taken for granted by many of the developmental theories of his time, in which the perception of others is made comprehensible by supposing a psychogenetic stage in which the child is not yet explicitly aware of the distinction between self and other.[47] According to this view, as portrayed by Merleau-Ponty, development begins with a phase "in which there is not one individual over against another, but rather an anonymous collectivity, an undifferentiated group-life," and it is followed by a phase in which, along with the gradual objectification of one's own body, the other is slowly segregated and constituted as a distinct individual—this process, Merleau-Ponty adds, "is never completely finished."[48] Accordingly, the idea is that the self and the other initially form a *system*, and what distinguishes different theories is their understanding of the status of self and other in this system. In his lecture course, Merleau-Ponty focuses on theories that introduce the initial system radically in terms of "symbiosis" or "syncretism," in terms of "indistinction between me and the other, a confusion at the core of a situation that is common to us both."[49] Focusing on Merleau-Ponty's discussion concerning this view will bring out important phenomenological aspects concerning the genetic constitution of the self–other relation.

For the newborn, Merleau-Ponty explicates, a full-fledged external perception is not yet possible: "In the earliest stage of the child's life, external perception is impossible for very simple reasons: visual and muscular control of the eyes are insufficient."[50] It is noteworthy that Husserl, too, opts for a view according to which empathy is not initially possible for newborn infants: "it is quite late in development that the infant comes to grasp space with spatial objects in it, and the mother as a particular body in the spatial field," and this grasping is necessarily required for empathy—while discussing this matter, Husserl even sometimes talks of a pre-empathic "continuity with the other" (*Kontinuität mit den Anderen*), while suggesting that this phenomenon resembles the temporal "fusion" (*Verschmelzung*) between the constituents (impression, retention, and protention) of a subjective living present.[51] In general, our sensibility is not initially fixed on the extra-bodily world. Instead, the child's first contact with the environment equals her immediate experience of her own body: "the body begins by being interoceptive."[52] Moreover, in the beginning "the interoceptive body functions as exteroceptive."[53] That is to say, before external perception is sufficiently developed, the experiential boundaries of our own body outline the limits of our "world": the frequent, constantly repeating bodily rhythms, such as heartbeat and "the whole respiratory apparatus, [give] the child a kind of experience of space."[54]

Following this line of thought, we may think accordingly that it is in the sense of interoception that *others*, too, come to exist for us in the first place. For instance, if the infant starts to cry when her caretaker lays her down and leaves the room, this allegedly does not mean that the infant would externally perceive a particular person leaving, but rather that she feels an unpleasant change in her bodily experience: rather than actually perceiving those who are there, the child "feels incomplete" when someone goes away.[55] The caretaker, the "maternal body,"[56] is not initially explicitly experienced as a distinct other, with whom the infant may establish a relationship of empathy, but rather as a *constituent* of the infant's familiar bodily atmosphere of warmth, scent, voice, movement, and rhythm of breathing—the sudden absence of which makes precisely the *interoceptive* system feel incomplete, thus constituting an experience of unfamiliarity, strangeness, or vulnerability. According to this view others are initially present as nuances in our interoception, as complementary moments of the bodily system, and no explicit differentiation between self and other occurs—the situation therefore somewhat resembles what I discussed in part 1 under the concept of incorporation.

However, if we would presuppose that, initially, there is no differentiation whatsoever between self and other, it would be impossible to understand and explain how differentiation could ever be established later on. Instead of undifferentiation, Husserl insists that we must recognize a fundamental and "insurmountable difference" (*unüberbrückbarer Unterschied*) between the self and the other.[57] To distinguish our own bodily movements and sensations from those of others is not something that we must first *learn:* after all, it is only "our own lived-body that is experienced in an immediate fashion, namely by the subject of embodiment," and hence there must be a difference—even if only an implicit one—between the self and the other(s) from the start.[58]

Merleau-Ponty himself also subscribes to this Husserlian view. While appraising Wallon, Guillaume, and other psychologists, Merleau-Ponty is not neglecting the subjectivity of pre-reflective consciousness. The fact that selfhood is not reflected upon, or thematized as such, does not mean that there *is* no selfhood. What pre-reflective consciousness lacks is not selfhood per se, but only a thematic or explicit selfhood: "the first *me* is . . . virtual or latent, i.e., unaware of itself in its absolute difference; consciousness of oneself as a unique individual, whose place can be taken by no one else, comes later and is not primitive."[59] That is to say, according to Merleau-Ponty, consciousness is not initially simply unaware of itself, but rather unaware of itself *in its absolute difference,* unaware of itself *as a unique individual.*[60] The distinction between oneself and others is deeply embedded in our incarnate being: one's own moving hand is given differently than the moving hand of the other, and despite the fact that this difference is not reflected upon and not thematic, it remains in the background and it also conditions our subsequent reflective awareness of ourselves as individual beings. As already argued, the anonymity of experiences does not abolish their essential "first-personal givenness": anonymous experiences are still lived experiences and, as such, they are subjective experiences.[61] In this sense, experiences are subjective already before they are thematically constituted as subjective. As Daniel Stern puts it, "first comes the formation of self and other, and only then is the sense of merger-like experiences possible."[62]

Our primordial embodied self-awareness not only originally *distinguishes* us from others; at the same time, it also *relates* us to others. Both Husserl and Merleau-Ponty argue that perception of others presupposes perception of one's own body, and Husserl specifies that this precedence must be understood not only in the static but also in the genetic-temporal sense.[63] Merleau-Ponty, too, writes: "the perception of one's own body is ahead of the recognition of the other, and consequently if the two comprise a system it is a system that becomes articulated in time."[64] That is to say, the self–other relationship originates along with the gradual development of bodily self-awareness. Before illustrating how the genetic constitution of the self–other relation goes hand in hand with bodily self-constitution, let me explicate this a bit further.

As we saw earlier, the intersensory environment and intersensory things are in a constant movement of becoming, and this emerging unity is the correlate of emergent bodily self-awareness. That is, experiences are temporal events: we experience not only the *result* of intersensory synthesis but also *the process of* emerging organization. Stern argues in detail that this process begins at least from birth: he introduces the notion of an "emergent sense of self," arguing that, in this minimal sense, infants must have *self-awareness* already at birth.[65] Husserl, too, argues that "for the infant, . . . the process of formation of constitutive unities is constantly in progress," although thereby "no surrounding world as world of things . . . is yet experienced": "in early childhood, the pre-giving perceptual field does not as yet contain anything that, with a mere look, could be explicated as a thing."[66] The emerging intersensory environment is the correlate of bodily experience—and the "consciousness of one's own body is incomplete at first and gradually becomes integrated; the corporeal schema becomes precise, restructured, and mature little by little."[67] Although infants immediately live through precisely their own hyletic-kinesthetic sensations, they do not initially grasp one externally sensed body as their own or as something that they can immediately move. Referring to William Stern, Merleau-Ponty explicates that "it is only between the third and the sixth month that a union occurs between the interoceptive and the exteroceptive domains. The different neural paths are not yet ready to function at birth. Myelinization, which makes their functioning possible, is late in taking place."[68] According to this view, it is not until the period from three to six months that an infant is able to experience the unity of her perceived body and the body as it is given in interoception—it is only around three or four months that the child starts to pay special attention to her own body parts, and around six months that the child begins to actively explore her own body, say, palpating her one hand with the other.[69] Merleau-Ponty further illustrates:

> Around the sixth month . . . the child is perplexed at the sight of a glove placed next to his hand. He is seen comparing the glove and his hand, looking attentively at the moving hand. With such experiments, the child comes to familiarize himself with the correspondence between the hand which touches and the hand which is touched, between the body as seen and the body as felt by interoception.[70]

> The first beginnings of an observation of others consist in fixations on *the parts of the body*. The child looks at the feet, the mouth, the hands;

> he does not look at the person. . . . The scrutiny of the parts of the other's body considerably enriches the perception that the child can have of his own body. We see him systematically relating to himself, after six months, the different things he has learned about the other's body from looking at him. Still at five months there is no fraternization with children of the same age. At six months, at last, the child looks the other child in the face, and one has the impression that here, for the first time, he is perceiving another.[71]

In short, it is only when our bodily self-awareness has developed to a certain point that we can perceive others as others.

Accordingly, the constitution of our concrete experience of others goes hand in hand with our bodily self-constitution. Even if a clear-cut difference between *myself* and the *other* has not yet occurred, there is initially a qualitative experiential difference between what is and what is not *mine*; from the start there is an experiential distinction between those perceived movements that are kinesthetically sensed, on the one hand, and those that are not accompanied by immediate kinesthetic sensation. The former are given as our own, whereas all movements lacking this immediate self-affection appear as alien.

Only one external body is actually given to us in immediate self-manifestation, namely our own body. And yet several external bodies are constituted for us as sensing and perceiving beings. How should we describe this "miracle of the other"?[72]

Apparently, the other's experiential interiority cannot be immediately present to us just like our own—otherwise the other's interiority would be part of our own interiority, and the other would actually be part of our self.[73] Husserl argues that "it is only through intertwining with exteriority that interiority can be objectively posited, i.e., that an *alter ego* can 'exist' for me."[74] Others can be experienced only "through" their perceived bodies. When seeing our *own* hand, we not only experience it as something that has other aspects, but as something that is also experienced from within; we *see* our hand as a *thing that senses*, we perceive its movements as *performed* movements. The alien body appears in a somewhat similar manner: the perceived body becomes "appresented" or "co-posited" as a *perceiving* body. The alien perceived body is not experienced by us from within, and this is precisely what makes it an *alien* body, and yet our perception of it involves appresentation, not only of other simultaneous perceptual appearances, but also of a simultaneous experiential interiority.

However, we do not perceive all moving bodies as living beings, and what has been said until now does not explain why we experience only *some* bodies as living bodies. Husserl emphasizes that "this is a peculiarity of empathy. My externally appearing corporeality is continuously bound to an impressional interiority (through association and apperception); and so, the fact that alien lived-bodily exteriority is of the same phenomenal type with my lived-body, accomplishes that a corresponding [lived-bodily] interiority is . . . intentionally co-posited."[75] The crucial question is the following: what exactly is the shared "phenomenal type" that motivates us to co-posit another lived-bodily interiority? The only body whose posture and movement is immediately given to us without external perception is our own body, we have a "privileged experiential consciousness" (*ausgezeichnetes Erfahrungsbewusstsein*)[76] only of our own interiority, and we are therefore unable to *compare* it with the alleged bodily interiority of others. One is thus tempted to argue that the other is gained by way of "reasoning by analogy." Let me briefly recapitulate this argument in order to distinguish it from the phenomenological argument.

The "reasoning by analogy" argument proceeds through the following inference: our own lived-body and the perceived alien body are similar externally, and since our *own* body is equipped with consciousness, the similar alien body must be likewise equipped with consciousness. This argument is problematic at least for two reasons. First, insofar as infants, as well as many animals, seem to discern the difference between living and lifeless beings, then how can we at the same time consider this difference as being established through an act of inference that requires developed intellectual abilities? Surely, we are not willing to assume that already around the age of six months children are able to carry out such acts of inference—to say nothing of animals. Second, we recognize, for example, cats, elephants, and crows as living beings even though they look very different from us, and even have organs we do not have (e.g., a tail, a proboscis, wings). That is, the argument from analogy cannot make intelligible our experiences of lived-bodies that are different from our own—moreover, we are unable to see our own eyes, for instance, and yet (from very early on) we recognize the other's look "in" her eyes.[77]

While arguing that other lived-bodies initially stand out as such due to their familiar "phenomenal type," Husserl is not referring to mere external similarity. He explicitly denies that our experience of others would involve inference, deduction, or reasoning, and separates the phenomenological account from the "reasoning from analogy" model.[78] The other moving body is paired, not with my body as an external thing, but with my *lived-body* as a whole. For instance, when I reach for something in front of me, I am not first and foremost aware of *either* the immediately sensed bodily interiority *or* the seen external movement of my hand, but rather of their union. My own moving hand stands out in my perceptual field in a manner that seems to defy causality; its movement appears as if not generated by an external cause, but by itself, which is another way of saying that the movement of one's own hand appears as an *expression of spontaneity*. The perceptual contrast between spontaneous movement and causal movement is what originally distinguishes living beings from lifeless beings—not our own body exclusively, but also other perceived bodies. That is to say, we originally recognize some bodies as organs of spontaneous movement,[79] and it is this peculiar *style* of the perceived movement, this harmonious "bearing" (*zusammenstimmenden "Gebaren"*), that motivates the associative pairing of our lived-bodies.[80]

Furthermore, motivated by such pairing, an "apperceptive transfer" (*apperzeptive Übertragung*) occurs, whereby our sensory-motor schema is tacitly "inserted" (*hineinstecken*), "transferred over" (*übertragen*), or "cast" (*entworfen*) into the perceived alien body.[81] As a result of this "analogical apperception," as Husserl also calls it, we perceive the hands of others as organs of grasping, the eyes of others as organs of seeing, and so on. Thus, in perceiving someone moving spontaneously, she is forthwith experienced as *another* spontaneous being, and the other is therefore constituted as my "analogon." Hence, in the sense of constitution, the alien lived-body is necessarily a *second* lived-body, whereas our lived-body serves as the *primordial* body.[82]

To summarize, the other is perceived as an other, as another perceiver, and, in this sense, the other is constituted as my analogon, as *similar* to me, but this experience—that is, empathy (*Einfühlung*)—includes no inferential leaps.[83] As Husserl argues, pairing is purely passive, it takes place "without further ado," it is "a primal form of that passive synthesis we designate as 'association.'"[84] As Husserl puts it, in empathy "there arises the peculiarity that, *while grasping her experiencing, I normally extend my experiencing, through her experiencing, into what she experiences.*"[85] The perceived bodies move and react in manners that are more or less similar to our manner of moving and reacting. Yet the apperceptive transfer of our body schema is only *more or less* successful. Correlatively, empathy comes in levels. For instance, humans, snakes, birds, apes, and insects all appear as spontaneously moving beings, and on this motivational basis, their style of movement is paired with ours, but at the same time it is true that our style of movement is closer to that of other human beings than to chimpanzees, and closer to that of chimpanzees than to that of birds or snakes. To be sure, insofar as the environment always already appears as being there for anybody, our empathic experience of others necessarily involves an initial, naive, expectation that others are able to experience the environment in a similar manner—this insight will be developed further in the last part of this work.

Empathy and A Priori Intersubjectivity

Let me now connect the idea of a priori intersubjectivity with my explication of empathy. I would want to suggest here that the empathically experienced body necessarily amounts to a *particular exemplar* of the anonymous anybody that is implicated in all our perceptions. As I have already illustrated, to see something as something graspable is to see it as a correlate of organs of grasping, but this is not limited to one's own organs exclusively: the thing originally appears to me as being graspable to *any* body. In this manner, shortly put, our concrete experience of others serves as a partial fulfillment of a priori intersubjectivity:[86] the actual other appears as somebody who can grasp the thing, and hence the appresented tactile appearances of the thing gain a properly intersubjective significance. Namely, the thing no longer appears merely as being there for *anybody*, but it now also appears as existing there for *this particular other*.[87] In empathy, the other is not given as a mere emptily intended possibility, but as another *actual* transcendental life, as an actual appresence (*reelle Appräsenz*)—as Husserl also phrases it, in empathy others are given as "other fulfilled immanent temporalities" (*anderen erfüllten immanenten Zeiten*).[88]

In this way, actual others, so to speak, come to fill in the slot that was a priori prepared for them by perception itself. And, accordingly, the appresentation pertaining to all our perceptions is thereby "fulfilled" in a peculiar manner. To be sure, this "fulfillment" does not mean that we gain an immediate access to the other's experiencing, but this by no means designates a failure of our experience of others. To approach the problem of intersubjectivity by demanding that others' experiences must be given in a manner like our own would be a misunderstanding. After all, it is precisely the "immediate inaccessibility" that makes our experience of others an experience of *others*. The empathically experienced lived-body appears precisely as an *alien* lived-body, as a lived-body that is *not our own*.

Empathy is, accordingly, not established ex nihilo: it presupposes, and refers back to, a priori intersubjectivity of perception, which, as already argued, amounts to a "certain lived-bodily intersubjectivity."[89] According to Husserl, only a bodily subject can experience others: "*empathy presupposes embodiment.*"[90] That is to say, the experience of others has a necessary motivational (genetic-constitutional) basis in the experience of one's own body: "It is only when I have constituted my lived-body that I can apperceive other lived-bodies as such. This apperception is necessarily a mediated one; insofar as it associates the alien body with a co-presentation of this body as experienced from within, it already requires an antecedent apperception of my lived-body."[91] This insight is adopted and developed further by Merleau-Ponty:

> Unless I learn, within myself, to recognize the junction of the *for itself* and the *in itself*, none of those mechanisms called other bodies will ever be able to come to life; unless I have an exterior, others have no interior.[92]

> My right hand was present at the advent of my left hand's active sense of touch. It is in no different fashion that the other's body becomes animate before me when I shake another man's hand or just look at him. In learning that my body is a "perceiving thing" . . . , I prepared myself for understanding that there are other *animalia* and possibly other men.[93]

That is to say, it is our self-relation that originally makes room for the other. As Zahavi nicely condenses, "it is the intra-subjective alterity that makes the experience of inter-subjective alterity possible."[94]

As bodily beings, we originally have an exteriority: our kinesthetic effort, as well as our perceiving more generally, is not closed off from the world, but present to us also in mediated ways. This is why it is not problematic for us to perceive other external bodies as other perceiving beings. In contrast, it is difficult *not* to perceive others in this manner. In everyday experience, no question arises whether a perceived body has a mind or not, no more than there arises the question of whether others can see only my *body* (the body that I have) or *me* as well. Merleau-Ponty suggests that the question rather ought to be posed in the following manner: "If my consciousness has a body, why should other bodies not 'have' consciousness?"[95] Alien bodies move spontaneously, and thus—without inference, deduction, simulation, or reasoning—they are experienced as others. To perceive others as mere physical things is based on an abstraction and is not original. Merleau-Ponty further illustrates that whereas the perception of other people and the intersubjective world is problematic for adults, children instead live in a world which they unhesitatingly believe to be accessible to all around them.[96] Empathy is fundamentally a bodily relation with the other: the presence of the other is originally a bodily presence, a presence "in flesh and blood" (*leibhaft*).[97] And insofar as intersubjective objectivity is established in and through concrete experiences of others, the first intersubjective object is the lived-body of the other.[98]

Before explicating the constitutive consequences of empathy, a brief summary should be offered. It should be clear by now that empathy (i.e., concrete experience of particular others as others) is not phenomenologically the most fundamental form of intersubjectivity.[99] Already before we perceive others, our perceptual consciousness is characterized by an a priori intersubjectivity.[100] That is to say, before others are constituted as others, they are already tacitly implied, emptily intended, in the form of appresentation, as co-perceivers that we implicitly take to be constituting the environment with us.[101] As Merleau-Ponty formulates it, "our perspectives merge into one another and we co-exist through a common world."[102]

This union of constituting co-subjectivity is what Husserl calls *transcendental intersubjectivity* (*transzendentale Intersubjektivität*): it does not refer to an awareness *of* others, to a particular intentional relation, but to an essential feature of intentionality itself.[103] As Husserl also puts it, concrete empathic experience of others is preceded by "transcendental 'empathy.'"[104] In the words of Waldenfels, the other "appears within myself and on my side before appearing in front of me."[105] Our experience of others as objects is preceded by "the *Urgemeinschaftung* of our intentional life, the *Ineinander* of the others in us,"[106] and the actual other is a particular exemplar of this anonymous anybody implicated in our perception. I believe this is what Husserl has in mind while claiming that before others become objects of our intentions they are appresented as co-constituting, "transcendental others" (*transzendentalen Anderen*), "pure others," or "others who as yet have no worldly sense."[107]

5

Reciprocity and Sociality

The transcendence of others is originally implied in the transcendence of the perceived environment, but this does not mean that empathy only reveals what was implicitly there already. To be sure, insofar as the other is taken to perceive the same environment, she is experienced as an exemplar of "anybody." Yet, on the other hand, the other is a *unique particular* who does not experience everything exactly in the manner that we do. Husserl emphasizes that the actually encountered other designates "a *completely new kind of transcendence*"—more precisely, "the first true transcendence" or transcendence "in a proper sense."[1] Namely, our concrete experiences of others have peculiar constitutive consequences. For one, empathy enables what Husserl calls *social intersubjectivity:*[2] *reciprocal* relations with singular others, relations where others are confronted face to face.[3] However, empathy is not, in itself, a *reciprocal* relation with others. To merely observe other sensing beings, for instance, to perceive them from a "third-person perspective," is a one-sided relation to others.[4] However, insofar as we understand that others can perceive us, we can establish a reciprocal relation with them. I will here employ the term "sociality" in the Husserlian sense, and thus take social relations to mean reciprocal intersubjective relations between *I* and *You*.[5] And, like Husserl, I am here interested in the *constitutive* dimension of social relations—or, as Husserl also puts it, in "transcendental sociality" (*transzendentalen Sozialität*).[6] I will set off by clarifying the sense in which embodiment serves as a condition of possibility for reciprocal relations, and argue that all communication—non-linguistic as well as linguistic communication—is based on bodily reciprocity.

Embodiment and Expressivity

Like other things, our own body, too, appears to us as something that can be seen, touched, and so on: our body, too, is constituted as being perceivable to *anybody*. Insofar as we perceive our body, the latter is constituted as also being present for possible co-perceivers. Moreover, as already argued, the perceived movement of one's own hand, for instance, appears as an externalization (*veräusserlichung*) of the immediately effected kinesthetic self-movement, as an "exteriority of interiority."[7] In other words, our perceived body appears as an *expression* (*Ausdruck, Kundgabe*) of our subjectivity: the lived-body amounts to the primordial field of expression (*erstes ursprüngliches Ausdrucksfeld*).[8] And, accordingly, to realize that others can perceive our body is to realize that others can perceive *us*.

Moreover, our own perceived bodily movements originally appear to us as intentional and meaningful, and likewise it is not difficult for us to perceive the movement of other bodies as intentional. For instance, in order to grasp something, we reach for it with our hands, and therefore, when seeing someone else's hands moving toward something, we perceive her *as reaching for something*. It is not the case that perceived body movements originally appear as meaningless physical distortions, and that they somehow indicate a subjectivity beyond them,[9] but it is rather the case that body movements originally appear *as actions, gestures, postures, and facial expressions*.[10] Of course, this does not mean that subjectivity can be simply identified with the *perceived* body. As already argued, we must distinguish between *having* a body and *being* a body: our perceived, external body is the body that we *have*, and it is an *expression* of our bodily holding-sway (most fundamentally: of our factical hyletic-kinesthetic self-affectivity).

Moreover, what is expressed in bodily movements, postures, and gestures—as well as in uttered and written words—is not only a fleeting act, but also the *motivational context* of the act. The motivational context may be unclear, but still it is necessarily given with the meaning of the expression. For instance, the movement of grasping a cup of coffee *in order to drink* is remarkably different from grasping a cup *in order to prevent a child from getting burned*. Accordingly, what is perceived is not only the bodily movement, but also its motivating context. If this context is completely obscure, the meaning of the perceived event remains unclear. For instance, we are most likely puzzled or perhaps even terrified if someone suddenly seems to laugh without any reason. Laughter is normally experienced as a reaction to a certain occurrence or event— for example, to something that somebody says. To laugh is to laugh in certain experienced circumstances. Therefore, what is expressed in our perceivable actions is not an isolated intentional act (to say nothing of "states of consciousness"), but structures that transcend the act: traits of character, and eventually, personality as a whole. I will return later on to this theme.

Insofar as we constitute ourselves as perceivable to anybody, we can express our wishes and desires to others[11]—and in this sense, bodily self-relation is a necessary condition for reciprocal intersubjective relations. It has been argued that reciprocal relations with others can be established already in the pre-linguistic phase.[12] For instance, if a child wants her father to hand her the toy she cannot reach herself, she looks at the toy and at the father in turn and acts as if trying to reach for the toy. Here the complex of the child's bodily movements serves as an expression of her desire for the toy: it is a primitive request the child addresses to her father. Insofar as the child sees the father as someone who sees her and is able to fulfill her will, this counts as a primitive form of communication: namely, the intention of reaching for the toy is a shareable experience.[13] Moreover, insofar as there can be pre-linguistic communication, there can also be pre-linguistic communities.[14]

Here one might want to argue that whereas the body obviously plays a major role in communication prior to the development of language, in verbal interaction the role of the body becomes less relevant. However, bodily reciprocity also has an important role in linguistic communication. To be sure, embodiment is obviously involved in the sense that written passages can be expressive only as seen (or touched, as it is with the blind), and uttered sentences only as heard, and in this sense, as Husserl puts it, words have a "linguistic body" (*Sprachleib*): "Each expression is the lived-body of a meaning."[15] Still, one might insist that in verbal communication the body no longer has the role that it has in gesticulation. After all, on a daily basis, we exchange e-mails with persons on the other side of the world, and this kind of communication does not seem to presuppose that we can perceive each other. However, even if the other may not be actually perceived, the possibility must remain that the other can be perceived. Namely, if we are to speak of a reciprocal relation with others, the receiver of our e-mail must necessarily be taken as someone who could be perceived and who could also perceive us. That is, it is only seemingly that language could make communication purely virtual. Mediated relations with others refer back to the possibility of an immediate bodily encounter, an experience of the other in "flesh and blood"—bodily interaction is a condition of possibility for mediated communication. In this sense, communication and language are based on the possibility of bodily interaction. As Husserl puts it, "the possibility of sociality, the possibility of comprehension, presupposes a certain lived-bodily intersubjectivity."[16] Moreover, since communities are established in and through communication, it can therefore also be argued that there can be no purely virtual communities: all communities are fundamentally bodily communities.

Social Intersubjectivity and Spatiotemporal Orientation

In and through reciprocal relations with others, the environment is constituted as shared. An experience of others is, as Carr writes, first of all an "encounter with another perspective upon the world, a perspective that is not my own,"[17] and our experience of others transforms our experience of the environment: the environment is constituted as a shared horizon. In the case of a priori intersubjectivity, one cannot yet speak of "sharing": the environment appears as being there for anyone, but not for anyone in particular—horizonal others are "any *alter egos* whatever" (*irgendwelche alter ego's*).[18] It is only through concrete experience of (particular) others that a shared environment is constituted. For example, if I desire an apple I see on the table, move toward it, and realize that another person is also reaching for it, the apple not merely appears anonymously as being there for anybody, but precisely as being there for me and for this particular other. This particular thing is present as a possible telos of the movement of the other: someone else is reaching for the apple that I was planning to grasp, and hence the apple appears not only neutrally as being there for anyone, but in a charged manner as being there for us with the practical intention of grasping. The situation might harbor a conflict of interests, which could not emerge insofar as the apple only appears as "being there for anybody." The apple can be constituted as a disputed object only from the basis of more fundamental sharedness: it appears as being there for us. And likewise, not only the spatial thing but also space itself is constituted as shared.

It should be emphasized that the fundamental being-for-anybody is not replaced by this being-for-us. While being constituted as an object for us, the thing is at the same time constituted as being perceiv*able* to anybody—although this horizonal otherness normally[19] remains unthematic and anonymous. Therefore, we are never fundamentally astonished if someone says, for instance, that she heard our conversation or saw us conversing, and this is because our words and gestures are not experienced as being audially and visually accessible only to the ones having the conversation. That is to say, singular others do not replace the "anyone," but are exemplars of the latter—and there is always the possibility that new perceivers show up. In this sense, the intercorporeal nature necessarily lies at the horizon of social world-constitution; the social environment is constituted within the horizon of the environment-for-anybody.[20]

As a particular realm within the environment-for-anybody, social space necessarily involves a certain *exclusion*, in the sense that a particular social space is not constituted for anybody, but only for the members of a respective social unit.[21] A home, for instance, is constituted as the social space of a family. To be sure, the furniture and other familiar things are perceivable to anybody, but they appear as familiar only to the members of the social unit. Likewise, a restaurant table that gathers a group of friends together is visible to anybody, but the meanings of this social space are shared only by those who are involved. In negative terms, a social space is not shared with those who do not participate in the social unit: for others, *our* home appears not as *their* home, but as an apartment, as someone else's home (like their apartment appears to us). A social space is the correlate of a particular social unit—and not of "anybody."

Moreover, the social space is oriented not according to the individual members of the social unit (community), but according to the unit itself. To be sure, the embodied subjectivity is still the zero-point of primordial orientation, but, on the other hand, others appear as other primordial zero-points of spatial orientation: the other in front of me is experienced as someone who sees me in front of her. Neither the self nor the other serves as the absolute center of orientation: the intersubjective space is rather oriented in relation to *us*.

Husserl argues that groups themselves have "a certain I-centering or an analogy thereof."[22] Let me illustrate this with an example. While conversing in a group of friends at a restaurant, I stand up, leave the table in order to get a drink from the bar, and then come back to the table. My experience in this case is not that the group of others is first "here," then "over there," and then "here" again, but precisely that I *leave* the table and *return* to it. Namely, the space of this social situation is not centered only around my body, but neither is it oriented first and foremost around the bodies of others; instead, I am "here" with friends, and this "here" is oriented not only in relation to me, but in relation to us: the social space is centered around the *group* sitting at the table—and it also serves as the center during the time that "one of us" temporarily leaves it. Social intersubjectivity is not destroyed by the temporary absence of a particular member.

According to Husserl, social units have a characteristic identity in a manner similar to the personal identity of a particular subjectivity.[23] Associations such as matrimony, family, friendship, church, or nation have concrete characteristics: Husserl attributes to social groups as such "faculties," a "character," "subjectivity," and "attitude," and qualifies them as "personalities of a higher order" (*Personalitäten höherer Ordnung*).[24] Moreover, social associations have, according to Husserl, "something like a corporeality" (*so etwas wie Leiblichkeit*), or even "a collective corporeality" (*kollektive Leiblichkeit*).[25] These characterizations are not purely metaphorical. The members of a group form a unity analogous to the singular organs of a unitary body. The individual players of a football team, for instance, are constituted for themselves as members in a larger whole, so that it would be misleading and one-sided to state that individual players on the home team won the match. The players of a team have a status somewhat similar to the status of organs of a body. For instance, it is not only my hand, but my whole body, that reaches for something: the movements of my hand are supported by the movements of my arms and shoulders, and these, again, are supported by my upper back, and so on. In a somewhat similar sense, communities as such have corporeal characteristics: they are oriented spatially. Instead of a *collection of individuals*, the "We" refers primarily to a concrete *whole*, to a personality of a higher order.[26] Yet, the corporeality of such a group is constituted by its individual members—although it is not reducible to them—and thus primordial orientation cannot be replaced by intersubjective orientation.[27]

Our temporal orientation, too, is transformed through social intersubjectivity. Husserl characterizes sociality as the *simultaneity* of subjective world-horizons,[28] meaning that, in social-communicative acts, an alien temporal horizon becomes intertwined with mine, so that I come to experience a shared time. For instance, if someone confronts me with a wish, the wished action comes to appear in my futural horizon. That is to say, this future in which I am wished to do something is not a determination of merely my own primordial temporality, but refers to the future of the other as well. The wish that motivates me from within is neither merely my own wish, nor is it merely an external wish of the other—it is rather *a wish of the other in me*.[29] In this manner, "what is my own, is impressed by others,"[30] and regardless of whether I intend to do what the other asks me to, the wish synchronizes our primordial temporal horizons. The other's wish has become one of my own motivations, an alien anticipatory horizon has become sedimented into my own, and I experience a shared time.[31]

More generally, by engaging in common tasks and projects, the future of subjectivity becomes intertwined with the future of others. In a common endeavor, like building a house, for instance, my acts and the acts of others have a shared goal. Together we aim to finish the house, and so our particular acts project a shared future.[32] Similarly, we have a shared past, a social past consolidated by shared experiences. The constitution of the social time also involves exclusion: past experiences or futural goals are not shared with anyone, but only with the members of a particular social unit.

In this manner, the living present is reoriented in and through social intersubjectivity. Social temporality is not oriented according to the subjective living present: in the subjective sense, our movements always take place "now," but in the social sense our actions can also be late or come in advance. The example of dancing illuminates this duality: if we are skilled, our bodily movements are in harmony with the movements of the other, continuing and anticipating them, and likewise the movements of the other are experienced as continuing and anticipating our own movements, and in this sense the self and the other are intertwined into one temporal act of dancing. If our movements come late, or are too fast, the unity of our intertwined movements is disturbed, but if we are well in sync, our subjective past and future are easily and seamlessly intertwined with those of the other, and we almost, so to speak, form one organism in which our bodies are two organs.

Social meanings thus transcend the meaning-giving possibilities of the particular subject. Not only do some meanings have their factual origin in the acts of particular others, but social objects originate—and refer back to—the meaning-giving powers of social units themselves. A shared home is a social environment par excellence: its meaning is constituted not by the self and the other as two individuals (in this sense, social units do not *consist in* particular subjects), but by the self and the other as a social unit, as an association of persons (*Personenverband*),[33] as a We-subjectivity. A shared home, for instance, is *our* home, and as such it transcends the meaning-giving abilities of the individual.

Here we can recognize that *a priori intersubjectivity* is both a static and a genetic concept. On the one hand, it amounts to a necessary structural feature of perception, but on the other hand, the sense "anybody" is *sedimented* in time.[34] "Horizonal others" are still intended in an empty manner, but this manner of intending is sedimented: the horizonal others, so to speak, gain features of the members of the respective social community, so that we pre-reflectively expect things to be perceivable to possible others precisely in their social meaning. In this manner, through our mundane encounter with others, the manner in which we tacitly co-posit others in our perceptions is transformed. In other words, horizonal others are tacitly taken as co-members of our social community. Nevertheless, "anybody" in its primordial sense is not thereby *replaced*. Instead, the social environment is constituted in the horizon of the environment for anybody—and as we participate in many social units, there is, correlatively, a multiplicity of social environments that partly include and partly intersect with one another.[35]

Personal Self-Constitution

Sociality also alters the manner in which we constitute ourselves. As already argued, perception is originally given in a "first-personal" manner, but not thematically as my perception, which is another way of saying that the subjectivity of perception remains anonymous. Husserl explains that it is not until we actually confront others that we can thematically constitute ourselves *as persons*[36]—and in this thematic sense, personal self-constitution has its origin in social relations. However, the Husserlian account differs, for instance, from the Hegelian account in the sense that, in Husserl's view, sociality does not *give rise* to personal individuation, but rather *discloses* individual subjectivity as such. In the phenomenological sense, independent of others, the constituting subjectivity is sedimented with habitualities and inclinations, although it is only in and through social relations that subjectivity can thematically constitute itself as having these "personal" features. On the other hand, social relations not *only* disclose what was there already, so to speak, but by interacting with others, subjectivity also gains *new* features and adopts intersubjective habitualities. This will be clarified in the following.

Husserl argues that to experience oneself *as an individual* is to experience oneself *as one among many*, and that, in this sense, "self-consciousness and consciousness of others are inseparable."[37] Accordingly, the notion of "I" is relative insofar as "the I requires the Thou, the We, the other," and therefore, "living as an ego . . . I am necessarily an 'I' that has its 'thou,' its 'we,' its 'you'—the 'I' of personal pronouns."[38] In his manuscripts, Husserl summarizes the phenomenological view:

> [The primordial subject], the center of . . . affections and actions, . . . becomes an ego, and therewith gains a *personal* "self-awareness," becomes a *personal subject*, in relations between I and Thou, that is, when it takes part in a community.[39]

> *The origin of personality* lies in empathy and in *social acts* which are rooted in the latter. For gaining a personality it is not enough that the subject is aware of herself as the center of her acts: personality is rather constituted only when the subject establishes social relations with others.[40]

In other words, personal individuality can be realized—that is, thematically constituted—only in and through reciprocal relations with others.[41]

However, as already mentioned, the concrete experience of others does not *create* personhood, but *discloses* subjectivity for itself as an individual person. Before, and independent of, experiencing others as others, subjectivity is not only individuated, but it also has certain sedimented habitualities. Personhood is not merely something *empirical*, but also a transcendental issue—so that, as already noted in the introduction, one can also speak of "transcendental persons" and "transcendental personality."[42] Husserl talks about the "modes of behavior" of the *pure ego*, emphasizing that "this concept . . . is totally different than the one which applies to the sphere of reality."[43] He clarifies: "Each pure ego . . . has its determinately specific modes of relating to its surrounding world, its *determinate way* of letting itself be motivated by it in active and passive kinds of comportment; and everyone who has developed to maturity apprehends himself in that way, is aware of himself as a person."[44] That is, in Husserlian phenomenology, personality resides in the habitual structure of motivations; it resides in the *habitual manner* in which we are motivated in our experiences.

Both Husserl and Merleau-Ponty compare the temporal unity of person—"personal identity"—with the unity of a melody and rhythm.[45] Melody is not a collection of separate sounds of some preestablished objective whole; rather, it is a living unity, a temporal complex of sounds, a unity that unfolds in time. The identity of a melody resides in the way the sounds are attached to each other, in the way the musical expression proceeds or develops. Personal identity is comparable to the unity of a melody in that personality too transcends its singular expressions: personality resides in the way that subjective experiences are temporally interconnected, in the way acts motivate each other, in the way expression proceeds. Moreover, when comparing personality and melody, Husserl and Merleau-Ponty both employ the notion of "style" (*Stil, style*). As Husserl puts it, a person has "his style of life in affection and action with regard to the way he has of being motivated by such and such circumstances."[46] Merleau-Ponty similarly specifies: "a style is a certain manner of dealing with situations, which I identify or understand in an individual or in a writer . . . even though I may be quite unable to define it."[47] In other words, the concept of style here refers to a personal manner of being, namely, to an individual way of relating to the world, to others, and to oneself.

Accordingly, personality does not *consist* of particular experiences or singular expressions. However, as already said, what is expressed in our bodily movements, for instance, is not merely a fleeting kinesthetic self-affection, or a "state of consciousness," but also its motivational context. According to Husserl, the lived-body serves as expression for a "person and his spiritual activity" (*Person und ihrem geistigen Verhalten*):[48] "facial expressions, . . . gestures, and the individual's intonation, express the spiritual life of persons, their thinking, feeling, desiring, [and finally] their [whole] individual spiritual character."[49] What is expressed in laughter, for instance, is not only the present state of amusement, but also a sense of humor, and yet the sense of humor cannot be reduced to the act of laughing. More generally, personality on the whole appears as something that goes through and permeates the singular expressions, gestures, utterances, and intonations of the subject, but is not reducible to them.

Experiences are not isolated, but constitute a unitary motivational structure, and personality resides in the *manner* in which singular experiences are interconnected. Experiences occur in a temporal horizon, and so through a single act we are presented with the way this particular act is attached to other acts. The passing notes of a melody carry in themselves an implicit reference to notes just passed, and they tacitly anticipate those to come, so that every particular moment of the melody presents us with a recognizable *direction, mood,* and *shape* of the melodic flow, and, in a somewhat similar fashion, as Merleau-Ponty formulates, a person is "wholly present in every one of its manifestations."[50] That is, although expressions do not exhaust personality, they nevertheless are expressions *of* personality.

However, one should refrain from considering personality as something complete or fixed. Our ways of acting and reacting are indeed, to a certain extent, outlined in advance, but we are not compelled to yield to our habitual motivations: we can also modify and resist[51] them, and by doing so we come to *reshape* our preestablished rhythm of comportment—and hence ourselves as persons. Nevertheless, a person remains identical, even if "the 'experiences' . . . of the person grow and the domain of his pre-givennesses changes as a consequence."[52] As Husserl also phrases it: "personal life . . . is a constant becoming through a constant intentionality of development. What becomes, in this life, is the person himself. His being is forever becoming."[53] Accordingly, personality reveals itself not only in the way we are motivated by our established habitualities, but also in the way we institute new ones. Personal identity is therefore not an unchangeable unity, but rather *a unitary way of changing*. Husserl formulates this idea in the following manner:

> In its conscious relations to the environment . . . , the [pure] ego maintains a peculiar individual style. The ego-pole does not merely have its changing sediments [that is, habitualities]; rather, it has a unity which permeates the process of sedimentation and which is constituted according to this style. [In other words,] the ego has its individuality, its whole individual character, which permeates every decision and determination as something identical. . . . [And therefore] these decisions express traits of character and, eventually, individuality on the whole.[54]

That is to say, even if the subject appropriates and develops new habitualities, the occurring transformations usually remain intrapersonal changes, changes that are typical or characteristic of this person: "Style is something permanent, at least relatively so in the various stages of life, [it is] something that normally [also] changes in a characteristic way, so that [even throughout the changes] . . . a unitary style manifests itself."[55] That is, even if some habitualities change, some remain, and hence personality persists through time like a melodic flow. As Husserl argues, personal identity resides in the "rhythm" of experiencing,[56] in the transcendental style that concordantly pervades the subject's modes of comportment. In short: "The Ego is a unitary *person* . . . insofar as it possesses a certain pervasive unitary style."[57]

As an infinitely complex motivational structure, personality is absolutely *unique*. Husserl argues: "personal life manifests typicality, and each personal life manifests a different one."[58] Yet, on the other hand, persons necessarily have general typicalities as well. Even though others cannot have my personality—even if they can never experience "what it is like" to be me—I do, on the other hand, "share" certain aspects of my personality with others. After all, smiling and laughing is not only *my* personal way of expressing amusement; others "employ" similar gestures as well when they are amused—and, to be sure, if we expressed our amusement in a "purely unique" manner we would not be understood.

Personality, accordingly, involves a certain generality. Yet, general and individual typicalities have a different constitutional status. Individual type is a *variation* or a *modification* of a general type.[59] For instance, my peculiar way of moving is individual, but it is nevertheless a modification of a general style of moving (e.g., with two feet, in an upright posture, in a masculine manner, and so on). General features do not annihilate personal identity, but are rather required for it.[60] Our personal style is shaped by the ways in which we appropriate, modify, and "particularize" (*besondern*) general typicalities.[61] In other words, we become individuals not by getting rid of the general features of our existence, but by appropriating these general features in a unique personal manner. Accordingly, the paradox of personality is that as individuals we are "made out of" suprasubjective features and yet are absolutely unique. I am the only one who *is* this person, and my life can be immediately lived by me alone; and yet my personal style of relating to myself, to others, and to the environment appears a modification of intersubjective features—and it is indeed true that, in certain regards, someone else can understand me better than I myself.

By entering into reciprocal relations with others, subjectivity thus constitutes itself as an individual person, as one among many, as an "I" within a "We." Moreover, as such, the subject constitutes herself in a world that not only exceeds her meaning-giving abilities, but her whole existence. Until now, I have been discussing only social associations that are established in our encounter with others. However, many social units have already been established before we enter into them and become their members.[62] This "entering into" involves appropriation of intersubjective norms. Namely, when social meaning is already established, one becomes a member of the respective community by adjusting oneself to the intersubjective manners of being. Moreover, the community predates us, and before we start contemplating it, we have already habituated ourselves to many of its respective norms, meanings, and language. This brings forward the themes of *historicity and generativity*.

6

Historicity and Generativity

Until now I have been discussing two types of intersubjectivity: *a priori intersubjectivity*, originally implied by the horizon-structure of perceptual consciousness, and *social intersubjectivity*, a reciprocal empathic experience of others—and I have argued that both, in different senses, presuppose embodiment.

Moreover, I argued that through our reciprocal interaction with others, a priori intersubjectivity is sedimented. Namely, through sociality, the intersubjective world gradually becomes familiar, and the meaning of the co-constituting "anybody" gains special features. The world originally appears as being there for anybody, but the sense of "anybody" is sedimented in time. In respect to the social environment, I argued, the co-constituting others are not anybody whatsoever, but anybody in the respective social community: co-members. That is to say, in social world-constitution, "anybody" is a restricted notion. Yet, due to the essential openness[1] of intersubjectivity, the environment at the same time still appears as being *perceivable* to anybody. In this sense, the social world is constituted against the horizon of the perceptual world—and this world of bodily experience is always present in our experiences of the familiar world of socially shared meanings.

Husserl's concept of familiarity (*Vertrautheit*) has a special sense that refers to *intersubjective habituality*, to an intersubjectively normal[2] manner of experiencing the environment.[3] The correlate of intersubjective familiarity is what Husserl calls a "homeworld" (*Heimwelt*): thus understood, the homeworld is our intersubjectively habituated environment, our "common, already familiar world" (*eine gemeinsame schon vertraute Welt*).[4] Husserl argues that the lifeworld of an alien culture cannot be made comprehensible otherwise than by making it one's homeworld; the homeworld is accessible only to those who live in it, to those *whose* homeworld it is.[5] In other words, a homeworld cannot be familiar "from the outside." An alien lifeworld is not valid for us as a homeworld. Nevertheless, alien homeworlds are given to us and, in this sense, are *accessible in their inaccessibility*.[6] like someone else's apartment appears to us as someone else's home, an alien lifeworld appears to us as an alienworld (*Fremdwelt*), as an alien homeworld. In this sense, we can share an environment perceptually, empathically, and even socially without sharing an intersubjectively familiar world. In encountering persons from an alien culture, we may, for instance, recognize their religious rituals as religious rituals, and even communicate with them, without sharing an experience of the cultural meaning of the ritual.[7] Regardless of the empathic and reciprocal relation, we might be "worlds apart" in the sense that we do not share the presently appearing environment in its intersubjective-historical saturation.

With the concepts of homeworld and alienworld, we are introduced to a third type of intersubjectivity: in addition to *a priori intersubjectivity* and *social intersubjectivity*, we now distinguish what Husserl calls *generative intersubjectivity* (*die generative Intersubjektivität*).[8] As already stated above, social intersubjectivity is not abolished by the temporary absence of a particular member: in order to pertain to the same social unit, two subjects do not have to experience each other all the time, but the possibility of an actual reciprocal encounter is nevertheless presupposed. However, with past persons and persons to come we cannot establish reciprocal relations, and hence these others are not members of our social intersubjectivity, and yet they can be members of our tradition, of our historical community—and, precisely as co-members, they are not just anybody either. Hence intersubjectivity is not exhausted by "a priori intersubjectivity" and "social intersubjectivity."

What is now needed is an explication of this generative intersubjectivity. In the following, I will illuminate how the embodied subjectivity constitutes itself as a member of historical traditions, and elaborate the constitutive consequences of this self-constitution. This examination will pave the way for raising the important question concerning the relation between the primordial and the intersubjective self-constitution of the embodied subjectivity.

Genetic Constitution of Historical Self-Awareness

Historical communities preexist the individual subject who enters into them. Here one must be careful not to slide into the naive natural attitude by declaring that a subject is simply born into a community. To be sure, others are "mundanely primary"[9] and in the objective sense we "belonged" to a community already as fetuses—and, in this sense, being born means "being born *into*" (*Hineingeborenwerden*), and to die is to "die *out*" (*Heraussterben*).[10] However, as Carr notes, we must distinguish between objective membership and membership by participation.[11] Consciousness of historical meanings, practices, and norms is not something innate, or established in the instant of birth. In the phenomenological sense, membership in a historical community is established in a temporal process of *appropriation* (*übernehmen, aufnehmen, zueignen*). It is a series of experiences whereby the subject gradually inhabits and familiarizes the intersubjective space of meanings, and thus makes it her *own*.[12] In the words of Steinbock: "Appropriation is a form of sense constitution that takes up pregiven sense as stemming from a homeworld and its unique tradition."[13] As appropriated, intersubjective historical norms and meaning-structures come to motivate subjectivity from within. However, appropriation is a temporal process; we become a member of a community by *entering into* it.[14] If historical intersubjective meanings are to mean anything for subjectivity, and if traditional norms are to gain their normativity, these meanings and norms must first be constituted in the life of subjectivity: they must have a *genetic constitution*.[15] Let me now examine this *genesis of historicity*.

For the initial sphere of familiarity, "family" is an apt name.[16] As was clarified earlier, regardless of the fundamental mineness of all experiencing, infants may not be thematically and explicitly aware of others as other distinct subjects—caretakers rather appear as constitutive elements of an atmosphere of protection, warmth, nurture, nutrition, care, and so on. However, the caretaker is not *anybody* either: a scent, way of holding, tone of voice, rhythm of walking, breathing, the perceptual figure, and so on constitute the infant's original sphere of *familiarity*—even if it is only gradually that these different elements of familiarity are thematically identified as properties of distinct persons. Accordingly, animals—pets, domestic animals (*Haustiere, Tiere der Heimwelt*)—can also serve as constitutive elements of familiarity, and in this sense animals can be members of the original "family."[17]

An important constitutive element of familiarity is "predictability." By habituating certain patterns, the subject comes to expect that *if* this-and-this happens *then* this-and-this should occur—and insofar as the subject's expectations are not constantly disappointed, a certain "everydayness" (*Alltäglichkeit*) is formed, a mode of experiencing in which everything unfolds, more or less, as it is expected to.[18] For instance, to put it slightly mechanically, if the infant is taken into the arms every time she cries, this pattern becomes familiar to her, whereby crying is expected to result in being taken into a caregiver's arms. If the expectation is disappointed—if things do not go as they "normally" do—the subject finds herself in an unfamiliar situation. Experiences of something unfamiliar are constitutively significant: when expectations are not fulfilled, the subject does not simply remain in a state of perplexity, but a revision of expectations occurs, and thereby a transformation in the subject's experience of the environment.

Accordingly, homeworld is a dynamic concept. In the course of time, our sphere of familiarity is modified: when our experiences grow and when we gain new abilities, our environment becomes expanded (*erweitert*), and as our abilities diminish, our environment is narrowed.[19] Correlatively, the sense of "We" is expanded.[20] The expanding of the "We" can happen in two ways. On the one hand, what is not originally included in our sphere of familiarity can become part of it, thus effecting a modification of the familiar patterns. On the other hand, the sphere of familiarity can also be expanded in the sense that a *new* "We" is constituted alongside the old "We." For instance, whereas younger siblings become part of the sphere of the family and alter *its* expected patterns, friends constitute another and partly separate sphere of familiarity that has its own patterns, norms, and meanings. However, family and friends are not completely disconnected spheres of familiarity—provided that we are not dealing with a pathological case of dissociation, for instance. That is to say, the subject normally constitutes herself as a member of both "communities," and this implies that together they constitute a larger community that includes the two minor ones. In this manner, in the course of our experiences, our sphere of familiarity—our "We"—is expanded. The subject constitutes herself as a member of a family, of the "close ones," of a city, of a nation, of a cultural region, and so on—and, *ultimately*, by saying "we," we refer to humanity. As Husserl puts it, "the universal 'We' is a generatively . . . closed nexus of human beings."[21]

In this manner, the "We" is genetically constituted in the sedimentation of a priori intersubjectivity. The horizontal others that are constitutively implied, or "co-posited," in our experiences of the human world are not just any perceiving beings, but human beings: "anyone" (*jedermann*) is a name for a normal human being.[22] On the other hand, in our experiences of the cultural world, horizontally implied others are co-members of our tradition, and in this sense "'anyone' does not mean all 'human beings.' Each closed community of life has its normality."[23] In generative intersubjectivity, the co-constituting others are our "home-comrades" (*Heimgenossen*),[24] namely, those past, present, and future subjects with whom we share an intersubjective familiarity, and—correlatively—a homeworld.

Our ways of moving, gesticulating, and speaking are rooted in these communities and traditions. I argued above that personal identity resides in transcendental style, and that an individual way of being (related to the world, to others, and to ourselves) is a unique combination of more "general" typicalities. Let me now specify: the *generality* of personal features lies in their *historicity*.[25] Our personal features are passed on over generations, they are appropriated and, in this active sense, "inherited" from our predecessors—and insofar as we constitute ourselves as persons, we are already involved "in the generative nexus, in the concatenation and branching of generations."[26] Although in this process we modify these features and thus make them unique, they are nevertheless initially generatively handed down—they are *more or less* traditional. Our unique personal ways of moving, our peculiar gestures and postures, are individual modifications of manners of moving characteristic to our kin, nation, class, age, profession, culture, and so on—eventually to humanity.[27] As Husserl notes, "The human being lives in the norm, insofar as he becomes aware of it as norm. The normal style of life as the style of communal life is not only a fact for her, but an obligation of being."[28] In this sense, the historical intersubjectivity *normatively regulates* our ways of being. We are "raised into the form of the tradition" (*in die Form der Tradition hineinerzogen*),[29] and this form tacitly serves as the guideline of how one is expected to act and behave in particular situations, but also of how one *ought to be experiencing* the world, others, and oneself.

By appropriating and modifying historical ways of moving, perceiving, acting, thinking, and so on, the subject comes to carry the tradition within her being.[30] Even if some ways of movement and expression, for instance, can be inborn, "natural," or "instinctual," our way of moving and expressing is nevertheless modified in the process of appropriation.[31] What we appropriate is the "style" (*Stil*) of the tradition, which, according to Husserl, makes up the latter's "historical substance" (*historische Substanz*), and as appropriated, historicity is found within subjectivity.[32] As Husserl puts it, transcendental subjectivity understands *itself* as transcendental intersubjectivity:[33] "Thus transcendental subjectivity expands into intersubjectivity, or rather, more precisely, transcendental subjectivity does not expand, but only understands itself better. It understands itself as a primordial monad that *intentionally* carries within itself other monads."[34] By becoming aware of ourselves as bearers of traditional manners of being, we constitute ourselves as representatives of a historical tradition. And, in this manner, we constitute ourselves as historical beings, as beings in intersubjective historicity.[35]

Linguistic Intersubjectivity

Social intersubjectivity presupposes empathy and (at least potential) reciprocity, and it is therefore limited to *contemporary* subjects. However, intersubjectivity is also diachronical; the "We" reaches over generations. In generative intersubjectivity, *language* plays a central role. Husserl argues that humanity is necessarily a linguistic community in the sense that the constitution of a "human homeworld" is "fundamentally regulated [*bestimmt*] by language":[36] "Civilization is, for every human being whose we-horizon it is, a community of those who can reciprocally express themselves, normally, in a fully understandable fashion; and within this community anyone can talk about what is within the surrounding world of his civilization as objectively existing."[37] That is to say, the intersubjective world is a horizon that we not only can perceive together, but about which we can discuss, and hence the intersubjective world is the realm of linguistic expressibility. Let me investigate this more closely.

Empathy without communication—pre-social or "one-sided empathy" (*einseitiger Einfühlung*), as Husserl calls it—does not establish a community in the proper sense.[38] In one-sided empathy we could experience the other as perceiving the same things that we do, but without communication this experience would, according to Husserl, remain "an inauthentic experience, empty understanding of others and their experiential situation."[39] That is to say, without reciprocity and communication, intersubjectivity is not yet an *inter*-subjectivity: in the constitution of the intersubjective world, Husserl argues, we must, first of all, be "vitally at one with the other person [*mit dem Anderen Lebendig-einig-sein*] in the intuitive understanding of his experiencing, his life-situation, his activity, etc."[40] Moreover, Husserl continues:

> From there one proceeds to communication through expression and language, which already is an interrelation of egos. Every sort of communication naturally presupposes the commonality of the surrounding world, which is established as soon as we are persons for one another—though this can be completely empty, inactive. But it is something different to have them as fellows in communal life, to talk with them, to share their concerns and strivings, to be bound to them in friendship and enmity, love and hate. It is only here that we enter the sphere of the "communal-historical" world.[41]

Pre-linguistic sharing is necessarily limited to the present: in empathy and pre-linguistic communication, we share the environment with present others. Through linguistic communication, environment is expanded temporally:[42] language enables *sharing over time*.

With language, our pre-linguistic sphere of familiarity, our homeworld, gains a "new kind of validity, accessibility, recognizability."[43] Husserl writes: "Clearly it is only through language and its far-reaching documentations, as possible communications, that the horizon of civilization can be an open and endless one, as it always is for human beings."[44] That is, language lifts communication to the level of ideality, so that the *meanings* of things and events can be "restored" and "passed on" to new subjects—as "possible communications." Here Husserl assigns a crucial role to *written* language: "The importance of written, documented linguistic expression is that it makes communication possible without immediate or mediate personal address; it is, so to speak, communication become virtual. Through this, the communalization of humanity is lifted to a new level."[45] With writing, a tradition can be "preserved" even through phases of interruption of personal address: without writing, "what is lacking is the *persisting existence* of the 'ideal objects' . . . , what is lacking is their continuing-to-be when no one has [consciously] realized them in self-evidence."[46] There could be, and indeed factually have been, traditions that are transmitted purely orally, and that are carried over in the form of practices, but such traditions (and their respective homeworld) are tied to actually existing persons. Through writing a tradition is freed from its boundedness to its current members. That is to say, whereas spoken language invests the objective world with a supratemporal existence, but one that is still tied to particular individuals, writing detaches ideal meanings from the existence of particular persons, and hence it enables persistence through times when the meanings are not self-evidently realized. It is precisely by clothing our experiences and thoughts with ideal meanings that communication and language enable sharing over time.[47]

However, Husserl warns us about the *"seduction of language"* (*Verführung der Sprache*).[48] Namely, as already pointed out, written and spoken expressions have their meaning only as "possible communications" (*mögliche Mitteilungen*).[49] To express one's thoughts and perceptions in language is to clothe them with ideal meanings,[50] but this does not mean that one could simply *hand* meanings to others. For instance, to hear someone uttering words and sentences is not sufficient to grasp their meaning—as I have already argued, sensuous sharing is necessary but not sufficient for social and cultural sharing. Instead, the original meaning (or intention) of the words must be actively reawakened. That is, written and uttered sentences offer themselves to us, not as realized, but as possibilities of intuitive realization. To "understand accordingly" (*nachverstehen*) is to "*quasi-*perform" (*quasi-vollziehen*): to understand the written or spoken words of others amounts to *as if* carrying out the original act of meaning.[51] As we *express* our lived experiences in our gestures, words, and sentences, the intersubjective meaningfulness that we are thus communicating to others resides precisely in the possible subjective realization. In this sense, "in the contact of reciprocal linguistic understanding, the original production and the product of one subject can be *actively* understood by the others."[52] In order for another person to understand our expressions, she must actively reawaken the "content" that we express in our gestures and sentences.

The required content, however, cannot be materially the same, since this would imply that we have the same experience. Instead, what is shared is not the content per se, but its ideal meaning, of which the content serves as an appearance. For example, when someone tells us that she "saw a dog chasing its tail," in spontaneously quasi-performing the act of perception we may have a different kind of dog in mind, and we might visualize the movement of the dog differently, but the meaning of the sentence can nevertheless be transmitted and reactivated. In this manner, through language, we can share, for instance, the ideal meaning of the factual event of "a dog chasing its tail," even if we were not present when this happened. This sharing may well transcend our present, and even our personal life. We can be informed about the past experiences and thoughts of others—even from times before we were born.

Therefore, the intersubjective world is expanded through language. The world is not only a horizon that we can share with those who are, or could be, present at the moment; as a horizon that we can talk, read, and write about, the world is constituted as the historical world.[53] However, we not only share a familiar homeworld, with a particular language, but eventually the multilingual and multicultural world of humanity.[54] To be sure, with the representatives of an alien culture, we do not share a language, but the alien language can nevertheless be understood as another language, as another ideal system of meanings—and there are means of interlingual communication.[55] Namely, we can learn the other's language (and thus "make ourselves at home" in a language that formerly was alien to us), and likewise others can learn our language, and therefore intercommunal communication becomes possible. With this, our world "expands," so that eventually a "world for a communicating humanity" is constituted.[56] Husserl argues:

> The objective world is from the start the world for all, the world which "anyone" has as a world-horizon. Its objective being presupposes human beings, understood as human beings with a common language. . . .
> Thus human beings, fellow human beings, world—the world of which human beings, of which we, always talk about, and can talk about—and, on the other hand, language, are inseparably intertwined; and one is always certain of their inseparable relational unity, though usually implicitly, in the manner of a horizon.[57]

That is to say, in the constitution of the objective world, the co-constituting "anyone" is tacitly taken as a human being—moreover, as a normal human being with a language.

From "I" to "We" (and Back Again)

Intersubjectivity is initially realized in relation to contemporary others, and, in this sense, generative intersubjectivity genetically presupposes social, reciprocal relations (that, again, presuppose a priori intersubjectivity). For instance, one's own parents are at first experienced as contemporary subjects, but as experiences grow, parents are constituted as having once been children, having (had) their own parents and grandparents, who preceded our times.[58] Consequently, we have come to realize that we and our family are situated within a historical continuum of a kin. Apparently, with past persons we cannot share a world in the sense of reciprocity, but our deceased relatives do not cease to belong to our kin. Rather, they are constituted as having witnessed the same world as we do now, and in this temporally extended sense, we share the world with them. More generally, all past persons are constituted as having walked the same earth, having witnessed the same sun and moon, and in this sense, we constitute ourselves as members in a historical continuum of humanity. As Husserl puts it, this "transcendental . . . connection of human beings" constitutes "my normal 'We,'"[59] my "transcendental 'We'" (*transzendentale "Wir"*).[60]

The intersubjective world is the historical world, and as such it is the correlate not only of contemporary subjects, but of past and future subjects as well: our predecessors and successors are constituted as subjects that have experienced, or will come to experience, the one and same world that we ourselves are witnesses to. In this sense, we "generatively" relate to one another through our experience of the intersubjective world.[61]

Husserl argues, moreover, that the generative dimension is operative within our experiences before we become conscious of it. To be sure, generativity is gradually realized in the course of subjective life, and, in this sense, *generativity necessarily has a genetic constitution*.[62] Certainly, in the beginning of our individual genesis, generativity remains "out of the question" (*unbefragt*), and the genesis of generativity is a matter of subjectivity "understanding itself better."[63] Husserl writes:

> In my childhood the meaning of the generative existence of mankind and history were still closed for me, I knew nothing of [the] tradition, for me there was no tradition. Others alone knew that my games and stories, etc., are passed on to me—through others, who belong to the respective tradition—from an age-old tradition. Of birth and death I had no idea, not even when I had already learned to use these words. . . . As grown up I can say: of "the" world I had a conception, but only a very imperfect [one].[64]

That is, even though as children we were completely unaware of the historical dimension as such, we *retrospectively* constitute the tradition as the generative source of the meaning of our games: "Reverting back, I see straight away that the world that was valid for me had already for its part constituents that stem from a tradition."[65] In this sense, we come to understand that we carried history in the core of our existence, in our actions and in our behavior, already before we knew it or became aware of it: "I eventually experience a world that was there already, lived-bodies and subjects that were there before me myself."[66] A code of conduct and a manner of speaking and writing are not something one is born with. Similarly, to recognize something *as* a tree, *as* a car, or *as* a game is a capacity gained in and through our interaction with others, whereas others have likewise inherited these meanings from their predecessors, and so on. Therefore the perceived things, events, and actions (e.g., playing of games) are from the start historical—even if it is only subsequently that we become aware of the generativity of meaning. In the words of Husserl: "We stand in a historical horizon, in a horizon in which everything is historical, even if we may know very little about it in a definite way."[67]

We exist within a tradition, within a history, which means that *our genetic constitution takes place within a generative framework*. Husserl emphasizes that "subjectivity is what it is—an ego functioning constitutively—only within intersubjectivity."[68] To be a constituting subjectivity is not only to be a member of a community of contemporary subjectivities, but to be a member of a "generatively and socially united civilization."[69] To be an intersubjective subjectivity is to be aware of the world in the form of "We." However, as sedimented, the awareness of the intersubjective-historical world does not presuppose that others are present all the time. Husserl repeats the example that intersubjectivity would not vanish even if all other living beings except me would disappear—the world would still appear as the historical human world, as our world.[70] "We"-awareness is accordingly an intersubjective self-awareness; it is an awareness of oneself as a representative of a community.

Husserl emphasizes that "we"-awareness is a type of self-awareness. He argues that different types of "we-hood" (*Wirheiten*) designate "different modes of I-subjectivity."[71] "Each 'We' . . . involves a centering in me who has this we-consciousness and perhaps utters it."[72] Carr condenses the Husserlian view: "It is in each case *I* who say 'we,'" and thus the "we-subject cannot be considered in abstraction from the individuals that make it up."[73] In other words, the fact that communities are not *intra*-subjective does not make them *supra*subjective, and we must not lose sight of the fact that the plural "we" is a *first-person plural*.[74] Accordingly, generative intersubjectivity does not make the questions of subjectivity vanish.[75] Even if subjectivity comes to understand itself as intersubjectivity, the latter does not substitute the former: "inter*subjectivity*" has literally no meaning without reference to subjectivity.[76] Therefore, as Husserl argues, it would be "wrong, methodologically, to jump immediately to transcendental intersubjectivity and to leap over the primal 'I.'"[77] Husserl also specifies that this is not only a methodological warning: "At all events, however, we must—for the most profound philosophical reasons, which we cannot go into further, and which are not only methodical in character—do justice to the absolute singularity of the ego and its central position in all constitution."[78] Namely, as I have already argued, historicity essentially has a genetic constitution: it is revealed in the life of individual subjectivity. It is only in and through individual subjectivity that historical communities have their existence, and this means that intersubjectivity essentially "refers genetically back" (*weist genetisch zurück*) to a constituting subjectivity.[79] Intersubjective experiences are necessarily, at the same time, also subjective experiences; experiences of the historical world are necessarily someone's experiences.[80] Therefore, when one constitutes oneself as a historical being, one is not detached from the *primordial-subjective present*. The historical world is necessarily revealed in and through the living present. More precisely, it is our living present that reveals itself as historical. Husserl argues that the historical world "is historical only through the inner historicity of the individuals," namely through their genetic self-constitution.[81] The historical world can reveal itself only in a subjective life, and from a first-person point of view, and, therefore, what is "historically primary in itself is our [own] present."[82] In short, as Husserl also phrases it: "The 'Us' or the 'We' extends from me to the past, present and future others."[83]

However, although intersubjective experiences are fundamentally oriented according to the individual and refer genetically back to the subjective living present, on the other hand intersubjectivity entails a certain self-objectification. Namely, our subjective life is constituted as a particular thread within a historical intersubjective life, and, in this manner, objectified as a "monad": subjectivity constitutes itself as a finite member in the historical intersubjective community, in the "functioning all-subjectivity" (*fungierende Allsubjektivität*).[84] For instance, a scientist may constitute her research as continuing the work of other thinkers, and as laying the foundations for a work to be made by scholars in the future, and in this manner the researcher indeed experiences the historical unity of researchers as being oriented according to her, but on the other hand she also situates herself in this historical continuum: she experiences her living present as a possible past for future others.

In this manner, by constituting herself as being "factually within a generative framework, in the unitary flow of historicity,"[85] the subject not only constitutes her ways of thinking and writing as continuing certain traditions, but she also constitutes herself as participating in the intersubjective continuum that exceeds her subjective life—and goes on independent of it. Historical self-constitution thus relativizes our subjective existence. Paradoxically, therefore, historicity is revealed in the course of our subjective genesis, but once revealed, it relativizes our subjective genesis. We are here dealing with a genuine paradox, since our subjective genesis is not *replaced* by the intersubjective-historical self-constitution: by being objectified for itself as a particular thread in the generative nexus, subjectivity does not cease to be the being that constitutes generativity in the first place, the dimension to which generativity refers back to, and yet the generative dimension relativizes the dimension of subjective-genetic constitution. We can shed more light on the paradoxical internal relation between genetic and generative self-constitution by studying the finitude of the embodied subjectivity.

Birth and Death

In its "expanded," generative-intersubjective self-constitution, subjectivity comes to grasp its own natality and mortality.[86] I will here first introduce death and birth as the limits of genetic (primordial-subjective) self-constitution, and, following Steinbock, I will then explicate the generative-intersubjective significance of birth and death.

As Heidegger famously argues, there is a decisive difference between one's own death and the death of the other.[87] Husserl, too, emphasizes this difference. The death of an other, Husserl writes, entails a complete loss of the expressivity of her body, which renders empathy impossible: "The lived-body dies, the lived-body is transformed in a corporeal manner so that the conditions of possibility of empathy are abolished. Even if it still looks like a lived-body, it thereby no longer expresses a soulful existence. This is what everyone knows from everyday experiences."[88] The other no longer gesticulates, moves, or breathes, and so on—and is thus not experienced as an expressive, living being. In short, what used to be a *Leib* is transformed into a mere *Körper:* "bodily being dies—it becomes a mere corpse."[89] In the case of one's own death such a transformation obviously cannot be experienced. One's own death does not appear as an event or experience among others—we have many perceptions, but we have only one perceptual life and one death. Husserl argues that one's own death cannot be experienced, because to actually experience one's own death would presuppose that one "lives through" and thus "survives" one's death—and this is contradictory because in this case one would not actually die.[90] As Merleau-Ponty puts it: "Neither my birth nor my death can appear to me as experiences of my own, since if I thought of them thus, I should be assuming myself to be pre-existent to, or out-living, myself, in order to be able to experience them, and I should therefore not be genuinely thinking of my birth and my death."[91]

Awareness of one's own mortality apparently has a different structure than any other experience of mortality. One's own death is unthinkable (*unvorstelbar*):[92] we are un*able* to die, we *can*not die. Nevertheless, as Husserl puts it, "I myself will die—like I was once born, developed into adulthood, and got old. But what this means—that is the question."[93] Elsewhere Husserl specifies: "I have once been born and will once cease to be, to exist in the world, with the breaking down of lived-bodilyness."[94] That is to say, even if the transformation of my *Leib* into a *Körper* cannot be experienced by me, death is still experientially a bodily issue. Namely, death is the "limit" of our bodily possibilities: the *limes* between lived-body and mere material body.[95] What distinguishes these two, is first and foremost that a *Körper* cannot do anything, whereas the lived-body, as already explained, is the field of "I can." Although the transformation cannot be experienced, the limit can be experienced *as a limit.*

In the course of our ontogenesis, we gain abilities like that of walking, we acquire skills like that of riding a bicycle, and as our experiences are thus sedimented, our subjective horizon of possibilities is correlatively subjectively widened. However, we can not only gain new abilities, but we can also lose some. If we suffer an injury, for instance, our horizon of possibilities, our "world," may be radically narrowed. For example, if my knee is severely injured, along with the narrowing of my possibilities of movement several sectors of my life are shut off or prohibited from me: this concerns not only the sectors that immediately involve bodily movement (such as daily walks or athletic exercises) but also those that mediately require movement (such as working at the office or meeting with friends). Therefore, as our bodily possibilities ("I can") are experientially narrowed down, we literally experience our "world" as limited or restricted.

Moreover, not only do we experience the outcome of the narrowing, but also the *process* of narrowing. We are retentionally aware of our possibilities, and we experience ourselves as *dis*abled and *in*capable precisely through contrasts to this awareness. Therefore our experiential life is revealed to us as having a *direction:* toward being more able or toward being less able. When we learn new things and acquire new skills, for instance, we experience the opening of new possibilities; on the other hand, when our abilities and skills are experientially weakened or ruptured, we experience a downward movement, a movement associated with the closing down of possibilities. Furthermore, this experiential narrowing down of possibilities has an ultimate limit, a borderline between our being-able and our not-being-able-at-all: a point where our bodily possibilities are completely nihilated, a comprehensive "I cannot," in which our body would become a mere *Körper*. Reaching this ultimate end cannot be experienced, since to experience oneself as a *Körper* is possible only for a *Leib*—and this is what Husserl has in mind when employing the mathematical term *limes*. The world is the correlate of "I can," and in the case of a comprehensive absence of the latter, no world could appear.[96] Therefore, the correlate of this limiting idea is for us, quite literally, the "end of the world." This is how Husserl describes death in the context of genetic phenomenology. Heidegger's formulation echoes Husserl's explication: one's own death designates the "possibility of the impossibility of every way of comporting oneself towards anything, of every way of existing."[97]

To tacitly experience this limiting idea does not presuppose that the narrowing down of possibilities is very radical: even when we are hungry, thirsty, or tired, and thus experience our strengths weakening,[98] we are aware of a *direction* whose ideal terminus is the comprehensive impossibility of being able. Moreover, just as in feeling hungry, thirsty, or tired we do not have to be explicitly (say, reflectively or cognitively) aware that we are in need of food, water, or rest, so too the possibility of the comprehensive "I cannot" as the limiting idea does not have to be (and usually is not) given explicitly—as Merleau-Ponty puts it, the possibility of one's own death is present like an atmosphere (*atmosphère de mort*).[99] When our need is fulfilled, when we gain strength, get better from a sickness, or recover from an accident, we experience the broadening of the horizon of life: new possibilities open to us, whereas the limiting idea of not-being-able-at-all becomes more and more distant. Yet, in this sense, death remains one of the constant tacit reference points of our experiential life.

In this manner, we can be aware of the possibility of our death even if we can never experience our death. In a similar manner, the fact that we cannot experience our birth does not prevent us from experiencing our being-born.[100] As with death, Husserl makes a phenomenological distinction between one's own birth and the birth of an other. While discussing the latter, he states: "Procreation is a process of life in which out of lived-bodies new lived-bodies emerge; new lived-bodies—not new organs of the parental lived-body, but organs of other subjects."[101] The birth of an other is accordingly the birth of a new lived-body which is separate from the body of the mother. However, even if "my lived-body as an organic body must have had a beginning,"[102] one's own birth has a different meaning. One's own birth, too, is a limit, but it is a different kind of limit than one's own death. At birth, embodied subjectivity is "poor" (*arm*) in abilities.[103] Even though the newborn does not yet *master* its body movements, it *can* move, and in this sense, we can speak of original and even inborn abilities. Our abilities are sedimented and each sediment tacitly indicates its foundation, so that ultimately our acquired abilities refer back to our original or inborn abilities—or, as Ricoeur puts it, to our "preformed skills."[104] Although it may remain unnoticed, this reference is experienced: should we not be aware of our ability to move ourselves, we would not constitute ourselves as being able to ride a bicycle, as being able to converse with others, and so on. Our actual and potential wakeful experiences and actions indicate our subjective-genetic history: each ability and experience points to less specialized ability—and our beginning (*Anfang*) is given as the limit of this impoverishment (*Limes der Verarmung*).[105] Thus, by tacitly indicating our original abilities, our experiences and actions ultimately indicate our being-born, our "becoming alert" (*Wach-Werden*).[106]

The life of subjectivity is a constant being in between the limits of birth and death: we are "already born" and "still alive."[107] Accordingly, *our sedimented experiencing fluctuates between our inborn capacities and the possibility of comprehensive impossibility*. In this sense, birth and death are not symmetrical limits of our life—and our life, accordingly, is not like a circle that begins and ends at one and the same point. Viewed from within (*von inner gesehen*),[108] from the point of view of subjective genesis, birth and death cannot be experienced as temporal events: they are the limits of genetic constitution or "subjective sense constitution"—and, in this sense, to quote Steinbock, birth and death "escape the parameters of a genetic transcendental phenomenology."[109] For subjectivity, her own death designates the "end of the world," and she is unable to experience her death as an event that is preceded and succeeded by other events.

However, as already said, intersubjective historicity reveals our subjective existence as a finite thread within a generative context. In entering into communion with others, we constitute ourselves as communal human beings, and we come to realize that human beings are essentially, "not only accidentally," finite beings that are born and will die.[110] As an "I" within a "We," subjectivity constitutes the world as an intersubjective horizon, the validity of which is not merely dependent upon *one's own* experiencing. Therefore, when Husserl asks "does the world disappear when I die?" he can go on to answer in the negative.[111] Namely, as subjectivity constitutes itself within the continuum of generations, it grasps its own birth and death as intersubjective events, as events in intersubjective time, in the "immanent common time of the respective 'We'":[112] The world... as such presupposes transcendental intersubjectivity.... Therein lies generativity, therein lies all having-been-born, having-been-a-child, as well as [the necessity of] dying at some point."[113] The world is our horizon, the horizon of transcendental intersubjectivity. Therefore, the possibility of one's own death does not coincide with the possibility of the end of the world—my death designates the end of the world for me, the end of my "world."[114]

Within a genetic context (i.e., for the primordial subjectivity) birth and death appear as the ultimate limits; but within transcendental intersubjectivity, birth and death reveal themselves as breaks (*Bruch*) or pauses (*Pausen*) in intersubjective constitution: "All beginning is a 'break' within a streaming continuity.... Likewise all ending."[115] That is to say, my experiential life is intentionally interwoven with that of others, and in this sense *our* existence exceeds *my* existence. In this intersubjective sense, there is life after death, just as there was life before it.[116] This implies that within the historical monadic community, subjectivity constitutes its individual existence as finite, not only from within (i.e., against the *limits* of birth and death), but also in relation to the historical life of intersubjectivity.[117] The subject constitutes herself as a representative of a "We" for which the world existed before she was born and to which it continues to exist after she perishes.[118] In this manner, subjectivity is "relativized" (*relativiert*): subjects are constituted as "limited unities of life" (*begrenzten Lebenseinheiten*) relative to historical intersubjectivity.[119]

However, as I have already argued, the subject does not thereby lose its individuality—historical intersubjectivity can exist only as the generative nexus of individual subjectivities. Therefore birth and death still loom as the limits of subjectivity. That is, on the one hand, the limits of genetic self-constitution are for us the ultimate limits, whereas on the other hand, our genetic self-constitution takes place within a historical-generative framework in which the birth and death of individuals are but "breaks" or "pauses." All our possibilities (of perception, of thinking, etc.) still refer back to our own beginning—even if we have learned, inherited, and appropriated them from others. Even though we realize that the world continues its existence despite the fact that some constituting members disappear and new members enter into the constituting intersubjectivity, the possibility of a complete "I cannot" still designates, for us, the end of the world. The intersubjective does not replace the subjective—the generative does not replace the genetic.

Intersubjective Subjectivity

Three basic senses of intersubjectivity have now been distinguished. We started with *a priori intersubjectivity*, ventured through *empathic-reciprocal* or *social intersubjectivity*, and ended up with *generative intersubjectivity*. In the first form of intersubjectivity, others are emptily implied by the horizonality of perception: the co-constituting others remain anonymous, and the perceptual environment appears as being there for *anybody*. In the second type of intersubjectivity, the other is present as a *concrete, singular other*—and the environment correlatively appears as being shared by the two of us, or more generally by the contemporary members of the respective social unit. In the third type of intersubjectivity, the environment manifests itself as our familiar historical world: the co-constituting others are *home-*constituting others, they are our *homecomrades*. Whereas in a priori intersubjectivity the embodied self remains anonymous, in social intersubjectivity the self is constituted as an embodied person among other persons, and in historical generative intersubjectivity the embodied self is constituted as a member of historical community.

It is important to realize that the three forms of intersubjectivity are not mutually exclusive. When we are engaged in an empathic-reciprocal relation with others, we simultaneously constitute ourselves as members of a historical community, and as being perceivable to anybody. Likewise, when someone appears to us as a *singular* other, she is at the same time constituted as a possible perceiver (as a particular exemplar of *anybody*), and she can also be constituted as a co-member of our historical community (as a *homecomrade*). And even if the environment is constituted as a social environment that is shared by me and you exclusively, the environment simultaneously appears as being perceivable to anybody, and, on the other hand, the social environment is constituted within a historical horizon.

Yet there is a certain constitutive hierarchy. Empathic-reciprocal intersubjectivity presupposes a priori intersubjectivity: the empathically experienced other is a particular exemplar of the horizonal other ("anybody") that is emptily implied in our perceptions, and in this sense a priori intersubjectivity serves as a transcendental foundation for empathy.[120] Moreover, in and through empathic-reciprocal encounter with others, subjectivity is sedimented with intersubjective meanings that have been inherited from past subjects. In this manner, the historical-generative dimension is gradually appropriated in the course of the genetic self-constitution of subjectivity. In other words, in order to constitute itself as a member of a historical community, subjectivity must enter into reciprocal relation with others, which is possible only insofar as subjectivity is embodied and hence tied to a certain perspective at the time, while intending the other perspectives as being simultaneously perceivable. In this manner, the generative intersubjectivity is constituted in the becoming of an individual subjectivity. However, the "genesis of historicity" has a retrospective effect. Namely, when the historical dimension is revealed, it is revealed as having been there already before we constituted it as such. The games we played as a child, the stories we were told, and the whole rhythm of the day are subsequently recognized in their "generative density,"[121] although at the time they did not appear as historical to us. In this manner, historicity and generativity are retrospectively constituted as having already been effective before they were revealed to us as such.

I have frequently emphasized here that subjectivity (and subjective-genetic self-constitution) is not replaced by intersubjectivity (and intersubjective-historical self-constitution)—rather, as I argued, "we"-awareness is a type of self-awareness. Historicity is revealed gradually in the course of our subjective genesis. When we realize, for instance, that our childhood games were already historical, we do not think that they become historical through this realization, but we should neither neglect the phenomenological fact that, back then, they were not constituted for us as historical. In short, the first-person perspective can never be neglected. In this manner, in the course of our individual self-constitution (in which historicity was revealed to us in the first place), the process of genetic self-constitution itself is grasped as having already been historical. In this manner, the genetic constitution of intersubjectivity eventually leads to a certain "relativization" of the process of genetic constitution—but at the same time the subjectivity still serves as the constituting foundation for this intersubjective relativization. That is, paradoxically, genetic constitution takes places within a generative framework, but the generative framework has a genetic constitution.

By explicating the primordial (part 1) and intersubjective self-constitution (part 2) of the embodied subjectivity, we have thus arrived at *the paradox of subjectivity*. It may first seem that this paradox forces us to make a choice: to maintain either that subjectivity becomes an intersubjective subjectivity in the course of its primordial genesis, or that we are "always already" intersubjective in the concrete historical sense. In other words, it first seems that we are forced either to render intersubjectivity absolute and subjectivity relative, or vice versa, since holding on to both alternatives seems impossible. However, as should be clear by now, subjectivity has both genetic and generative self-constitution, and making a choice between these would result in a one-sided view. The paradox of subjectivity cannot be undone without falling guilty to such one-sidedness. By being constituted in the intersubjective space, our lived-body does not cease to be the "absolute Here"—and, more generally, by being objectified for itself as a particular member in a historical community, subjectivity does not cease to function as the primordial subjectivity in the life of which intersubjective historicity is revealed in the first place.

Therefore, paradoxically, there seem to be two absolutes: the genetic-primordial and the generative-intersubjective. How is this possible? How are the genetic and the generative dimensions interrelated in the constitution of objective reality? I will investigate this problem in the final part of my treatise by explicating the normative structures involved in primordial and intersubjective constitution. This explication will not only enable me to clarify the internal relations between genetic and generative constitution—and hence to shed new light on the paradox of subjectivity—but it will also enable me to complete my explication of the constitutive role of embodiment. It will be argued, namely, that the relation between primordial and intersubjective self-constitution of the embodied subjectivity unfolds as a "normative tension."

Part 3

Normality and Objective Reality

7

Primordial and Intersubjective Normality

Thus far we have been discussing subjectivity *in relation to itself* and *in relation to others*, and the centrality of embodiment in both relations has been highlighted. This final part focuses on the significance of embodiment in the constitution of *objective reality*.

The preceding part was concluded with the claim that even though subjectivity is sedimented and even though it constitutes itself as an intersubjective being, subjective-primordial awareness is not thereby replaced by the intersubjective one: intersubjective constitution cannot lack first-person perspective. Accordingly, primordial self-constitution cannot be subordinated or reduced to intersubjective self-constitution. The phenomenological relationship between primordial and intersubjective constitution must be investigated in detail, since this will enable the clarification of the significance of embodiment in the constitution of objective reality.

It is striking, at first glance, that while Husserl elaborates the features of intersubjective world-constitution, he *excludes* the "anomalous" and the "abnormal" from the constituting intersubjectivity. However, as will become clear later on, the "exclusion" (*Ausschaltung*)[1] in question is not an act of discrimination or devaluation: it is not a result of an act of deliberation, and it involves neither degradation of, nor disrespect for, the subjects in question. Husserl is not claiming that we should decide to exclude the anomalous, but he is instead describing one particular structural feature of our experiencing, a mode of constitution.

The problem of normality arises already at the level of primordial experience. Namely, when for instance we hear something, we take this something as being there for anybody, but precisely thereby we tacitly "restrict" these horizonal, co-constituting others to those with *a proper sense of hearing*. Accordingly, one only needs to consider the deaf in order to realize that normality has a role to play in the constitution of the objective world. In general, "anybody" does not mean all sensing beings whatsoever, but exclusively *normal* perceivers. This brings to light the essential *asymmetry* or *dissymmetry* of intersubjective experiences: it is never quite the same to constitute a perceived thing as something that others should be able to perceive as well, and to constitute what others claim to perceive as something we ourselves should be able to perceive.[2] In the first instance, the "measure" of perceiving the thing in the right manner resides in the abilities of the self, whereas in the latter this "measure" is defined by the abilities of others.

Along with the essential asymmetry, we also find the constitutive hierarchy that was discussed already in part 2. Just as the intersubjective-historical dimension is essentially constituted for subjectivity in the course of its individual genesis, and refers back to it, so too the norm as defined by the abilities of others—the "intersubjective norm"—can be constituted only on the basis of, and in relation to, the norm as defined by the abilities of primordial subjectivity—this is the "primordial norm." This asymmetry and duality can be further illustrated with an example. As we come to know that there are blind subjects, this does not motivate us to think that we ourselves experience features (e.g., colors) that do not actually exist. On the contrary, we immediately—before reflecting upon the issue—consider these others as constitutively anomalous or "deviant" in the sense that they do not perceive the visual environment which is there for "anybody." In other words, the perceptual abilities of the blind do not rule out our intersubjective experience of the colors, which means that—in respect to the constitution of the *visual* realm—the experiences of such subjects are not "normatively significant" like those of the seeing ones. On the other hand, it should be emphasized that the blind, as well as other anomalously perceiving subjects, can nevertheless be "constitutively significant" in many other respects: they contribute to the constitution, say, of the tactile world, the auditory world, the practical world, and the historical world, and in this sense they are participating members of transcendental intersubjectivity.

In this sense, as I will argue in detail, the constitution of the objective world involves normative structures: the world appears as being there for anybody, but "anybody" does not refer to all perceivers whatsoever, but only to *normal* perceivers. Yet, as I will also clarify, due to certain essential structures of empathy, the sense of "anybody" remains bound to the experiencing self and its experiential potentialities, and the normative structure of world-constitution should hence be understood as twofold, and it ought to be introduced in terms of a tension between what I will call primordial and intersubjective normality.

Before presenting my argument for this view, it is necessary to explicate the phenomenological concepts of normality, and clarify the relation between normality and objectivity. The correlation between normality and objectivity—both intersubjective and intercommunal objectivity—will also be discussed. My main argument here is that both intersubjectivity and primordiality have a normative role in the constitution of the objective world. By explicating this twofold normativity, I will shed new light upon the internal relation between primordial and intersubjective world-constitution.

Phenomenological Concepts of Normality

In general philosophical discourse, the word "norm" is taken to mean "a standard, rule, [or] principle [that is] used to judge or direct human conduct as something to be complied with."[3] "Normality" and "normativity" have importantly different meanings: something is normal insofar as it accords with a norm, whereas something is normative insofar as it posits, reveals, or institutes a norm. In Husserlian phenomenology, this basic significance is sustained, but the concepts of normality and normativity are employed in a special manner that differs remarkably both from everyday discourse and from the respective biological and sociological notions—at least in three respects that should be explicated.

First, in phenomenology "normality" and "abnormality" do not refer to objective features; normality is "not merely a fact" (*nicht nur ein Faktum*).[4] Accordingly, it is not the body, behavior, factuality, or objectivity, but the constitution of the body, of behavior, of factuality, and of objectivity that is here considered as normal, abnormal, or anomalous.[5] Husserl stresses that "normality is a mode pertaining to constitution," and as such it should be addressed as a philosophical, constitutive problem.[6] Second, the difference between normality and abnormality is not, therefore, regarded as a *quantitative* but as a *qualitative* one: it is not the number or frequency of experiences but the *manner* of experiencing that appears as normal or abnormal. This is the reason why, unlike in many sociological, biological, and physiological theories,[7] in phenomenology normality is not defined, for instance, through a statistical average. In the words of Georges Canguilhem, the "norm is not deduced from, but rather expressed in the average."[8] This brings us to the third point: norms are not something immutable, fixed, or eternal; they have a temporal constitution, they are dynamic and fluid. Namely, experiences can be "normative" not only in the sense that they point to, reveal, or revalidate an already existing norm, but experiences can also establish or institute new norms that guide further experiences. Hence "the normal" cannot be identified with the "natural" or "original" over against something "acquired," "developed," or "artificial."

In brief, phenomenology deals with normality as a transcendental, qualitative, and dynamic issue. However, phenomenology offers and employs several notions of normality.[9] Husserl first characterizes normal experience as "*a lawful experience that is concordantly integrated into the context [of experience] and maintains the identity of the experienced thing.*"[10] Concordance (*Einstimmigkeit*) pertains to an "orthoesthetic body"—that is, to a body sensing in a unitary and continuous manner—and thus concordance is the basis of sensuous normality.[11] For a person with a burnt right hand, for instance, the environment appears in a *discordant* manner: a conflict (*Widerspruch*) surfaces between the sensations provided by the right and the left hand (water, e.g., may feel lukewarm or hot depending on whether it is explored with the burned hand or the healthy one).[12] When the hand is healed, sensuous concordance is restored, and this particular discordance is subordinated to concordance as an exceptional and deviant state, as an anomaly.

It is important to distinguish between *anomaly* and *abnormality*. What is anomalous is not in itself something abnormal or pathological, but an individual deviation within the bounds of normality.[13] In this sense, as Husserl stresses, normality precedes anomaly: "Anomaly is initially given as a break in the concordance of experience."[14] Namely, it is through a contrast with the concordant experiencing that a definitive awareness of anomaly and normality arises.[15] Discordance, in other words, is essentially discordance within concordant experiencing.[16] And since "*anomaly is a modification [Abwandlung] of normality,*" "total discordance is not, of course, possible."[17] Instead, abnormality is not a break within normality, but something that exceeds it, and as such, unlike experiences of anomaly, experiences of abnormality are normatively significant (I will come back to this later).

Husserl distinguishes two kinds of discordance: discordance through anomalous perception (as in the case of a burned hand), and discordance as an experience where the system of perception has no inner conflict, but the experienced thing instead proves to be something other than what we expected.[18] For instance, when what we took to be a human being turns out to be a tree, the "previous perception suffers in its continuation a doxical annulment" and thus our sensuously continuous perception manifests itself as discordant or "heterological" (*heterologisch*).[19] Accordingly, discordance can be subordinated to the *old* concordance (e.g., when the hand is healed), but it can also lead to the establishment of a *new* concordance, or to a higher-level concordance (*höhere Einstimmigkeit*), under which the old concordance is subordinated.[20]

Concordance, accordingly, is not sufficient for perceptual normality: as purely descriptive notions, concordance and discordance alone are unable to explain why discordance sometimes institutes a new normality, and sometimes not. This difference can be made intelligible by adding that in order to be normal, constitution must satisfy two conditions: it must not only run concordantly but also constitute an object or event in the "optimal" (*optimale*) manner.[21] Perceived objects appear *better* or *worse* depending on the perceptual circumstances such as distance, lighting, perceptual medium, and the status of the perceiving body, and the optimal manner of appearing is preferred since it reveals the most of the concordantly constituted thing: the thing in "its greatest richness of differentiation" and with a "maximal clarity."[22] What we intend as the thing itself is the thing given in an optimal manner, the thing in an "optimal continuity of appearances."[23] This *optimum* is also what we are tacitly referring to when saying that the thing appears worse if it is too far, too near, obscure, and so on.[24] Accordingly, Husserl claims, "normal embodiment means one that produces or enables a circle of optima; with a burned finger, I feel 'badly,' with myopic eyes, I see the distance badly, etc."[25] Correlatively, the features pertaining to the thing itself are the optimal ones: "The optimal designates the true, the full optimum, the real itself, the [thing] 'as it is.'"[26]

Yet, as noted already, norms are not fixed but essentially dynamic and this in two related senses. When trying on new glasses, the things perceived suddenly appear differently, and the optimal distance of perceiving things is altered: this new, more elaborate way of appearing is constituted as the norm of perception, to which—in a retrospective manner—the earlier normality is subordinated.[27] That is, norms are not fixed. To give another example, the requisite perceptual circumstances of reading a map become transformed if we notice that the paper includes hidden figures that can be seen only in an ultraviolet light. In this manner, the previous normality becomes subordinated and relativized by the new one: the appearances of the map in daylight gain a reference to the new optimum so that, from now on, an optimal perception of the map involves the presence of ultraviolet light. In this sense, perception itself is not merely optimal or non-optimal, but it can also be *optimalizing*—that is, perceiving can revise the already existing norms and even institute new ones.[28] Given the possibility that a more optimal manner of givenness may always present itself, ultimate optimality remains an ideal.[29]

Moreover, as such, the bounds of normality cannot be defined exactly. Normal perception is one that takes place under normal circumstances,[30] but these circumstances or this "framework [in which we perceive things] is a *typical idea*, a necessarily approximate idea that gives no geometrical form . . . , a typical schema."[31] As Merleau-Ponty puts it, the perceptual distance from me to the object is not "a size which increases and decreases," an "objective magnitude," but "a tension that fluctuates round a norm," or "the degree of precision of my gaze's hold on the thing," which is another way of saying that the thing itself is the correlate of a perception from the "'best' point of observation."[32] In the words of Husserl: "I have ontic certainty of this thing [as that] to which all the sides at once belong, and in the mode in which I see it 'best.'"[33] However, the boundaries of normal thing-constitution can be exceeded, whereby the thing itself no longer appears. When it comes to perceptual distance, for instance, a tree no longer appears as a tree when it is in contact with one's retina; other human beings no longer empathically appear as others when they are viewed from an airplane high up; and if one approaches a painting in an art gallery, there is a point after which one no longer see the painting as a piece of art, but as a material thing like any other. Whenever the parameters of normal circumstances are thus exceeded, the materiality of the things gains prominence so that the concrete meaning, the thing itself, is concealed. The disparity between the world of experience (the lifeworld) and the world of objective sciences is here also illuminating: when we are marveling at the sky at nighttime, despite our best knowledge we do not *perceive* stars as faraway suns, and if we look at our own hand through a microscope, we do not *perceive* it as a functioning organ.

Like objective circumstances, such as distance, subjective-bodily conditions can also be anomalous even if they are concordant. A constant and perfectly continuous migraine, for instance, may bring about an uneasiness of perception in such a manner that things are not perceived as well as they would be without the constant headache. In short, constitution is not necessarily optimal even if it is concordant, and therefore, although necessary, concordance alone is not sufficient for perceptual normality: "Every normal subject occasionally has anomalous deviations of her normal experience, and thus something given in an anomalous manner. Yet, the subject nevertheless identifies the same given, the same thing, as merely appearing differently."[34] That is to say, it is normal to experience accidental discordances.

Moreover, as optimal perceptual circumstances are preferred, in time this preference becomes habitual and develops into "a certain typical constancy" (*eine gewisse typische Konstanz*).[35] In this sense, optimality becomes typicality. Moreover, as Steinbock argues, it is the "concordant repetition" that endows optimality with normativity.[36] Without a temporal background one could not constitute certain circumstances as those in which this particular type of thing or event would give itself in the best possible manner. In other words, optimality gains its normativity from its "genetic density."[37]

However, as already argued, in our genetic self-constitution we are intimately related to others. What we habitually prefer as the optimal circumstances are not only our individual norms, but intersubjectively shared norms; they are intersubjectively preferred circumstances, and this is not a mere empirical fact. The preference of certain circumstances is established and appropriated within a tradition, within a generative nexus, and optimality is thus eventually bound to a historical lifeworld. In encountering persons from alien cultures, we may recognize a certain consistency and a habitually preferred, typical manner of being,[38] and yet their manner of being appears as alien and "abnormal" to us. A certain typical manner of being can appear normal only insofar as it has been appropriated, taken in, and hence only insofar as it is something familiar to us. Accordingly, what makes a particular habitual system of optimality normative is its intersubjective familiarity (*Vertrautheit*).[39]

While regulating the life of an individual from within, normality also assumes the form of a cultural principle of action: "The normative ideas of civilizations and their culture . . . , as the "oughts" . . . , [determine] the life of humans, both as individuals and as variously organized into communities."[40] In this manner—in a non-quantitative sense— normality gives rise to averageness: what is normal is what "one" does.[41]

As intersubjective familiarity, normality is ultimately bound to a generative setting, to a historical homeworld. Therefore, objectively speaking, there can be several different normalities (*verschiedene Normalitäten*), "different 'best' intuitive environments" (*verschiedene "beste" Anschauungswelten*)—and hence "many averages" (*viele Durchschnittlichkeiten*).[42] However, as should be clear by now, it is only our familiar normality that functions normatively in our experiences: alien homeworlds with their alien normality appear to us precisely as alien, and hence their norms do not regulate our experiences from within.

As I have stressed, primordial constitution cannot be subordinated or reduced to intersubjective constitution. Within primordial constitution, normality can be subordinated to new normality, but this primordially constituted normality cannot be reduced to intersubjective normality. Instead, in the words of Husserl: "Also the individual subject has therefore its normality within which anomaly . . . occasionally arises": a "solitary normality" (*solitäre Normalität*) or "subjective normality" (*subjektive Normalität*).[43] By elaborating the structure of this *primordial normality*, as I will call it, it will become possible to explicate how intersubjective objectivity originates in a tension of normalities.

Primordial Normality and Its Relevance in the Constitution of Others

As has been argued, without intersubjectivity, things could not explicitly appear as things for me: "The introjection of sensations and appearances into a subject, or a conception of them as merely subjective, comes from intersubjectivity."[44] However, already in the primordial sphere of experience—within the "private environment" (*private Umwelt*) or "primordial 'world'" (*primordialen "Welt"*), as Husserl also puts it—perceptual circumstances can appear as *exceptional* in regard to previous experiences, and thus deviations can be experienced.[45] Through such experiences a distinction originally arises between "the thing in such and such perceptual circumstances" and "the thing itself" that remains identical through the change of circumstances.[46] For example, a tree appears differently in bright daylight, in the reddish light of the sunset, and at nighttime, but the tree is experienced through these changes as something identical.[47] Moreover, it is not a formal, mathematical-logical "X" that we thus intend in our pre-scientific life, but precisely the *tree* itself with all its qualities.[48] The thing itself does not lack perceptual content. As Husserl writes:

> *The object itself is nothing more than the ideal unity of . . . maximal aspects of content*, [the ideal unity] that bring these aspects together and combines them in a manner that is demanded by the synthetic unity of the perceptual intention. This unity is an ideal one since it is always only something meant, something that is actually given neither in a particular perception nor in a complete perceptual context.[49]

That is, the thing itself, the intentional object, is an ideal unity of optimal appearances.[50]

This has major consequences for the phenomenological account of intentionality. Namely, the appearances of the thing gain a "conscious relation to the optimum" (*Bewusstseinsbeziehung auf das Optimum*), which means that they henceforth "refer phenomenologically to" (*weist phänomenologisch auf*) an "optimal manner of givenness."[51] Accordingly, the thing itself, the thing as it would appear in optimal circumstances, serves as the intentional object of perception. In the words of Husserl:

> In the series of possible appearances, a particular manner of givenness of the thing is privileged insofar as with it *the thing manifests*, relatively, *the most of itself*, and this manner of givenness acquires the character of what is *especially intended*: it is the predominating focus of the "interest," it is where the experiential tendency *terminates* in, is *fulfilled* in.

> The other manners of givenness become intentionally related to this "optimal" one.[52]

In perceiving a tree, for instance, what would fulfill our intention is the tree in its optimal givenness. Moreover, optimality cannot be defined from the point of view of an isolated sense. Husserl illustrates: "With regard to the visual mode of givenness . . . , a privilege attaches to *clear daylight,* such that there not only does the form become visible in a particular favorable way up to its finer details, but also in this light such global characteristics are visible through which properties of other sense spheres are co-announced at the same time."[53] Accordingly, if we explore the bark of a tree in pitch-darkness, for instance, our tactile sensations also refer to other senses (say, to possibility of vision), so that what we *perceptually intend* while merely palpating a tree, is a multisensory object that *should* also be visible in proper lighting.[54] The thing as it appears intentionally refers to its own optimal givenness, to "its maximum articulation" (*maximum d'articulation*),[55] which is another way of saying that the optimum intentionally regulates our perceptions of the thing.

Optimality also plays an important role in motor intentionality.[56] If, for instance, the numbers on a timetable at a train station appear blurry, we grasp the perceptual distance as non-optimal—and we *move* accordingly. Namely, our bodily movements are not motivated only by the things as they happen to appear at the moment, but also by their intended optimal givenness—which, of course, is relative to our current interests and goals. When we want to write something down, and see a pen on the other side of the room, the visually perceived pen refers to the possibility of tactile givenness, to its givenness within reach, and until the pen is within reach our intention is not fulfilled.[57] Similarly, we squint and narrow our eyes because we want to see something better, and we turn toward a person who is talking to us in order to gain a multisensory and thus more optimal perception of her. What our perceptions intend is the optimal givenness of the thing, and our bodily movements are orchestrated and arranged accordingly. In this manner, normality quite literally guides our perception: the optimal manner of givenness of the thing directs our bodily movements.

Accordingly, insofar as in the primordial sphere of experience (i.e., independent of the constitutive effect of others) a difference arises between the thing itself and the thing as it appears, *already primordial constitution involves normative structures.* If we were unable to distinguish between the thing itself and the thing as it appears at the moment, we could not experience others as those who perceive the same things from different perspectives: at best, we could expect them to simultaneously witness the same appearances as we do—as children up to a certain age seem to.⁵⁸ Accordingly, in the sense that our appearances intentionally refer to the thing itself, to the thing in its optimal givenness, a primordial system of normality must already be constituted. As Husserl puts it: "In the first place, I have a normality within my solitary ego."⁵⁹

This idea has remarkable consequences for the theory of intersubjectivity. Namely, to perceive a foreign body as a lived-body, as another embodied subjectivity, is to experience it as having an affective-perceptual relation with an environment. But the environment, to which we expect the other to be related, is precisely that environment that we ourselves intend in our perceptions.⁶⁰ Husserl: "What I come to know in my concordant experience as qualification of the world that is already valid for me, concerns also the world that the other experiences. He is constituted for me as being related to this same world."⁶¹ We saw above that when exploring a tree in pitch-darkness, our tactile sensations refer to possible visual ones, so that the tree is experienced as something that could also be seen in appropriate circumstances. What was left unsaid is that this is not the case for everyone. For example, for persons blind from birth the touched tree does not intentionally refer to its possible visual givenness. The thing itself, to which the other is expected to be intentionally directed, is initially constituted in relation to our own perceptual abilities, and thus our own perceptual abilities have a certain initial constitutive priority.⁶² Our own perceptual abilities primordially outline what counts for us as the "natural thing 'itself'" (*Naturding "selbst"*).⁶³

This is what Husserl is referring to also when he states, in a striking manner, that "I myself [am] constitutionally the original norm for all human beings" and "constitutionally the primal monad."⁶⁴ Let me quote a slightly longer passage:

> I, with my whole habitual structure and world that is already valid for me, and valid in an intersubjective manner, function thereby, by virtue of my being in the form of being-for-myself and being-in-connection-with-others, as primally instituting for the apperception of others as my kind. . . . Everyone newly entering into my circle [of experience] . . . counts as *normal* insofar as the general prefiguring of his horizon [of experience] . . . attunes with mine in the general structural style; that is to say, insofar as [the other] is experientially ratified as . . . similar.⁶⁵

Accordingly, the "first normality" is outlined in relation to the perceptual abilities of oneself and of "those who are similar to me" (*meinesgleichen*).⁶⁶ In this sense, as Husserl puts it, "*my 'internally experienced' lived-body . . . is the original apperception, and provides the necessary norm. Everything else is a* modification of this norm."⁶⁷ What Husserl is saying in such paragraphs is that how we anticipate others to experience the world is initially motivated within the limits of our own perceptual abilities. For example, a person blind from birth does not originally expect others to see the world, and neither does a seeing person originally anticipate others to be blind to it. Or, when seeing someone else approaching a closed door, we expect her to be able to see the door (just as we would in her position), and this anticipation pertains to our experience of the shared objectivity. If the other simply bumps into the door, what we first question is not the objectivity of the door but the other's perceptual abilities. And, as the anticipatory horizon involved in our encounter with others is initially pre-delineated by our own possibilities, the other is tacitly expected to manifest similar abilities. In this sense normality is originally relative to the constitutive powers of the self: the embodied subjectivity with certain perceptual abilities initially functions as the norm while experiencing others, and thus we can speak of *the normative relevance of primordial constitution.*⁶⁸

Intersubjective Normality as the Tension Between Primordialities

However, an encounter with an other is always an encounter with another primordial system of normality. In such encounters an *intersubjective normality* is established: an ideal normality in respect to which the *primordial normality* is relative. Let me now clarify how this takes place.

When confronting the other, we encounter another primordial normality: "empathy poses an 'alien lived-body' and thereby a second normal ... lived-body."⁶⁹ This appresented "second normality," however, is constitutively related back to the "first normality" which again is relative to one's own experiential abilities: "the normal other is essentially related to me as the normally existing ego, although, to be sure, *after* [*nachdem*] his being is established for me, my being is likewise related to his."⁷⁰ That is to say, others are initially expected to be capable of perceiving the same things, and this presupposes that the other's system of appearances, namely her lived-body, is taken to be similar with ours: "Empathy ... appresents a presented lived-body as a subject with an appearing world that is not only generally the same [world], but appears in the same aspects and [same] sensuous things. ... The *normal case* is accordingly that each joint subject factually has the same orthological multiplicity of appearances (multiplicity of aspects)."⁷¹ The other's intentional experiences are appresented as according with our own intentional experiences. Consequently, "in the confirmation of empathy the alien normality must coincide with our own."[72] The intersubjective thing must likewise coincide with the thing as it is primordially given: if the other is to be recognized as an other, there must be an intersection of our systems of appearance—an alleged alien system of appearances that does not coincide at all with ours is not experienced as an other.[73] Therefore, the similarity of the systems of appearance—and therefore the similarity of the perceiving bodies considered in their *Innenleiblichkeit*—is a necessary component of intersubjectivity.[74]

When the "second normality" proves "similar" to the "first normality"—that is, when our primordial normalities coincide—an intersubjective, shared normality is established. However, Husserl emphasizes, the *identity* of systems of appearance of two or more subjects is an *ideal possibility* (*ideale Möglichkeit*).[75] We can perceive and think of other concordantly sensing subjects with whom we could switch places and thus have the same appearances and aspects that they did a moment ago, but our systems of appearances are in fact never absolutely identical or alike (*absolut gleich*), and therefore, in the sense of "identical orthology" (*identische Orthologie*) or "like-sensing" (*gleichsinnlich*), *intersubjective normality is an ideal*.[76] As Steven Crowell puts it, "what counts as objective—i.e., as real intersubjectivity—is only that which would be the same for all; and in principle nothing immediately intuited can fit the bill."[77] The intersubjective thing itself is a "rule of possible appearances" (*eine Regel möglicher Erscheinungen*),[78] and the intersubjective world is a normatively regulating system (*Regelungsordnung*) of intersubjective appearances.[79] But the rigorously objective thing or world can only be given "in thought" (*durch Denken*); it is graspable only by understanding (*verstehbar*).[80]

Moreover, there are different degrees of similarity between systems of appearance: "intersubjective normality involves a multifarious gradation-ideal."[81] Namely, it is not necessary that the bodily abilities of others are identical with ours, but they must nevertheless be similar enough (*genug*) for the identification between our perceptual correlates to be possible.[82] If our systems of appearance were perfectly identical, and our perceptions could be simply replaced by those of others, intersubjective normality would be nothing else than an extension of our primordial normality. This is not the case; intersubjective normality is rather constituted from the basis of factual differences and dissent between primordial subjectivities.

Moreover, being constituted on the basis of factual differences, intersubjective normality—and, correlatively, the intersubjective world—

is not fixed once and for all, but is in a constant process of becoming.[83] In this temporal constitution of intersubjective normality, individual subjectivities function normatively insofar as they participate in establishing, revising, or instituting intersubjective norms. When we recognize that someone else is able to perceive the same things that we do, and thus take her to have a similar system of appearances, her experiences are taken as constitutively significant. When a person seems to suddenly notice something behind us, we experience (although in an empty manner) something indefinite behind us, and when we turn and see that there is something going on behind our back, our intention is fulfilled. In this manner, the other is constituted for us as a like-sensing subjectivity, and she is taken to participate in the constitution of the one and the same world. Instead, if we cannot perceive what the other seems to notice behind our back, the other is not constituted as constitutively significant in this respect, but perhaps as delirious or paranoid: although such persons are experienced as constitutively significant in many other respects, they are not taken as world-constituting subjectivities in the same sense as the subject whose perceptions we can accord with.

In respect to normality, the implications of our experience of others are multifarious. First of all, "each experience-system with its level of normality can be transgressed by a more complete one."[84] For example, we may come to realize that someone else is able to clearly see the timetable at the train station from where we stand, whereas we ourselves will have to move closer to the board in order to see it properly. Such experiences have normative relevance for our experiential life in the sense that the timetable henceforth appears for us as something that can—with an optimal sight—be read from further away than where we ourselves are able to read it. That is to say, even if it refers back to my primordial normality, the intersubjective normality—once established—can be revised by our experience of others: "When my lived-body functions anomalously, the other's lived-body can function normally," and hence, "in particular matters I can enter into contradiction with others, into doubt and negation of being, similarly to the way I do this with myself."[85] Whereas in primordial experience the normal givenness of the object was identical with its primordially optimal givenness, once an intersubjective normality is established, the status of our own perceptual abilities as the standard or measure of perceptual normality is called into question:[86] that is, to continue the example, our own perceptual abilities come to appear as non-optimal, and so we come to regard ourselves as "nearsighted."

Therefore, through intersubjective encounter we not only constitute the environment as shared, but such encounters can also transform or revise the manner in which this shared environment is concretely perceptually intended: namely, the thing itself as the "rule of possible appearances" can gain features and determinations that we ourselves do not primordially constitute. However, to realize that someone else can see better than I do, to realize that one's own perceptual abilities are not optimal, is not to obstruct one's access to intersubjective objectivity—on the contrary, it is precisely to confirm this access. The intersubjective thing itself is not postulated beyond one's own subjective experiences, but it is rather that which is intended all the time: an ideal pole in respect of which our perceptions can be better or worse. Two perceiving bodies cannot be "absolutely alike" (*absolut gleich*), but insofar as their perceptual abilities remain on the scale of better or worse, their individual differences (as well as the occasional anomalies) remain within the bounds of an "intersubjective concordance" (*intersubjektive Einstimmigkeit*).[87] This is another way of saying that the appearance-systems of these two subjects are similar enough for the constitution of shared objectivity. On the other hand, along with the establishment of intersubjective normality, the normativity of the primordial is "relativized": instead of being simply relative to subjectivity, normality is now constituted as *relative to intersubjectivity*—and hence to perceptual abilities that I myself may not have.

In this manner, the intersubjective norm, like the primordial norm, guides our intentional experiences. But what is the status of the primordial norm in intersubjective experience? In what sense is primordial normativity "relativized" in intersubjectivity? As I have repeatedly stressed, the primordial is not simply overcome by the intersubjective—and, accordingly, *primordial normality cannot be replaced by, or subordinated to, intersubjective normality*. For instance, it is not that after realizing her disability, a person blind from birth would henceforth constitute herself merely as an abnormally perceiving subject; after all, such a person never actually comes to experience the lack of a particular sense-field—any more than we experience our "lack" of an echo-location system or of a lateral line system. Hence, it is rather that, for her, those who speak of a visual realm are referring to an alien dimension to which she has no direct access, and even if she would come to "know" that other people can sensuously experience visual features such as colors, the tactile sensations of the blind never gain an intentional reference to the visual givenness of things.[88] Such reference is simply beyond their constitutive possibilities, and thus intersubjective agreement is not established in this regard. For a person born blind, there is no experiential reference to intersubjectively optimal visual perception, no visual normality, and hence her system of perceptual normality is qualitatively different from that of those who see. Although they participate in many other respects, the blind are unable to participate in the intersubjective constitution of the *visual* world.

However, even if it is emphasized that the normative structures of primordial constitution are not subordinated to the normative structures of intersubjective constitution, the other extreme must be avoided as well—that is, the idea that intersubjective normativity would be subordinated to primordial normativity. To continue my earlier example, the nearsighted person seeks for a place where she herself can best discern the timetable, where it appears in an optimal manner for her; but on the other hand she can also realize herself as nearsighted, and she does not expect others to seek for the place where she herself can best discern the timetable. In other words, what appears as optimal in the intersubjective sense is not subordinated to what is optimal in the primordial sense. Yet, even if the primordial has been constituted as intersubjectively relative, the primordial is still operative. Let me clarify this issue through an analogy. My experience of a drinking glass on the left is not annulled when I realize that for a person facing me, the glass appears on the right. There is no rivalry, no conflict between our systems of orientation, and this is because they are both relative to a shared intersubjective space, that is, both are appearances of it:[89] the glass appears at *our* disposal, within *our* reach, between *us*, and thus our primordial views have a common ground. However, the glass can appear to me as being "on the right from the point of view of the other" only insofar as I already perceive it (and the other) in some direction, and it can appear as being within *our* reach only insofar as it appears within *my* reach.[90] Likewise, primordial normalities are still operative in intersubjective normality. The appearances of the world still refer to optimal givenness *in the limits of my own* abilities. Despite the reference to intersubjective normality, the primordial normality has not vanished.[91] In other words, just as the primordial system of orientation is necessarily involved in the constitution of other primordial systems of orientation and in the constitution of an intersubjective space, so too the constitution of intersubjective normality necessarily includes a reference to primordial normality.

Accordingly, the primordial norm and the intersubjective norm are not mutually exclusive notions. Instead, *each concrete experience involves two kinds of normativity:* the primordial-subjective (i.e., what is optimal in the limits of one's own perceptual abilities) and the intersubjective (i.e., what is shared among the optimally perceiving members of our intersubjective community). Our perception of the timetable refers to its possible optimal manner of givenness, and this optimality is defined in relation to both one's own factual abilities and the possible abilities of others. That is, the ideal intersubjective normality does not solve the factual tension between primordial systems of normality—and, as said, it is this tension that gives rise to the ideal intersubjective normality in the first place. Intersubjective experience is an experience in the first-person perspective. And as the perceptual systems are never quite identical, the constitution of intersubjective objectivity is established against the background of a tension between primordial normalities.

However, as already emphasized, if the other is to be normatively significant, she cannot be completely different: disagreement can only take place within the horizon of a more fundamental agreement, in regard to something shared.[92] Namely, like in the case of a nearsighted and optimally seeing person, so too in the case of an encounter between a blind person and a seeing one, a shared ground is constituted: even though the perceptual reference to the visual is not shared, the environment can be intersubjectively verified as to its tactile, auditory, olfactory, and taste-related features, and in this limited sense the blind and the seeing can experientially share the perceptual environment.[93] Again, nearsighted persons take part in the intersubjective constitution of the visual world, but in this constitution their perceptions are not *normative* (optimalizing). Accordingly, there are levels in the shared normality, levels of agreement, and levels of intersubjectivity—and correlatively, there are levels of objectivity: "The levels of normalities and anomalies correlate with the levels of the constitution of being, from relative being in relative appearances, up to objectively true being of the truly existing world."[94] In the following section I will elaborate this correlation in more detail. This is important because my general task in this part is to argue that the constitution of objectivity is fundamentally relative to the bodily-perceptual abilities of individual subjects. Let me first offer a brief summary.

To experience an other is to experience a second normality, and in such encounters an intersubjective normality is established. Primordial constitution is normatively relevant in two senses. First, it is relevant in the sense that what we pre-reflectively expect others to be able to perceive is initially outlined by our own perceptual abilities. Second, it is also relevant in the sense of revising and transforming intersubjective normality. Both primordial normality and intersubjective normality are present in our concrete experiences: *each experience involves two interrelated normative structures*. My awareness of what is intersubjectively normal is mediated by the awareness of what is normal for me—and intersubjective normality is hence necessarily something that more or less coincides with my primordial normality. If it does not coincide with mine, I do not experience it as *our* intersubjective normality, but as an alien one—as abnormality.

Particular Lifeworlds and the Underlying Nature

Experiences of alien normality have constitutive consequences. Namely, encountering alien cultures and traditions gives rise to the relativization of our familiar homeworld. The levels of objectivity must now be clarified and their interrelations explicated. This will later enable me to illuminate the manner in which primordial normality is operative in the constitution of the objective world. In order to clarify how alien cultures are constituted, and how their alien normality appears to us, I will start with a more general discussion of normality in cultural context: this illustrates the manner in which the alien culture presents itself, and as such it serves as an introduction to my analysis of the constitution of intersubjective nature.

In the course of our genesis, we have grown into an intersubjective system of normality, which, as appropriated, has become a habitual part of our subjectivity. As such, intersubjectivity regulates our perceptions, experiences, and actions from within—it is a "norm of the will" (*Norm des Willens, Willensnorm*).[95] Yet norms are not present as something explicit, say, as "rules," "rights," or "conventions." For instance, when addressing someone, we tend to say that we have the right to get a response, but as Husserl points out, this is an "inauthentic turn of phrase," since norms are "not present categorically" as conventional rules, but rather "have their exclusive authority in [the form of] 'conscience.'" In other words, before norms are reflected upon and objectified as particular rules or conventions, they have "a sensed validity (a felt, recognized [validity])."[96] As "consciously valid norms" (*bewusst geltende Normen*), norms are not mere objective facts, but something we perceive and act according to: they are like a general transcript of the respective perceptual and practical situation, a "default" manner of moving and comporting that regulates our intentional life—in perceiving, behavior, and acting. Our ways of experiencing tend not only toward subjectively habitual and typical manners, but toward intersubjectively familiar ways of experiencing.

Accordingly, the culturally defined manner of conduct is expressed in the acts of individuals and, in this sense, individuals *represent* the tradition and community they are part of—even if not necessarily in an explicit manner (which is the case, e.g., when an activist functions as the voice of a particular minority, or when a leader of a nation represents the nation as a whole). The traditional style of thought, expression, and movement characteristic of one's own tradition manifests itself in the individual acts of thinking, expression, and movement. Hence our encounter with others is not only an encounter between primordial normalities, but at once an encounter between intersubjective normalities and their respective generative backgrounds. However, within a particular cultural sphere, the perceived actions of others express a familiar manner of being, and hence the generative aspect in the other's ways of being remains implicit. We do not pay attention to the intersubjective peculiarities that regulate the other's behavior if she acts more or less as we expect—and this is more or less the case in an encounter between homecomrades. Instead, the ways of acting and thinking of persons from different intersubjective contexts, alien cultures and traditions, express something unfamiliar.

The alien intersubjective context becomes particularly prominent and explicit in situations where mutual understanding is not reached. The thoughts of the other may reveal a set of alien presuppositions, an alien style of thinking, a foreign code of conduct—and the other may literally speak a language unfamiliar to us. We realize that the other shares these ways of acting and language with other members of her tradition, and she is thus experienced as a representative of an intersubjective context of meaning—although an unfamiliar one. In confronting others, we are therefore never faced only with a singular person, but at once with an intersubjective tradition.

Such encounters are not without constitutive effects.[97] Being faced with an alien intersubjective context of meaning, our scope of objectivity is transformed. What we until then had taken as *the* world turns out to be the correlate of our system of normality, a "homeworld" of a particular intersubjective community, and thereby our normality and correlatively our world is constituted as being one lifeworld among many. On the other hand, our homeworld and the alien homeworld are rooted in the one and only real world that serves as the ultimate horizon for all possible homeworlds. This relates to our earlier discussion about different forms of intersubjectivity. I have argued that transcendental intersubjectivity is essentially open not only to our homecomrades (the "We") but, at the same time, to anybody. Here I argue that our culturally specific homeworld (the correlate of the "We") appears in the horizon of nature (the correlate of anybody). By investigating the relation between homeworld and the underlying nature, and by connecting this exposition of nature with the notion of anybody, I will be shedding light upon the significance of embodiment in the constitution of objectivity.

In line with the distinction between the homeworld and the underlying nature, Husserl distinguishes between "objectivity as intersubjectivity," that is, objectivity as the correlate of a community of subjects, and "objectivity in the strict sense," that is, objectivity as the correlate of "the actual unrestricted 'universe,' the allness of all those cognizing subjects in general who stand in connection with the cognizing one."[98] Husserl stresses on the one hand that what is objective is identical for everyone (*jedermann*).[99] However, on the other hand he claims that these others, horizonally implied in our experiences, are "normal human beings" (*normalen Menschen*), and explains that the notion of *jedermann* does not actually cover all human beings:[100] "*Each closed community of life has its normality and for it 'anyone' has a special sense; and so the environment that anyone experiences as [the] world is not the idea of the world which is, in itself, the world of all human beings in unconditional commonality.*"[101] That is to say, our homeworld, our intersubjective lifeworld, has an objectivity in the sense that it is shared by "anybody" within it, and yet our homeworld is one particular lifeworld, and as such it is relative to the ultimate horizon of nature, to the perceptual world that is shared by "anybody" in the sense that is not restricted to our homecomrades. As I have argued, subjectivity is a priori open to others—to possible homecomrades as well as more generally to anybody. In the following I will analyze the constitution of nature—the real world that is objective in the strict sense—in order to be able to point out the central relevance of embodiment in this constitution.

Just as one's own primordial experience has a constitutive primacy in the encounter with others, so too in encountering alien communities the constitutional primacy resides in the "intersubjective sphere of ownness" in the sense that one's own culture is constitutionally primordial over against every alien culture.[102] That is to say, there is a structural similarity between the perceptual and the cultural: just as we pre-reflectively expect the other to be able to sensuously perceive what we do, we also tacitly expect her to share our habitual ways of thinking, our manners of expression, our set of presuppositions, our code of conduct—in short, we expect others to share our familiar intersubjective normality. We expect the other to act in a normal manner and the normality in question is relative to our intersubjective background. For example, we expect the other to reply or at least react if addressed: when asking the time from a stranger, we not only expect her to hear our voice, but also to realize that we are addressing her, and even to understand our language—and there is always a moment of surprise if she doesn't. That is to say, just as we expect the other to sensuously perceive our bodily movements and uttered sounds, we also tacitly expect her to understand their intersubjective meaning, and thus to witness the cultural significance of the perceived things and events. However, as differences then manifest themselves, we grasp that others do not share our intersubjective normality. In this sense, we initially experience their behavior as "abnormal."[103] This, of course, is not to say that we experience them as pathological cases: their experiences and actions seem to have an inner coherence that may be optimal and familiar to them. That is to say, the alien is not constituted as abnormal in itself, but as abnormal for us, as abnormal from the point of view of our intersubjective normality: as Canguilhem nicely phrases it, abnormality is not the absence of norms, but the presence of alien norms.[104] In confronting the alien, we find ourselves as confronted by a strange normality that is not our own. The experiences and actions of the alien other do not motivate us to *revise* our intersubjective normality, and neither can the alien normality simply be subordinated to ours. Rather, like in the individual level, there remains a *tension of normalities*.

Such experiences are not without constitutive significance. In encountering an alien normality, our familiar normality is constituted as one among many.[105] However, our "intersubjective sphere of ownness" does not thereby cease to function as the constitutive basis of objectivity. In other words, even though we can grasp that from the point of view of the alien, we appear "abnormal" like they appear to us, and even though the world is thus revealed as being divided into a multiplicity of lifeworlds relative to historical communities, we nevertheless do not gain a neutral, purely objective standpoint to the world. For each community, the purely objective world serves as the horizon of its respective homeworld, and is necessarily experienced through the latter—in this sense, we are never free of "relativism."[106] However, Husserl argues that through our encounter with the alien, and *only* through it, do we come to experience our lifeworld as *our* intersubjective world, as something that we share with other members of *our* community. Namely, once an alien community (e.g., an alien nation, folk, or culture) is constituted, "precisely thereby 'our own' association of homecomrades, association of the people in relation to our surrounding cultural world, is constituted for me and for us as the world of our human validities, of our particular validities."[107] That is to say, the objective world and homeworld are first distinguished from one another through the fact that there are several homeworlds.[108] In other words, it is not until a "liminal encounter"[109] with the alien that we become aware of ourselves as representatives of a particular "We." If we never experienced other cultures, our own culture could not appear to us as such. Like personal identity, cultural identity can be revealed as such only in relation to what is other.

Thus it turns out that our "community of homecomrades" (*Heimgenossenschaft*) refers to a *particular* "anybody" within a more general "anybody." Correlatively, what we simply took as objectivity is now constituted as relative to our intersubjective community: what we took as *the* world is now revealed as a particular lifeworld, as the correlate of a particular

"We," of a particular human community (*Sondermenschheit*).¹¹⁰ To experience another cultural sphere is to constitute an alien lifeworld. However, this alienworld is not constituted as an extension of the homeworld: the homeworld is not expanded in such encounters, and there occurs no synthesis between the homeworld and the alienworld.¹¹¹ Rather, there remains a tension: like inter*subjective* objectivity, inter*cultural* objectivity too is constituted through experiences of difference; it arises from the basis of an irreducible tension of (intersubjective) normalities. In this sense, experiences of abnormality (i.e., alien normality) are constitutively significant. Namely, the tension between intersubjective normalities gives rise to the constitution of a shared horizon.

Our lifeworlds and cultural environments can be remarkably different, and yet—insofar as we experience others as members of an alien culture—there is necessarily constituted a common horizon. How should one characterize this intercultural objectivity? The question can be reformulated into a question concerning the general features shared across all surrounding worlds. Husserl writes: "The multiplicity of the alienworld is given as oriented to mine [my homeworld], and is [given as] a world because it is constituted along with a common objective world . . . , and the spatiotemporal form of this objective world functions at the same time as the form that gives access to it."¹¹² What Husserl is suggesting is that there are certain *invariants* that pertain to each and every lifeworld, and that these are what enable a so-called external access to an alien lifeworld (or alienworld).¹¹³

First and foremost, we can experience the alien lifeworld as an alien lifeworld because our "worlds" share a spatiotemporal and, more generally, a *natural structure*.¹¹⁴ To be sure, what is shared between homeworlds is not a "mere nature" (*blosser Natur*), which is the correlate of the natural-scientific attitude, but rather nature as the correlate of human experience.¹¹⁵ Husserl specifies: "After all, [regardless of] how alien they may be, they have something in common [to us], earth and sky, day and night, stones and trees, hills and valleys, diverse animals etc.—all this [is] grasped through analogy, according to the most general type, although as alien."¹¹⁶

Thus we come back to the theme of embodiment. Namely, regardless of our cultural background, we are all sensing, bodily beings, we walk on the same earth and witness the same sky and stars, we all breathe the same air, eat and drink, organize our lives in relation to the shifts of day and night—and, in this sense, we all belong to the one and only world—regardless of the vast differences in our intersubjective-cultural systems of normality and the correlative lifeworlds. No matter how different the alien others might be, we experience them as bodily beings that are related to the one and only "spatiotemporal horizon" or "real world in general" (*reale Welt überhaupt*).[117] Husserl explains that alien others are experienced as "alien people, but still as people, realities, animated bodies, persons who live in a particular community with each other, building culture and specific community, being therewith interconnected through specific convictions (theoretical, axiological, practical), and specific (typically new kinds of) purposes in life, and thus shaping culture."[118]

In our encounter with another community, and hence with another possible lifeworld, a shared realm is disclosed, a "nonpractical horizon" (*unpraktischen Horizont*),[119] to which our historically separated lifeworlds with their practices ultimately refer back. Husserl writes:

> Through experience, a human being learns to exceed his relative environment, [and thus] he becomes better acquainted with *the* world. . . . In this relativity the concrete world is . . . established, in the living constitutive genesis, as the world for human beings that are normal in the most general and extended sense. He is no longer merely a normal [subjectivity] of his homeworld, but a normal [subjectivity] of human-cognition and world-cognition, that is established in the synthetic expanding of environments. Starting from my homeworld as a world of concordant intersubjective experience of my homecomrades, every alien [subjectivity] is for me and for us ultimately normal, insofar as he is understood like me and my homecomrades as a subject of her homeworld, i.e., as a comrade in her community of homecomrades.[120]

What is shared across cultural boundaries, and what is thus objective in the strict sense, is the realm of nature, the sensuous world "in its invariant general structure."[121]

> Essentially hand in hand with the constitution of [our] historical surrounding world goes the constitution of an infinite, open nature that exceeds the finitudes of the historical surrounding world, and this, as always preceding, *enables* the constitution of the open possibility of ever new, although factically inaccessible, historical totalities [i.e., alien traditions and correlative lifeworlds].[122]

That is to say, the ultimate horizon that fundamentally "bridges" our lifeworlds is nature, the world of bodily experience. Husserl emphasizes that "there can exist only one objective world, only one objective time, only one objective space, only one objective nature. Moreover, this one nature *must* exist if there are any structures in me that implicate the coexistence of other monads."[123]

As I have argued, the horizonal structure of perception tacitly implies, a priori, an open infinity of co-perceivers, of co-bearers (*Mittträgern*),[124] and therefore the perceptual environment is from the start taken as being there for anybody. The a priori intersubjectivity is not replaced by the culture we grow into: perceived objects are still tacitly taken to be shared, not only with our homecomrades, but with *anybody*. And it is this horizon that serves as the basis for our encounter with other persons as well as alien cultures. Accordingly, Husserl summarizes:

> The question of the transcendental constitution of the world that exists for me has levels: the first is the level of the constitution of a concordant *homeworld*. . . . The second is the problem of critique of the homeworld in the horizon of alien homeworlds, that is to say, critique of universal experience that should produce a unity across all synthetically unified homeworlds, that is to say, [should] produce a true world.[125]

In other words, we are not only members of local intersubjective communities (say, family, nation, tradition), but we are also members of a total community that reaches across our homeworlds.[126] And, correlatively, even if we do not share a historical lifeworld with everyone, we nevertheless share the real world with everyone, or rather, with *anybody*.[127]

However, there are certain necessary restrictions that must be made in respect to the "anybody." These restrictions must be brought to light in order to be able to explicate the constitution of the objective world and to understand its relation to the embodied subjectivity.

Subjects from alien traditions do not share our particular intersubjective normality, they are not constituting members of our intersubjective community and do not participate in the constitution of our homeworld, but insofar as they are concordantly related to the horizon of nature, they count as members of the total community of co-bearers of the world of nature. That is, even if we do not share the normality as familiarity, we share normality in the sense of orthoesthetic concordance—and correlatively we share the world of nature.[128] Similarity of appearance-systems is the minimum requirement for the intersubjective constitution of nature. Others are constituted as perceiving the environment only insofar as this requirement is satisfied.[129]

However, as already indicated, the identity of perceptual systems is an ideal possibility, whereas factually the similarity of appearance-systems comes in levels. Here I am interested in what I termed with Husserl "objectivity in the strict sense."[130] With other mature and healthy human beings, we do not necessarily share the "content" of our lifeworld, but we still share the world in the sense that our lifeworlds have a common "world-form," an invariant structure that is common to us both. But what about animals? They obviously do not share our world-form, and yet they are not like stones either.[131] Husserl argues that the total community of normatively significant, co-constituting subjectivities does not factually cover any perceiver ("anybody"):

> However, "other" subjects include also "the insane" and animals.... As intentional modifications of myself, *all* are accessible beings through "empathic" experience. *But not all, reduced in a transcendental manner, are co-bearers of the world* that is pregiven as my world and that "we" have as pregiven—and here the "We" is taken precisely as the open multiplicity of co-bearers that together in a community constitute the one and the same world (animals or insane "human beings" [are] in no way [such co-bearers of the world], although they are experienced by us as being related in their inner life to the world, to the one and the same "actual" world).[132]

Here Husserl argues that transcendental intersubjectivity does not in fact cover all possible perceivers. As he puts it elsewhere: "The constitution of material nature is first accomplished in relation to normal embodiment, that is, for normal subjects."[133] In other words, not only the constitution of a homeworld, but also the constitution of nature is inseparable from the problem of normality. There are infants, there are the blind and the deaf, there are persons who have lost their sense of kinesthesia, there are demented and schizophrenic patients whose experience of spatiotemporality is disrupted, and there is a vast range of non-human animals that are related to their environment in ways that are very different from ours.[134] Therefore, if every sensory being was equally constituted as a co-bearer of the natural world, we would have to maintain that the natural world lacks all intuitive content, since there would not be any concrete experiential point of reference that is common to each and every sensing subject—even if we can theoretically construct a point of reference, as the natural sciences do. However, nature is what we experience immediately: it manifests itself *in* the objects of our familiar lifeworld—not somewhere behind or beyond it. The book that I hold in my hand is also a physical thing and its materiality is experienced immediately: what is experientially shared across the homeworld and the alienworld is not a formal point of reference that cannot be given "in the flesh," but precisely the visible and palpable reality of things and events—regardless of how these are culturally defined.

In this manner, the discussion of normality and objectivity brings us back to embodiment. Namely, not only the constitution of "objectivity as intersubjectivity," but also the constitution of "objectivity in the strict sense" presupposes the similarity of orthoesthetic systems of perception—and, as I have argued, the experienced similarity has its "measure" or norm in the subject of such experience. Moreover, since nature is constituted in relation to our primordial normality, in what follows, I will argue that the constitution of the real world is tacitly restricted by our own embodied abilities. Let me first offer a brief summary.

The real world is constituted in levels and these levels correlate with levels of normality. There is first of all a *primordial normality*, outlined in relation to one's own abilities of perception and movement. An encounter with the other is accordingly an encounter with a second normality. As Husserl puts it, "in empathy different normalities collide,"[135] which is another way of saying that the "first normality" and "second normality" enter into a relation of tension. This tension motivates the constitution of an *intersubjective normality*, in regard to which the primordial normalities are constituted as relative, as "merely subjective." Correlative to this shared normality intersubjective objectivity is constituted.[136] Further, as soon as we confront representatives of alien homeworlds (i.e., representatives of alien normality) our intersubjective homeworld (and likewise our intersubjective normality) is realized in its particularity and relativity. Hence what we simply took as shared objectivity turns out to be objectivity-for-us, objectivity shared within a particular intersubjective community. In this sense, experiences of alien normality (i.e., abnormality) are constitutively significant: they reveal the natural world of experience that underlies and permeates the cultural world.

Accordingly, we can distinguish three levels of objectivity, correlating with the three levels of normality:[137]

(1) "Primordial objectivity," correlative to "primordial normality"
(2) "Intersubjective objectivity," relative to an "intersubjective normality"
(3) "Objectivity in the strict sense," the real world, objective nature, relative to "anybody"

In the course of my elaboration, I ended up suggesting that problems of normality reach even to the constitution of objective nature: whereas in respect to the constitution of intersubjective objectivity, the "normatively significant" members are our homecomrades who share our intersubjective normality in respect to the constitution of global objectivity—the nature underlying all homeworlds—the "normatively significant" members are those that have similar appearance-systems.[138] The fact that the constitution of objectivity is inseparable from questions of normality has remarkable implications. Our primordial perceptual abilities outline what is initially constituted as being perceivable to anybody, and in this manner the primordial lays the foundation for all further types of intersubjectivity. Thus, in the constitution of objective reality, embodiment plays a crucial and central role: embodied subjectivity is the original norm-generating being.

8

Transcendental Consequences

In the previous chapter, I studied the genetic constitution of intersubjective objectivity. I elaborated how an encounter between individual subjectivities (primordialities) gives rise to intersubjective normality, and how an encounter between intersubjective normalities (homeworlds) gives rise, in a structurally similar manner, to the constitution of the intercultural world of nature. I argued that in intersubjective encounters, the status of primordial normality is transformed in the sense that our own lived-body is now constituted as *one* primordial norm, as *one* original body (*Urleib*)[1] among others. In this chapter I develop the transcendental consequences of this analysis by clarifying the sense in which primordial normality is sustained in intersubjective world-constitution. By elaborating this in detail, I will disclose, within subjectivity, a structure that I call a "normative tension."

Empathy and the Limits of Intersubjective Constitution

What enables our reciprocal confrontation with alien cultures is ultimately the fact that we are all related to the same sensuous realm: even if we do not share a historical lifeworld, we nevertheless constitute ourselves as being related to the one and the same horizon of bodily experience, to the sensuous environment in its invariant, general structure.[2] This presupposes that our perceptual abilities coincide—and here the embodied self serves as the primordial norm. Even if the other is not familiar with the cultural meaning of the ice cream that we hold in our hand, for instance, we nevertheless assume her to perceive it as something in front of her, as something she could approach and grasp, and as something that would feel cold in her hands. That is to say, the other is constituted as having a similar system of spatiotemporal orientation, similar possibilities of kinesthetic self-movement, and a similar system of sensibility—similar, even if not identical. Now, insofar as our expectation is fulfilled, insofar as the other in fact proves to have the capacities we originally attribute to her, what is experientially shared is not a formal, theoretical object, but the thing as it is sensuously given.

The experientially shared thing can be neither constituted nor defined without reference to possible perceivers, and, consequently, the natural thing itself is necessarily constituted in relation to *a particular kind of* appearance-system. This influences even eidetic-phenomenological descriptions. To be sure, we can conjure and imagine remarkably different perceptions, but what we mean by "perceiving" is bound to our own—primordial and intersubjectively familiar—embodiment. In this sense, as Husserl puts it, the "possibilities of imagination as variations of essence do not float freely in the air, but are constitutively related to me in my facticity, [to me] with my living present that I factically live through."[3] To employ Husserl's example, if I am imagining a centaur, I am bound to imagine it as in a certain orientation and in a particular relation to my sense organs: whatever I imagine, "upon closer scrutiny, I *myself* am *thereby* co-imagined in a peculiar manner."[4] In this sense "*my normal being* [is] the bearer (the Archimedean footing) not only of worlds that are actual for me, but also of those that are conceivable for me."[5] The idea of the normative structure of primordial constitution, accordingly, has remarkable consequences. Namely, as this issue is investigated further, it will turn out that our factical embodiment has a central normative role in the constitution of objective reality. In order to clarify the normative role of the embodied subjectivity in the constitution of objective nature, we must return to Husserl's theory of empathy.

In perceiving the other, we empathically experience the environment from her point of view.[6] That is, before any deliberation, we empathically grasp the sensible situation[7] of the other. Of course, as Husserl adds, this does not mean that I would thereby feel myself "over there"; in the literal sense, there occurs no "feeling-into" (*Einfühlung*) or "transference" (*Übertragung*) and hence empathy must be distinguished from simulation.[8] Moreover, besides simulation, Husserl also distinguishes empathy from imagination. He tentatively characterizes empathy as "thinking-one's-way-into-the-other" (*Sich-in-den-Anderen-hineindenken*) and as "imagining-one's-way-into-the-other" (*Hineinphantasieren*), but specifies that, unlike imagination, empathy is "positional, and does not proceed in the 'as if' of pure fantasy"; others are given as being actually there, whereas "out of pure imagination no path leads to reality."[9] To merely imagine the world from the point of view of the other is not the same as to perceive something shared.[10] The other is experienced as someone who actually perceives; her perceptions are not merely imagined but posited. Yet, empathy presupposes imagination:

if we were not already able to imagine how the environment would appear from "over there," it would forever remain unintelligible how it is possible that a perceived body "over there 'reminds' me of my possible being and prevailing over there."[11] In this sense, the imagined possibility for the interchange of places is necessary for empathy. Husserl sums up: "To consider him [i.e., another ego] from the basis of empathy, this means necessarily: to consider myself and my motivations. However I think of him, he is for me an other, a modification of myself, my analogue, that can be intuitive to me only insofar as I retrieve myself in him or himself in me."[12] The other's "primordial nature"—a "second original world" (*zweite originale Welt*)—which is appresented in our empathic experience, must appear as "the same na-ture," as the same "world," and in this sense, as Husserl claims, it must appear "in the mode of appearance: 'as if I were standing over there, where the other's body is.'"[13]

In this sense, appresence refers back to primal presence.[14] Husserl characterizes pairing or coupling as "reciprocal overlapping": "should the pairing ones possess in themselves, each in their own manner, presumptive validities with appropriate abilities, this is carried mutually from one over to the other—passively, without further ado, in one go."[15] That is to say, insofar as the other is presumed to be related to the same nature, she is presumed to share our abilities, capacities, and faculties. This is another way of saying that the other is expected to share our primordial normality: "precisely this structure of normality . . . is thereby necessarily carried over into each actual and thinkable other."[16]

In short, through empathy, the appearance-systems of self and other, and thereby the environment that originally manifests itself in them, "come into synthesis."[17] The appresented perception of the other is coupled or paired with our perception, and these two elements become "so fused that they stand within the functional community of one perception, which simultaneously presents and appresents."[18] In this manner, successful empathy establishes intersubjective constitution:

> The coexistence of transcendental subjects, the coexistence of their immanent temporalities, the coexistence of their primordialities is no empty (upon closer inspection, unthinkable) being-together, but a being-for-one-another, which means: appresentive accessibility to one another, and therefore internal, comprehensible, self-demonstrating being-united and being-bound [with one another]. This enables intersubjective constitution.[19]

Accordingly, even though we cannot actually experience the other's experience, the appresented experience does not lack *content*. Husserl writes: *"Empathy* is, so to speak, *coincidence* of the ego and egoic life along with its appearances with those of the other. The alien appearances are an intentional modification, they are contentual variations, in the same sense that my own possible experience is a variation of my actual experience."[20] That is, the other's experiences are appresented not only as to their form but as to their content, and what we initially take her to perceive is what we ourselves perceive.[21] For instance, we intend the perceived landscape as something that the present other is able to perceive with us—and the appresented content refers back to the perceptual content of our own experience. In this sense the empathically appresented experiences are "contentual variations" (*inhaltliche Abwandlungen*) of our experiences and point back to our primordial normality.

Intersubjectivity and Humanity

This brief clarification will enable me to explain Husserl's claim that the totality of constituting intersubjectivity resides in mankind.[22] Husserl asks, "What about animals and animal environment? After all, we also relate animals . . . , along with their probably quite widely deviating sensuous intuitions, to the same things, to the same world, that we ourselves experience. Are we and our normal human embodiment thereby the norm, and the sensuous intuitions of animals, in contrast, anomalous deviations?"[23] Husserl answers this question in the affirmative: animals are "understood as modifications of the norm of the human" (*von der Norm des Menschen abgewandelt verstanden*).[24] However, this must be understood as a purely descriptive claim concerning the *constitution* of others: it is neither a devaluation of animals nor a claim that animals are like failed human beings. As already said, Husserl claims that, in the objective sense, there are several systems of optimal experience, several normalities—and it would be simply wrong to claim that in comparison to dogs, for instance, humans hear better. Husserl clarifies: "no species can claim *a priori* to possess in its system of experiencing the optimal manner of experiencing, in which *all* properties of things would manifest themselves."[25] Nevertheless, in the sense of constitution, humanity has a normative primacy—just as, analogically, primordial constitution has a constitutive primacy over the "second normality" of the other, and like one's own culture has a primacy over other cultures. Let us take a closer look at the problem of animals.

To be sure, as we perceive animals, we experience living beings: animals are constituted as self-moving and reacting beings that are sensuously related to their immediate environment—this is phenomenologically indisputable. For instance, if in the marketplace a seagull suddenly snatches our ice cream, we experience the gull as having "seen" the ice cream and, while grabbing the ice cream, as having "felt" its coldness and weight. In other words, even though the bird obviously has a remarkably different sensory-motor system, it is nevertheless experienced as being sensuously related to the same environment and to the same things that we are. To claim the opposite would be absurd: after all, we see the bird, which means that it does not live in a parallel universe, and there must be a point of intersection connecting our sensuous environments. However, the animal does not perceive things in their human meaning. To borrow an example from Heidegger: "When we say that the lizard is lying on the rock, we ought to cross out the word 'rock' in order to indicate that whatever the lizard is lying on is certainly given in *some way* for the lizard, and yet is not known to the lizard *as* a rock."[26] How, then, should we characterize this dimension of the environment that, allegedly, is shared with animals? To study this question is to explicate the manner in which animals participate in the constitution of the "sensuously common world" (*sinnlich gemeinsame Welt*).[27]

Let us weigh our options. We are unable to experience the environment from the animal's situation; we have no access to "what it is like" to sense like this animal.[28] Accordingly, there seem to be only three alternatives: the alleged shared environment must be either (1) the human environment as such, (2) an abstract level of the human environment as such, or (3) a species-neutral environment. First of all, animals do not perceive the environment in its human significance (they do not perceive ice creams *as* ice creams, rocks *as* rocks, etc.), and therefore the first alternative must be ruled out. Moreover, when it comes to the second alternative, we are forced to admit that animals cannot experience things as "mere things" (*blosse Sachen*): things can be constituted as "*mere* things" only insofar as they are originally something "more," and animals are hardly capable of such complex theoretical abstraction.[29] Hence the second alternative must be ruled out as well. However, the third alternative must also be ruled out: the environment is constituted, primordially, as the horizon of one's own subjective-bodily abilities (as the field of "I can"), and, intersubjectively, as the environment that can be experienced by others that have similar subjective-bodily abilities. For us, the shared environment is constituted as the correlate of our (human) type of corporeality—we are unable to "transgress" (*überschreiten*) our facticity, as Husserl puts it.[30] That is, nature is not constituted as a species-neutral dimension—to be sure, we can theoretically construct a species-neutral environment, but such theoretical constructions are human products, and they arise from the basis of our (human) lifeworld. As Husserl claims, "human existence as such is always related consciously to an existing practical world as a surrounding world already endowed with humanly significant predicates."[31] Hence we seem to end up in a puzzling situation, since all the mentioned alternatives seem to be problematic: animals cannot experience the environment as it appears for us, and we cannot experience the environment as it appears for the animal, and neither can we experience a species-neutral environment.

Nevertheless, it is indisputable that in some sense humans and animals are related to one and the same environment: animals are constituted as being related to the environment that we experience. Accordingly, our options seem to narrow down to the following: what we take the animal to be perceiving are the things that, for us, are endowed with human significance, and the environment is therefore not shared reciprocally but one-sidedly.[32] For instance, we experience a seagull as feasting on our "ice cream," a cat chasing a "mouse," a dog howling at the "moon," a mosquito sucking our "blood," and so on. To be sure, we do realize that the animal does not perceive these things *as* such (nor as "mere things")—but we do, and this is our necessary starting point in experiencing others, whether animals or humans.

Moreover, this does not only concern cultural predicates: already in its materiality, our familiar surrounding world has intersubjectively shared qualities that are correlates of a particular type of embodiment. Natural things of a certain size, for instance, appear as "graspable" and "movable," despite the fact that there are beings with no organs of grasping; as "graspable" and "movable," things are constituted as correlates of a particularly organized lived-body with certain abilities of sensation and movement. Accordingly, the constitution of objective nature has a normative structure: it is an achievement of certain kinds of lived-bodies. The animal is constituted as being related to the sensuous environment as it appears to us: "*Each species has its relative truth, its relatively true world . . . that manifests itself as one and the same. . . . But we call it 'the same,' since for us it is known as the same.* The most original knowledge of such identity we have on our own case."[33] In this manner, we ourselves, with a certain set of bodily-perceptual abilities, function as the norm in defining and constructing the "world" of animals. Husserl specifies: "*All interpretation is relative to us human beings.* All other organisms are to be understood . . . only as modifications of [the] human [organism], with all its mental products, psychophysical faculties, perceptual functions, and practical functions. Only as such do they have a sense for us."[34] Accordingly, we do "share" the environment with animals but, in the constitutive sense, only in a one-sided manner.

Husserl further clarifies this issue by distinguishing, in the following manner, between reciprocal and one-sided empathy:

> (1) a universe of possible subjects that are reciprocally related to one another in empathy, i.e., a universe of subjects that know themselves to be related to the same world, and experience themselves as such; [and] (2) a universe of subjects . . . that a particular subject can "gain" through empathy (a universe of *one-sided* empathy): he necessarily experiences or knows that these [other] subjects are related to the same world, i.e., that they have in their solipsistic environment appearances of the things of this same world. But this does not mean that they could empathically apprehend me and anyone else, and attribute this same world to all, etc.[35]

To be sure, in a certain sense, there are "reciprocal" relations with animals, that is, empathic relations in which we experience the animal perceiving us. Nevertheless, in the sense of constitution, such relations remain one-sided, since we naively expect the animal to perceive us like *we* would perceive other people. The animal's "world of experience" (*Erfahrungswelt*) is "an intentional modification of the world that we humans have."[36] That is to say, as we transpose ourselves into the sensuous and motivational situation of the animal, we take its experiences as variations of our possible experiences—and thus we "humanize" the animal.[37] In the words of Husserl: "We find animals in our world through a kind of empathy, which is an assimilating modification of the empathy that we have toward fellow humans"—yet the "animal knows nothing of the environment that we attribute to it in naive empathy."[38] Thus, although we naively take the animal to perceive what we do, this naïveté is abolished in the course of experience: the animal does not move like we do, it does not share our perceptual capacities, and the environment that we perceive must accordingly appear to it in a very different manner.

Perceptual empathy renders the other's appresented experience as a modification or variation of our own experience; how we assume the animal to perceive its spatiotemporal environment is founded on how we ourselves perceive the environment. In this sense, we "human beings in our sense of being precede the brutes"; in the constitution of objectivity, the human body serves as the "prototype" (*Prototyp*) or norm:[39]

> Relative to the animal, the human being is, constitutionally speaking, the normal case—just as I myself am the primal norm constitutionally

for all other human beings. Animals are essentially constituted for me as anomalous "variants" of my humanness, even though among them in turn normality and anomaly may be differentiated.[40]

> *The world that is valid for us* . . . is relative to us human beings, thereby *primarily to our corporeal organization.* . . . The *world, and first and foremost nature, is essentially relative to human organization.* . . . The world is accordingly not thinkable without a human organism with human psychic life, the life of experience.[41]

Accordingly, the total transcendental intersubjectivity that constitutes the natural world is a "restricted" community. Animals are constituted as non-human existents in the human world. In this sense, the ultimate nature that looms on the horizon of our experiences of cultural objects is fundamentally a "human" nature: it is the horizon of *our* bodily capacities, and this is what we naively take others to be perceiving as well. The world is constituted for us as the human world, and nature is likewise constituted as human nature.

In this sense, animals are constituted as part of the human world, but not as world-constituting subjects. They are, as Merleau-Ponty puts it, our "*quasi-companions*" (*presque compagnons*).[42] Our encounter with non-human animals therefore structurally differs from our experience of alien cultures. Both confrontations take place within the human world, but the transcendental consequences of these confrontations differ remarkably.[43] Animals are not constituted as representatives of an alien community, and the animal environment is not an alien lifeworld next to ours. Therefore, unlike the encounter with alien communities, what we have here is not a "liminal encounter" with an alien homeworld: instead, our encounter with animals is an encounter *within our homeworld*, within the limits of our normality. In this sense, animals are constituted not as abnormal but as anomalous.

This is not to say that our one-sidedly empathic experiences of animals could not have constitutive effects. Husserl exemplifies: "As we understand that a dog is picking up the scent of game, it so to speak teaches us something of which we did not know; it expands our world of experience."[44] However, as I have argued, this expanded world is not something that we reciprocally share with the animal.[45] Rather, animals can expand *our* world. For example, we "employ" sniffer dogs in the customs, trackers in hunting, and sheepdogs in herding, and thus animals can be constitutively significant members of our homeworld[46]—and, in this sense, animals can also "belong" to alien cultures. However, as Husserl puts it, our experience of the world cannot be "corrected" (*korri-*

giert) by the animal's experience,[47] which is another way of saying that there can be no normative conflict between the human and the animal. To be sure, in an objective comparison, dogs have a more sensitive and elaborated sense of smell than we do. Nevertheless, when we realize that a dog picks up the scent of game, we do not thereby constitute ourselves and our friends as perceivers that should be able to smell the game in these circumstances—that is to say, our experience of animals does not motivate us to constitute *ourselves* as anomalous perceivers.

To summarize all this in the words of Husserl, "the world as it is, the actual world, is the exclusive correlate of us human beings," "the normal world with its normal qualities is a correlate of the normal community of human beings (which is here defined through normal embodiment)," and in this sense "universal intersubjectivity, into which all objectivity, everything that exists at all, is resolved, can obviously be nothing other than mankind."[48] Hence the "dependency of all animal species on the human" and the "relativity of the world to human organization."[49] What serves as the measure in our experience of objective nature is an optimally perceiving human body.

Yet, the idea of an optimally perceiving human body is established in the encounter between primordialities: the constitution of the objective nature presupposes the similarity of perceptual systems, and the primordial measure for this similarity resides in one's own lived-body. In this manner, the constitution of the intersubjective world is ultimately rooted in the primordial facticity of the embodied subjectivity.[50]

9

Paradox of Subjectivity Revisited

My rather extensive elaboration on animals has brought to light the manner in which the constitution of the intersubjective nature is related to primordial constitution. In the following, I will clarify the simultaneous presence of primordial and intersubjective normative structures in the constitution of the world, thus explicating what I call the "normative tension." I will do this by focusing on the constitution of spatiality, and by arguing that space is ultimately oriented in relation to both our lived-body and an intercorporeally shared ground. The duality of the oriented space will exemplify and illustrate the normative tension between primordiality and intersubjectivity in concrete world-constitution. I will eventually argue that the "paradox of subjectivity" (i.e., the paradox that subjectivity is, at the same time, both transcendental and empirical) can be understood in terms of this normative tension between transcendental primordiality and transcendental intersubjectivity. Let me start with the constitution of spatiality.

The Two Origins of Space

In and through an encounter with others, our experience of nature is transformed. Others are experienced as being related to the environment from their standpoint, and thus, by perceiving other perceiving beings, we experience other zero-points of orientation.[1] Through our experience of others, the spatial orientation of the environment is therefore transformed: space is no longer merely a horizon projected by our own abilities (the "I can," the primordial norm), but a horizon projected by intersubjective abilities (the "we can"). In such intersubjective space, our own body, the primordial center of spatial orientation, is constituted as being "over there" from the point of view of the other—and so, through others, we constitute ourselves as intersubjective objects in the world.

It should be emphasized once again that our primordial system of orientation is not replaced by that of the other.[2] Rather, it is constituted as something subjective, as one standpoint among others. Again, this does not imply that the other's system of orientation is constituted as the absolute point of reference, to which our system is relative: we still perceive this alien standpoint from our point of view, and only in relation to it does the alien standpoint have a sense to us as such. The lived-body of the other is perceived in the same environment in which our perceiving body is localized, and we therefore constitute the other as being perceptually related to the same space as we are. This intersubjective space is not oriented according to any particular body in it. However, if movement is to have an absolute sense (instead of only being movement from a point of view), there must be a shared point of reference in regard to which our subjective experiences of space, as well as our subjective systems of orientation, are relative. Husserl names this absolute point of reference the *earth-ground* (*Erdboden*).[3]

The givenness of the earth-ground radically differs from all kind of horizontal givenness—namely from the type of givenness in which our lived-body serves as the norm. The ground is somehow already present in the constitution of space, and hence it cannot originally be present as a thing in space.[4] As such, the ground does not originally appear as being "left" or "right," nor "down," "below," or "beneath."[5] This would be to define the ground in relation to our body, which would thus be taken as the ultimate norm.[6] The ground does not originally appear as a huge thing beneath our feet, as something oriented according to our body. Rather, the vertical axis (up/down) is originally constituted in relation to the ground: the ground is a dimension that is tacitly present in our experiences of "down" and "up," and gives meaning to these words in the first place. But just as our own lived-body as the primordial center of orientation cannot be constituted as a horizontal object on the left or on the right, the ground, as the ground, cannot be originally present as a thematic or marginal object *on* the vertical axis. It is not originally given as a correlate of our intentional bodily experiences; it is not something that we can perceive better or worse: the ground as such is not included among the possible objects of our spatial experiences that are oriented in relation to the ground.[7] In short, as Steinbock puts it, the ground is not given "horizontally" but "vertically."[8]

Instead of appearing as something horizontal, something over and against our body, the ground is originally disclosed *within* our bodily self-awareness. Namely, whereas our lived-body serves as the norm for *horizontal* orientation ("left," "right," "upward," "downward," "forward," "backward," "near," "far" are relative to a perceiving body as the center of orientation), and whereas, in this sense, our lived-body is constitutive of space, *vertical* orientation is established in relation to the ground. By moving our body, we can modify the horizontal directions and, in this sense, we have a control over them, whereas in relation to the vertical we are powerless—by turning around, a thing on the left comes to appear as a thing on the right, whereas by standing on our hands, "up" remains "up" and "down" remains "down." In this case we find *ourselves,* and not the perceptual field, as upside down. The ground does not spread "under" our body due to the fact that we happen to stand in an upright posture, and it would not appear as spreading "above" our body if we stood on our hands; rather, it is owing to the presence of the ground that we can find ourselves in an upright posture or as being upside down. That is, in the constitution of space, the ground is given as an *absolute* point of reference: even our lived-body, the primordial zero-point of orientation, is oriented in relation to the ground.

Moreover, horizontal orientation is established in reference to vertical orientation: our intersubjectively normal, direction-constituting lived-body is itself oriented in relation to the intersubjectively shared ground. After all, when lying on the couch on our left side, we do not experience the sofa as being on the left: what is then "on the left" in the primordial sense is still "down" in the intersubjective sense. This is because the ground is given affectively: it reveals itself in the weight of our body. This experience further enables the constitution of an intersubjectively shared horizontal axis of orientation. Namely, "left" and "right" can be intersubjectively defined through the lived-body only insofar as we stand up straight and fix the upright posture as the norm. Yet, to gain an experience of "standing up straight" it is not enough that a person straightens her body, but experiences of "standing up straight" presuppose the ground in relation to which the posture is upright.[9] Moreover, insofar as the intersubjective space is oriented in regard to perceiving bodies in an upright posture, intersubjective orientation can only be established in relation to the ground: the intersubjectively normative upright posture presupposes the givenness of the ground, and hence it is only in relation to the ground that the lived-body serves as the primordial norm for "left" and "right."

In this sense, the earth-ground has a tacit normative function in the constitution of horizontal directionality: our intersubjectively normal experiences of space are dependent on the givenness of the vertical. That is to say, the ground is inseparable from normal bodily self-awareness: our normal bodily self-awareness is "earthly" (*irdisch*) self-awareness.[10] The ground is a dimension within our experiencing that normatively regulates and thus motivates our horizontal experiences.

What interests us here is the relation between the primordial norm and the intersubjective norm. The claim that horizontal orientation is ultimately established *in reference to* vertical orientation does not mean that the intersubjective norm (the ground) would overrule or replace the primordial norm (our lived-body). After all, the vertical can reveal itself only within our horizontal experiences, and only in them does it have its sense. Even if we are aware of the horizontal directions ultimately through the vertical ones, it must not be forgotten that the vertical axis cannot reveal itself without a reference to a lived-body that is somehow oriented in relation to it. *The ground cannot be constituted as such without a lived-body that is oriented according to it.* In other words, the primordial norm has not vanished—bodily self-awareness, as well, is a condition of possibility for the constitution of space. In this sense, the lived-body and the ground—the primordial norm and the intersubjective norm— essentially belong together: both are normatively operative in our experiences of space.

Moreover, it is not the case that we experience our body on the one hand, and the ground, on the other. Rather, as already said, the ground is originally revealed within our bodily self-experience of being "earth-bound" (*erdgebunden*).[11] We originally experience the ground by experiencing our body; and by experiencing our body we also experience the ground. As already said, when we lie on the sofa on our left side, the sofa does not appear as being on our left but as being beneath us—and yet, if we considered our body in isolation from the ground, we would have to say that the sofa is on our left. To give another example, when perceiving others, we at once constitute ourselves *both* as the primordial zero-point, according to which our perceptual field (including others) is organized, *and* as a perceivable object in the intersubjectively oriented space. The two normative "poles" in space-constitution are not competing, and one cannot choose between them. Both norms are indispensable for our experience of intersubjectively oriented space: the perceptual field is oriented in relation to the lived-body, while the lived-body is oriented according to the ground. In other words, both norms are simultaneously present: one vertically, and the other horizontally.

Yet, the ground is originally revealed within our bodily experiences, and hence there is a certain imbalance between the norms of space-constitution. To be sure, the ground is given as the *absolute* dimension in relation to which our bodies are vertically oriented (and thus *relative*), but our lived-body nevertheless outlines the manner in which the perceptual horizon is oriented. Ultimately, it "depends on the lived-body . . . *what it is that, as world*, stands against the subject."[12] Accordingly, since it outlines in advance what can be present to us in the first place, our lived-body cannot be given as a mere *relative* norm. In other words, our perceptions are not "merely" subjective, since it is only through them that the objective world comes into being for us. On the other hand, our lived-body is not simply given as the absolute norm: the perceptual horizon is not relative to our body alone. Accordingly, in the intersubjective sense, the lived-body serves as a *relative norm*, but in the primordial sense, the lived-body functions as an *absolute norm*. Hence, as both intersubjectivity and primordiality are present in the constitution of space, we must maintain that the lived-body is, paradoxically, both absolute and relative. Merleau-Ponty condenses this Husserlian view: "My body is the absolute 'here.' All the places of space proceed from it, not only because the location of other places is conceived starting from the place of my body, but also because my body defines the optimal forms; ... The I could then displace the norms, but the idea of norm has been founded by my body. *The Absolute in the relative* is what my body brings to me."[13] In other words, the lived-body is a subject-object; it is neither pure subjectivity, nor mere objectivity, but originally both.

This implies that space is constituted both as our primordial horizon for which our body serves as the primordial measure, and as an intersubjective horizon in which we locate ourselves as embodied beings in relation to the intersubjectively shared ground. In short, space is at the same time our primordial horizon and an intersubjective dimension; the spatial world is oriented in a double manner: "Universal world-experience accordingly has a peculiar structure: it is (1) oriented for each one in regard to himself, and the world is respectively given as oriented from here to there, from near to far, from the surrounding world to the worlds afar; (2) but [the world] is also oriented as the communal world of experience."[14] That is to say, each of our spatial experiences has two norms: the natural world is constituted in relation to our lived-body and in relation to the shared ground. Moreover, since the lived-body as well as the ground both have their *absoluteness*, there is necessarily a *tension* between them. On the one hand, the ground is revealed within bodily experiences and is thus relative to the latter, whereas on the other hand, bodily experience is intersubjectively oriented in regard to the ground, and is thus relative to the former. Since the spatial world is constituted not in relation to a lived-body on the one hand, and to the ground on the other, but simultaneously in relation to both, in relation to an earthly body, it can be argued that the constitution of space unfolds in a *normative tension*.

The Tension Between Primordial and Intersubjective Normality

What I have said above enables an analysis of the relation between primordiality and intersubjectivity in general. The "normative tension" presents itself not only in our experience of space, but it permeates throughout the constitution of the world: constitution is, in general, oriented both subjectively and intersubjectively. There are two normative poles in each concrete experience, and in this sense the experiential world has, as Crowell puts it, a "twofold source of meaning."[15] By explicating this tension within subjectivity, we can unearth the roots of what Husserl calls "the paradox of subjectivity."[16]

The manner in which transcendental, constituting intersubjectivity is revealed in our subjective experiences is comparable to the manner in which the ground is disclosed in our bodily experiences of space. The tradition provides us with an intersubjectively shared normal way of experiencing and acting, and we tacitly understand, measure, value, and organize our subjective experiences and actions against this background. In this sense, the tradition orients our subjective experiences in general—like the shared ground orients our spatial experiences. The tradition is not something over against subjectivity: as argued, intersubjective familiarity is not present as a set of "norms," "rules," and "conventions" thematically known as such. Rather, our subjective experiences and actions have an internal reference to the intersubjectively normal manner of experiencing and acting, and in this sense the tradition presents itself in the form of "conscience." As it is gradually appropriated, the normality of the tradition gains a normative status, which means that the tradition comes to orient our experiences and actions from within: culture becomes our "second nature." In this sense, our individual experiences, decisions, expressions, and actions are always already burdened by the tradition—and, therefore, somewhat similarly to the manner in which the ground reveals itself in the weight of our body, the tradition reveals itself in our experiences, decisions, and actions, in our particular personal ways of being.

Hence, besides the "earth-ground" (*Erdboden*), we can speak, as Husserl does, of "the ground provided by the common tradition" (*Bodens der gemeinsamen Tradition*).[17] Namely, as a member of a tradition, subjectivity is bound to a "*universal 'situation'*" (*universalen "Situation"*) which is carried over to it from the "We" (*Das überträgt sich von "Wir" auf das 'Ich"*), and which serves as the ground (*Boden*) for our acts and decisions, as well as perceptions.[18] Due to such structural similarities between the earth-ground and the tradition, the metaphor of "verticality" is apt: the tradition is something that is originally *handed down* to us.[19]

However, as I have already argued, the primordial cannot be subordinated to the intersubjective. While the world is spatially constituted in relation to the ground, and historically in relation to the tradition, the world is nevertheless, at the same time, the horizon of our primordial experience—fundamentally, of bodily experience. This is why Husserl states the following:

> *A human being's total [world]consciousness is in a certain sense, by means of its hyletic substrate, bound to the lived-body, though, to be sure, the intentional lived experiences themselves are no longer directly and properly localized.*[20]
>
> Each monad necessarily has a hyletic materiality... Each monad must constitute a lived-body, and this lived-body must be either actually given or horizontally implied in all world-experience.[21]
>
> In the streaming primal presence [*Urpräsenz*] we invariably always already have bodily perception [*Leibwahrnehmung*], and so throughout the temporalization of immanent time, my bodily perceiving continuously permeates time and constitutes my synthetically identical lived-body at all times.[22]

That is to say, the "*entire content of experiences . . . is dependent upon the respective particular organization of the lived-body*,"[23] and world-consciousness in all its complexity is hence ultimately bound to one's own lived-body.[24] Husserl stresses that this boundedness is not a matter of contingency but of necessity:[25] the intersubjective constitution of the world constantly presupposes primordial experience—the "cultural world too is given 'orientedly,' in relation to a zero member or [zero] 'personality.'"[26] Accordingly, on the one hand, experiences are oriented according to the tradition, which has become our "second nature" and which thus governs our experiences from within; on the other hand, the world is present as the horizon of subjective possibilities, as a field of "I can," meaning that our experiences are also oriented according to our own embodied subjectivity as the "zero member" of world-constitution. We cannot choose between these two, we cannot subordinate or reduce one to the other; both are inseparable elements in our experiences of reality.

The internal relation between these norms proves complex. To be sure, the tradition is given as a background against which our subjective experiences are internally determined, organized, and measured. However, insofar as the primordial is retained, the tradition cannot be constituted as the absolute norm to which the primordial is subordinated. This is particularly clear in cases of anomaly. For example, persons born blind come to "know" that the environment has features (e.g., colors) to which they have no experiential access, and hence they can constitute themselves as "lacking" something that others have. In this intersubjectively mediated sense, blind persons can constitute themselves as sensuously "deviant," as "intentional modifications of normal people."[27] Yet, persons born blind are unable to directly experience the lack of vision, and hence what is primordially constituted as deviant for them are not their own experiences, but the reported experiences of others.[28] Accordingly, even though the blind constitute themselves as *anomalous in the intersubjective sense,* they do not constitute themselves, in this regard, as *anomalous in the primordial sense.* On the other hand, even if those others who give reports of the visual are constituted as deviant in the primordial sense (i.e., as deviating from the primordial norm), they are not constituted as deviant in the intersubjective sense.[29]

More generally, both the primordial norm and the intersubjective norm remain operative in concrete experiences, but—paradoxically— *both are absolute and relative at the same time.* The intersubjective world is revealed in and through subjective experiences, and therefore subjective experiences cannot be constituted *only* as subjective-relative. In other words, subjectivity cannot constitute itself *merely* as a relative norm—this would allow for the absurdity, for example, that subjectivity could primordially constitute itself as *anomalous throughout.* On the other hand, subjectivity does also constitute itself as an intersubjective being, and from the intersubjective point of view, the primordial-subjective is something relative.[30] Accordingly, since intersubjectivity and primordiality are both necessarily involved in the constitution of the objective world, since the world is constituted as being there for anyone and still necessarily has a first-personal givenness, we must maintain that the *embodied subjectivity is both absolute and relative:* it is "Absolute in the relative," *an* absolute, *one absolute* among others.

This is why Husserl presents, on the one hand, one's own primordial constituting life as the "primal mode" (*Urmodus*) and, thus, "absolute life" (*absolute Leben*).[31] The world is constituted as our primordial horizon, as the horizon outlined by our subjective capacities ("I can"): "the world as the 'world of us all' is a world from my—the ego's—vantage point."[32] Therefore: "In my primordial purity—as transcendental ego— I am the absolute ground for the transcendental nexus of egos and the absolute bearer of validity and the bearer of validity-basis for everything that is."[33] On the other hand, the world is an intersubjective realm, which is handed down to us in "absolute historicity" (*absoluten Geschichtlichkeit*), "transcendental historicity" (*transzendentalen Geschichtlichkeit*), and, therefore, "what has precedence is [the] community, we human beings who are for one another in reciprocal understanding," that is, what has precedence is the "normally persisting community of normally experiencing beings."[34] However, by arguing on the one hand that subjectivity is the absolute, and on the other hand that intersubjectivity is the absolute, Husserl is not contradicting himself: paradoxically, *there are two absolutes.* "I am transcendentally primary" (*Ich bin also transzendental der erste*), and yet I am one subjectivity in the absolute intersubjective community.[35]

Correlatively, the world appears in a twofold manner, as if against two backgrounds. Let me illuminate this with an example of a paraplegic person perceiving a stairway. The injury does not prevent this person from perceiving the stairway in its intersubjectively shared practical meaning: it appears as something that enables movement between places. However, as the correlate of the factual capacities of the person in the wheelchair, the stairway appears as a construct that does not enable but rather hinders movement. If primordial constitution had, for the paraplegic person, a merely relative status, she would constitute the stairway fundamentally and absolutely as something that enables movement. This is not the case. Yet, on the other hand, if the primordial served as the ultimate measure in sense-constitution, the incapacitated person would experience the stairway as a mere obstacle, and she would accordingly grasp those who climb the stairs as persons surmounting an obstacle. This obviously is not the case either. Rather, the stairway appears simultaneously both as something that enables movement and as something that hinders movement—and the latter is not a mere subjective illusion. After all, the disabled person has no other reality than the one which is constituted as the correlate of her experiencing,[36] and in this sense the primordial constitution of the stairway as something that cannot be surmounted is, for the disabled person, *absolute* despite its subjective-relative nature: for the incapacitated person, the stairway at the same time appears absolutely as something that enables movement and absolutely as something that cannot be surmounted.[37]

I emphasized earlier that intersubjective normality does not overrule or replace primordial normality: there are two normative dimensions in each of our concrete experiences. Now I have asserted further that both norms have a kind of absoluteness. Our lives are determined by the shared intersubjective normality, which provides us with a "default" manner of perceiving, moving, comporting, and acting. But besides this intersubjective, shared normality, each of us also has a primordial normality, felt privately. Our lives are oriented *both* according to what is for us personally the optimal manner of being *and* according to the intersubjectively preferred manner of being—and these can also enter into an open conflict.

Moreover, as I have argued, intersubjective normality is an ideal, and there remains a necessary disparity between the primordial and the intersubjective norm. Therefore, since both the primordial and the intersubjective norm have their own absoluteness, since neither can be subordinated or reduced to the other, I argue that there is necessarily a certain tension between these norms: world-constitution necessarily unfolds in a "normative tension" between primordiality and intersubjectivity. This brings us to the "paradox of subjectivity."

What Husserl discusses under the title "paradox of subjectivity" has been introduced and elaborated by Carr, Dodd, Rinofner-Kreidl, and other scholars as the problem of how subjectivity can at the same time be both transcendental and empirical,[38] and this is also the manner in which Husserl himself portrays the problem: "human being, and in communalization mankind, is subjectivity for the world and at the same time is supposed to be in it in an objective and worldly manner."[39] What I have said above sheds new light on this paradox. Namely, as I have argued, the tradition is appropriated and thus sedimented into subjectivity in the course of its individual genesis, and in this sense the generative dimension has a genetic constitution. It is something *constituted*. Yet, as I have argued at length, the appropriated tradition comes to have a constitutive significance,[40] and subjectivity constitutes itself not only as an object in the world, but also as a member within a transcendental community. In this sense, subjectivity already constitutes itself both as absolute and as relative *within the transcendental sphere*. The paradox of subjectivity accordingly surfaces as the correlate of a transcendental experience that involves an internal tension between primordiality and intersubjectivity: it is due to this transcendental tension that we constitute ourselves both as intersubjective objects in the world and as primordial subjects in the experiential life of which the world comes into being. In this sense, the paradox of subjectivity is related to the problem of the normative tension: the problem of the relation between the transcendental and the empirical—between "transcendental interiority" (*transzendentale Innerlichkeit*) and "interiority that exists in the world" (*in der Welt seiende Innerlichkeit*)[41]—can be interpreted in terms of a tension within the transcendental, namely a tension between primordiality and intersubjectivity. That is to say, the paradox of subjectivity arises because the constituting subjectivity understands itself *both* as transcendental intersubjectivity *and*, at the same time, as the primordial dimension in which intersubjectivity reveals itself.[42]

In this manner, the paradox of subjectivity relates to the tension between *genetic and generative self-constitution*. Namely, as I argued in part 2, in the process of genetic self-constitution subjectivity constitutes its primordial constitutive life as a finite thread within an intersubjective continuum of life that goes on independently, regardless of this particular subjectivity, and in this sense, subjectivity is "relativized." But, as I have argued here in part 3, subjectivity cannot constitute itself as something *merely* relative. Accordingly, our genesis takes place within an intersubjective-generative framework, whereas the generative framework can be constituted only in and through our genetic self-constitution. We are intertwined, enmeshed, and entangled in a tradition,[43] but this does not mean that we cease to be the *Nullglied*, the primordial subjectivity in whose experiential life the tradition comes into being in the first place.

The paradox of subjectivity is not something that could be "solved" or "overcome" by subordinating one—primordiality or intersubjectivity—to the other. In the primordial sense, we are the subjectivity in whose constituting life everything that exists comes into being, whereas in the intersubjective sense, we are subjects with others, subjects for others, and thus we eventually constitute ourselves as beings in the historical world of the tradition. And we cannot choose between these two aspects without ending up with a one-sided understanding of subjectivity. To be sure, we *know* that our "lived-body must have had a beginning as an organic physical body; we have, after all, once been born."[44] Yet, as Carr notes, "man's objective being (as subject *in* the world) comes first in the order of knowing but not in the order of being," that is, in the order of constitution.[45] In the "order of constitution," we are at the same time both primordial subjects for the historical world and beings that are situated in the historical world; nature and history are constituted genetically within our subjective-primordial life, and yet at the same time we are natural and historical beings, situated *in* nature and history. Our actions, decisions, and judgments, for instance, are loaded with the burden of tradition, and yet they are our *own* actions, decisions, and judgments for which we are eventually responsible. Our individual peculiarities, our unique ways of thinking, acting, and moving are not created by us: they are modifications of historical manners of being, generatively handed down and passed on within a tradition—and yet they are our *own*, personal and individual manners of being. The "paradox of subjectivity" resides precisely in the fact that our existence takes place in the meeting point between "primordial" and "intersubjective" self-constitution—and hence in the fact that our self-constitution is both *genetic* and *generative*.

Bodily Roots of the Paradox of Subjectivity

The roots of the paradox of subjectivity reach all the way down to the level of sensibility. As I argued in part 1, subjectivity is originally aware of itself in a twofold way, hyletically and kinesthetically: it opens to the hyletic environment, whereas this environment appears in relation to the kinesthetic "circumstances." Fundamentally, as I argued, subjectivity is a lived relation between the constituting kinesthetic sequences and the hyletically constituted exteriority. However, as has also been shown, the sensuous environment is not originally something at a distance, something to which we first have to establish a connection, but a realm that is present to us immediately. Our sensings are localized, and by feeling our body, we feel something worldly. However, to be sure, as experienced originally, localized sensings are not part of nature: they are not found in a physical body, but they are something that constitute the connection between experiential interiority and physical exteriority in the first place. Tactile sensings as such are not processes on (or in) the hand, and yet they are localized.

As we have seen, the embodiment of subjectivity does not mean that subjectivity is "naturalized": even if our sensings are localized, this does not mean that our subjectivity is located in certain objective coordinates. As explicated in part 1, the localized body is not "the body that we *are*" but "the body that we *have*." Along with localization, subjectivity is constituted as *having* an exteriority; it constitutes itself in the realm of the *sensed*—but it does not thereby cease to *be* the subjectivity for whom this exteriority is constituted. In "double sensation," the lived-bodily exteriority receives a certain objectivity. Since the sensing subjectivity has an exteriority that can be sensed, the distinction between the constituted and the constituting is originally dynamic: the constituted can be reversed into the constituting, and vice versa. The constituting flow of sensing constitutes itself in the realm of the constituted. One's own perceived body is revealed as the exteriority of the constituting flow of sensing, as an expression of lived-bodily interiority. That is, due to the perceptual self-reflexivity of the lived-body, it is originally a subject-object: an expressive complex of lived-bodily interiority and lived-bodily exteriority. In the words of Husserl: "All acting is two-sided, and the original two-sidedness is that which is given in the lived-body and in comprehensive bodily experience."[46] That is to say, it is precisely as embodied that subjectivity is initially both constituted and constituting, and hence the paradox of subjectivity can be claimed to be rooted in what could be called the *paradox of embodiment.*

It is no coincidence that Husserl discusses temporalization and embodiment in similar terms. He examines, on the one hand, "the paradox that temporalization at once also temporalizes itself" (*das Paradox, dass auch die Zeitigung sich zugleich selbst verzeitigt*).[47] On the other hand, he writes that "an experience *of* the lived-body . . . always already presupposes the lived-body," and that the external manifestation of the lived-body refers back to its immediate self-manifestation.[48] This similarity is understandable since time consciousness is fundamentally actualized as a flow of kinesthetic-hyletic sensing. This is why awareness of time and awareness of space are inseparable, and this is equally the reason why Husserl speaks of the lived-body as "the bearer of the here and the now."[49] Temporality is fundamentally not only *lived* temporality, but *lived-bodily* temporality, and in this sense the paradox of temporalization is ultimately one aspect of the paradox of embodied subjectivity.

Moreover, as I argued in part 2, it is the original duality of embodiment that enables the constitution of intersubjectivity. As embodied, subjectivity is bound to perceive the world from a particular locus, and others are originally (although emptily) implied as co-perceivers in this horizonal structure of perception. Moreover, as one's own exteriority is constituted as that of an impressional interiority, the perception of other similarly moving bodily beings motivates the positing of another interiority: empathy presupposes embodiment, as we saw Husserl arguing. Entering into communicative relations with others, subjectivity constitutes itself as a member of a community, as intersubjective subjectivity—eventually, as one finite member in a historical community. Yet, the primordial remains, and there arises the problem of the internal relation between primordial and intersubjective self-constitution, a tension between genetic and generative self-constitution. This tension unfolds as the paradox of subjectivity. We are on the one hand absolute world-constituting subjectivities, whereas on the other hand we are beings in the intersubjectively constituted world—not only spatially and temporally, but also in the sense that we are situated within a tradition. As I have argued, in the constitution of the world, both primordial subjectivity and the intersubjectively handed down tradition function as norms of sense-constitution, and subjectivity therefore constitutes itself as a relative absolute.

Concluding Remarks

By introducing embodiment into the midst of the transcendental dimension, Husserlian phenomenology restores intuitivity to transcendental philosophy and revises the transcendental tradition on the whole. At the same time, this move makes phenomenology more responsive and open to empirical sciences. To be sure, Husserl consistently emphasizes that there is a limit to possible naturalizing: "the spirit can be grasped as dependent on nature and can itself be naturalized but only to a certain degree"; "subjects cannot themselves dissolve into nature for in that case what gives nature its sense would be missing."[1] Yet, while strongly holding on to this position, and without losing sight of its own unique transcendental character, Husserlian phenomenology succeeds in opening the needed dialogical connection between transcendental philosophy, naturalism, and the empirical sciences. As I see it, it is precisely a thorough phenomenological examination of embodiment that is able to clarify why subjectivity can neither be simply reduced to the world nor understood as something extra-worldly altogether, and this is what I have tried to contribute here.

The central task of this book has been to investigate the constitutive significance of embodiment in Husserlian phenomenology. I have focused on explicating the diverse roles of embodiment in the constitution of selfhood, intersubjectivity, and objective reality, and it is now time to recapitulate and develop further some of the most crucial achievements and consequences of these analyses.

The investigation commenced with an analysis of self-awareness. With Husserl, I introduced subjectivity as an affective dimension, as the realm of kinesthetic and hyletic self-awareness, and argued that due to its fundamental affective structure subjectivity originally constitutes itself in relation to something that is other to it. Conceived in this manner, subjectivity is not a closed immanence that would first have to find a way out of itself, but rather a lived relation between interiority and exteriority. This lived relation is originally realized in, or rather realized *as*, the lived-body, and to say that self-awareness and awareness of the environment are equiprimordial is just another way of saying that subjectivity is fundamentally embodied.

However, as I stressed repeatedly, the claim that subjectivity is embodied is not exhausted in the claim that subjectivity *has* a lived-body. Subjectivity is not only intentionally aware of a particular body belonging to it, but it is also embodied in the deeper sense of being kinesthetically and hyletically self-aware. I clarified the complex structures of embodiment by employing Husserl's distinction between *Innenleiblichkeit* (i.e., immediate kinesthetic-hyletic self-manifestation) and *Aussenleiblichkeit* (i.e., the lived-body as it is constituted in double sensation, the lived-body as an object for itself), and I argued that even though in the sphere of sensibility subjectivity necessarily localizes itself in the exterior, this by no means compromises its transcendental, constituting, character.

Having illustrated the indispensable constitutive significance of embodiment in the primordial self-constitution of subjectivity, the analysis was developed further and expanded by an investigation of the multiple and layered significance of embodiment in the constitution of intersubjectivity and intersubjective self-constitution.

I distinguished three kinds of intersubjectivity—a priori, social, and generative-historical intersubjectivity—and argued that, in different senses, each of these necessarily involves embodiment. First, the structure of perceptual experience implies, a priori, the co-positing of a plurality of anonymous co-perceivers. In this connection, I reinterpreted the Husserlian *Jedermann* as "anybody," and explicated the embodied foundations of a priori intersubjectivity. Along with Husserl I argued that social, reciprocal relations can be established only among embodied subjects: reciprocity presupposes that others are experienced as being able to perceive us. Moreover, I explained how empathy is essentially built upon a priori intersubjectivity, in the sense that the empathically appresented other is necessarily constituted as a particular "exemplar" of the anonymous "anybody." At the same time, I emphasized that this by no means compromises the alterity of the other. A priori intersubjectivity is, in this sense, a necessary but not a sufficient ground for empathy, and our factual encounter with others undoubtedly introduces our experiential life with something unprecedented—the actual other endows our consciousness with "the first true transcendence," as we saw Husserl arguing.[2]

Moreover, I investigated how, in and through social relations, subjectivity constitutes itself as a person among others and eventually grasps itself as a finite member in a historical tradition that "lives on" regardless of the "coming" and "going" of individuals. I argued that birth and death appear as ambiguous phenomena in the following sense: in the *generative-phenomenological sense* (i.e., from the point of view of intersubjective historicity, or the "We") birth and death are constituted as "pauses" or "breaks" within intersubjective constitution, whereas, in the *genetic-*

phenomenological sense (i.e., from the "egological," first-person point of view) birth and death appear as non-symmetrical limits of subjective potentiality ("I can"). That is to say, birth and death present themselves both as the limits of subjectivity and as events within the intersubjective continuum of life: my own death will be the end of the world for me, but not the end of the world for others. On a more general level, I argued further that the genetic-egological point of view cannot be reduced or subordinated to the intersubjective-generative one: both dimensions are operative and both have their own validity in the self-constitution of an intersubjective subjectivity.

The analysis of finitude not only served as a clarification of certain less well-known dimensions in the Husserlian analysis of embodiment and subjectivity, but it also served to exemplify the internal relationship between subjectivity and intersubjectivity, as well as between genetic and generative constitution. This theme was developed in the third part of the book in connection with a phenomenological analysis of normality and normativity.

The normative significance of primordiality in intersubjective constitution was introduced and highlighted first by studying interpersonal and intercultural encounters, and then by investigating the sense in which non-human animals do and do not participate in the constitution of objective nature. My central claim here was that the scope of what we always already take as being perceivable to "any-body" is primordially outlined by our own factical embodiment, and that, in this sense, primordial constitution has a normative status: the anonymous co-perceivers of a priori intersubjectivity are expected to prove similar (*meinesgleichen*). Moreover, I equally emphasized that generative-historical intersubjectivity does not and cannot replace a priori intersubjectivity. The latter is sedimented in time, but the founding layers are still operative in concrete intersubjective experiences. Accordingly, the world simultaneously appears *both* as being there for anybody (and hence constituted in relation to one's own perceptual abilities) *and* as being there for *us* as members of a particular intersubjective tradition (and hence constituted in relation to intersubjectively normal perceptual abilities). In other words, "intersubjective normality" does not replace what I called "primordial normality": both are necessarily operative in the constitution of objective reality.

In this sense, as I concluded, embodiment has (quite literally) a central role in the constitution of objective, intersubjectively shared reality. What subjectivity originally perceives, it takes as being perceivable to anybody, and this primordial constitution, with its peculiar normative structure, is retained in intersubjective world-constitution. Moreover, given that intersubjective normality is an ideal—that is to say, given that the subjective abilities of two individuals are never perfectly identical with one another—and given that our concrete experiences are always both subjective and intersubjective, the relationship between primordial and intersubjective normality unfolds as what I called a "normative tension."

My argument for an irreducible tension between intersubjective and primordial normality sheds light on the discussion of the relation between genetic and generative phenomenology, as it challenges all interpretations that render *either* the genetic-primordial *or* the generative-intersubjective as the one and only absolute. World-constitution involves both first-person singular and first-person plural, and neither of them can be reduced to the other. I have tried to argue that this irreducibility manifests itself in the "paradox of subjectivity."

In the light of what has been said here, the relationship between the subjective and the intersubjective must be recognized as being more complex than a simple one-way founding relation. We would of course hopelessly fall prey to subjectivism if we simply held that intersubjectivity is constituted by subjectivity, full stop. However, it would be equally misguiding, I believe, to maintain the opposite. After all, the tradition can figure as a constituting factor in our subjective experiences only insofar as it has been assumed by, and absorbed into, the constituting life of subjectivity. In this sense, historicity necessarily has a genetic constitution—paradoxically, we become historical in the course of time. On the other hand, however, as we constitute ourselves as intersubjective beings we realize that the tradition plays a normative role in our subjective life, and we also retrospectively posit that it has already played such a role before we knew anything about it. Thus we constitute our individual genesis as a process taking place within an intersubjective-historical framework. In this sense, subjectivity retrospectively constitutes itself as having already been historical before coming to know it. Yet, as I have repeatedly argued, this does not imply that subjectivity would be subordinated to the intersubjective. Rather, there remains a certain duality in experience, an inner tension. I further illustrated and developed this idea first by discussing the roles of Earth-ground and the lived-body in the constitution of spatiality, and then by arguing more generally that the constitution of the world is determined both by our intersubjective tradition and by our primordial-subjective abilities. Namely, somewhat similar to the manner in which the spatial horizon is experientially oriented *both* in relation to the ground *and* to our lived-body, all our concrete experiences are simultaneously oriented *both* primordially *and* intersubjectively. Each experience accordingly involves a twofold normativity, and there unfolds

CONCLUDING REMARKS

an irreducible normative tension between the primordial and the intersubjective.

The implications and consequences of this "dual normativity" were not thoroughly elaborated by Husserl himself, and neither have they been sufficiently explicated in the previous literature on Husserlian phenomenology. The phenomenological insight that primordial constitution involves normative aspects that are retained in intersubjective constitution has important philosophical consequences. The analysis of an irreducible normative tension between genetic and generative self-constitution opened the possibility of shedding new light upon the Husserlian "paradox of subjectivity." As I argued, this paradox—that is, the problem of subjectivity being both constituting and constituted—is intimately related to the tension between primordial and intersubjective normativity, to the normative tension between genetic self-constitution (individual facticity) and generative self-constitution (intersubjective historicity). Subjectivity is *both* the absolute dimension in and through which others come into being for it, *and* something relative, one subjectivity among others, a "relative absolute," and this duality can also be expressed by saying that subjectivity constitutes itself both as an intersubjective object in the world and as the primordial subject for the world.

Conceived in this manner, as should be clear by now, the paradox of subjectivity is ultimately rooted in the structures of embodiment: the paradox of subjectivity arises from the basis of a normative tension between primordiality and intersubjectivity, and this tension and hence the whole duality of subjectivity are ultimately rooted in the primordial interplay between hyletic and kinesthetic self-constitution. Time is originally a lived-bodily time, and the claim that besides external objects, the primal flow of temporality always already temporalizes (objectifies) itself as well, is owing to the fact that time-consciousness itself originally unfolds as a lived organization of two essentially different kinds of sensings, kinesthetic and hyletic, and because experiential time is always already "filled" by both. As my analysis of the essential unity of time-consciousness and sensibility has hopefully made clear, the body not only serves as our point of entrance to the world, but also as that which binds together time and space in the first place. It is due to the intimate entanglement of sensing and time-consciousness, that an awareness of time is inseparable from an awareness of space. In other words, insofar as we are embodied, space cannot be less original in our experiences than time.

Moreover, it is precisely the fact that subjectivity originates in the meeting point of kinesthetic interiority and hyletic exteriority that endows subjectivity with a fundamental ambiguity, and it is eventually owing to this incarnate duality of subjectivity that it is destined to be both constituting and constituted. In this sense, the origin of the paradox of subjectivity can be ultimately traced back to the structures of embodiment.

We may hence conclude by saying that it is ultimately due to our fundamental bodilyness that we constitute ourselves, at the same time, both as the primordial subjectivity whose possible death signifies an "end of the world," and as a finite being within the flow of intersubjective historicity; both as a unique individual and as a being whose personal life is throughout permeated by historical and intersubjective features; both as an autonomous, self-normative being, and as a being whose individual life is regulated by supra-individual norms that are passed on in a tradition.

Besides delivering phenomenological analyses of self-awareness, intersubjectivity, and world-constitution, and highlighting the role of embodiment in each of them separately, I have hopefully at the same time managed to illustrate how embodiment brings together these different dimensions of subjectivity. We can well conclude by saying that it is precisely owing to our fundamental embodiment that we are simultaneously related to ourselves, to others, and to the world. It is insofar as we are embodied that we are situated, and the irreducible ambiguity and paradoxicality of our subjective existence is a manifestation of our fundamental embodiment.

Notes

For a list of the works by Husserl cited in these notes and their abbreviations, see the bibliography, p. 221.

Introduction

1. Descartes's claims are often quoted: "I am really distinct from my body, and can exist without it" (Descartes 1984, 54, 119; Descartes 1970, 87); "the soul by which I am what I am, is entirely distinct from the body, . . . and even if the body were not, the soul would not cease to be what it is" (Descartes 1967, 101); "this I which is thinking is an immaterial substance with no bodily element" (Descartes 1970, 84). That is to say, Descartes argues, even though I have a body "which by some special right I called 'mine'" (Descartes 1984, 52), a "body that is very closely joined to me" (Descartes 1984, 54), this body is nevertheless a thing "without any of the attributes which belong to the mind" (Descartes 1984, 157), and it is only the mind that is qualified as oneself (Descartes 1984, 35; Descartes 1988, 163); "I am not that structure of limbs which is called a human body" (Descartes 1984, 39); the "body is by its very nature always divisible, while the mind is utterly indivisible" (Descartes 1984, 59; see also 17), and the difference between the human body and other things "consists merely in the arrangement of the limbs and other accidents of this sort" (Descartes 1984, 109)—the mind merely "uses" the body "like an instrument" (Descartes 1984, 245). To be sure, Descartes sometimes discusses the union of mind and body almost as a third ontological dimension, and it has been claimed that, instead of a "dualist," Descartes ought to be recognized as a "trialist" (Cottingham 1986, 119–34; see also Alanen 2003, 44–77). Nevertheless, neither Descartes himself nor the Cartesian tradition ever recognized embodiment as a *fundamental* problem, even if they considered it as being one of the most difficult and perplexing ones.

2. As Merleau-Ponty puts it in *Phenomenology of Perception:* "Thus, while the living body became an exterior without interior, subjectivity became interior without exterior, an impartial spectator" (Merleau-Ponty 1945, 68/64–65). When quoting Merleau-Ponty and Sartre, with the former page number I refer to the pagination in the French original text whereas the latter number points to the English translation listed in the bibliography.

3. In *Träume eines Geistersehers* Kant writes: "where I sense, there I am. I am immediately in the fingertips as well as in the head. . . . *My soul is wholly in my*

whole body, and wholly in each of its parts" (Kant 1954, 21). On Kant's discussion concerning the role of the bilateral body in the constitution of spatial directionality, see Woelert 2007.

4. Kant 1998, B409.

5. Throughout the work I will employ the feminine form instead of both feminine and masculine: this is simply to enhance readability, and what is said is of course suggested to apply to both sexes equally.

6. For example, Hua I, 71; Hua III/1, 122ff.; Hua VI, 254; Hua VIII, 163; Hua XXIV, 212ff.; Hua XXXIV, 90. Throughout this work, I refer to the volumes of the *Husserliana Gesammelte Werke* in the standard manner, "Hua R," where the Roman number ("R") refers to the volume in question. I have consulted the available English translations, but when paraphrasing Husserl I will not separately mention whether or not my own translation deviates from the published translations, and I will refer to the pagination of the original texts only. When quoting the as-yet unpublished manuscripts, I will provide the quoted text in German.

7. The word "attitude" (*Einstellung*) is slightly problematic since what Husserl aims to express is not a contingent type of relation to being, but something that essentially penetrates one's experiential life and all particular attitudes within it. See also Merleau-Ponty 1945, 66/62: "The tacit thesis of perception is that at every instant experience can be coordinated with that of the previous instant and that of the following, and my perspective with that of other consciousness—that all contradictions can be removed, that monadic and intersubjective experience is an unbroken text."

8. Merleau-Ponty 1945, 71/67–68: "But although it is of the essence of consciousness to forget its own phenomena, thus enabling 'things' to be constituted, this forgetfulness is not a mere absence, it is the absence of something which consciousness could bring into its presence: in other words consciousness can forget phenomena only because it can recall them, it neglects them in favour of things only because they are the cradle of things."

9. Fink 1933, 346–48; Merleau-Ponty 1945, 72/69; see also Hua IV, 180–85; Hua VI, 172–73.

10. Accordingly, it is a misunderstanding to treat the phenomenological reduction as a "special and detached reflection" that may or may not be executed in phenomenology, as for instance Hubert Dreyfus claims (see Dreyfus 1982a, 122). Such characterizations neglect the initiating role of the reduction.

11. For example, Hua XV, 70. Husserl's assistants, Eugen Fink and Ludwig Landgrebe, emphasize that the reduction cannot have an analogy *within* the natural attitude, since it is something that concerns this attitude on the whole (Landgrebe 1982, 32–33; Fink 1933, 344–46; Fink 1988, 35–41; see also Hua V, 148). However, it is equally important not to mystify the reduction. In everyday life, the sense-giving consciousness announces itself in particular instances—such as when one miscategorizes something. For example, when something that was taken *as* a house turns out to be a façade, the positing of the thing *as a house* is canceled, and the thing is experienced *as* a façade instead. Here we can recognize the sense-bestowing or positing activity of consciousness: the experienced thing gains its *experiential sense*—*as* "house" or *as* "façade"—from consciousness,

not from the alleged thing in itself. For the motivation of the reduction, see Lenkowski 1978; for the different "ways" to the reduction, see Kern 1977.

12. Hua XV, 20–21; Hua VI, 180; see also Hua XV, 23; Merleau-Ponty 1945, 71/68.

13. See, for example, Hua I, 59–60; Hua III/1, 120; Hua VI, 145, 155; Hua VIII, 167. In the *Crisis*, Husserl's account is univocal—"In the reorientation of the *epoché* nothing is lost, none of the interests and ends of world-life, and thus also none of the ends of knowledge (Hua VI, 179)—and he also explicates that to construe the *epoché* as a "turning-away" (*Abwendung von*) from natural human life-interests is a "very common misunderstanding" (Hua VI, 179–80). In a sense, Husserl thus also anticipated the (mis)interpretations by Føllesdal and Dreyfus, who present the reduction as a turning-away from worldly objects, and who accordingly strongly distinguish between objects and "noemas," while claiming that phenomenology is exclusively interested in the latter (see, e.g., Dreyfus 1982a; Føllesdal 1982a, 1982b, 1982c).

14. Accordingly, as Husserl's understanding of the reduction matured, he soon realized that "it is better to avoid speaking of a phenomenological '*residuum*' or of the '*exclusion of* the world'; such language use readily misleads us into thinking that from now on, the world would no longer figure as a phenomenological theme, and that, instead, the theme would only reside in the subjective 'acts,' modes of appearance, etc. of the world" (Hua VIII, 432).

15. Hua III/1, 120–21.

16. Hua VI, 263. Husserl even states that "the transcendental ego is nothing else than the absolute human person" (Hua XXXIV, 246). He explains: "all my human worldly acts are at once . . . acts of my transcendental life. . . . The one that ultimately thinks in all 'thinking' is the transcendental ego" (Hua XXXIV, 453). Therefore, "I, a human being in the world . . . , am nothing other than what I discover myself to be in the transcendental attitude" (Hua XXXIV, 200; see also Hua VIII, 430).

17. Hua III/1, 120–21; Hua VI, 52.

18. Hua III/1, 120.

19. Hua I, 117; see also Hua VI, 171: "meaning is never anything but meaning in modes of validity, that is, as related to intending ego-subjects which effect validity."

20. Merleau-Ponty 1945, xi/xviii.

21. Hua III/1, 120.

22. Hua I, 61, 67–70; Merleau-Ponty 1945, 71/67. See also Hua VI, 170, 166.

23. Hua XV, 20; Fink 1988, 179; Crowell 1995, 16; Zahavi 2003a, 68–77; Zahavi 2001b, 105–20; Carr 2002, 35.

24. Hua VI, 180; Merleau-Ponty 1945, 74/71; Hua VI, 248.

25. Hua VI, 169; see also Hua I, 65, 121.

26. See, for example, Hua XIX/1, 387. See also Hua XXXIX, 14.

27. Merleau-Ponty 1945, 381/385.

28. Carr 1999, 116.

29. Hua VI, 161.

30. Hua I, 66, 65.

31. Merleau-Ponty 1945, viii/xv. On Husserl's and Kant's concepts of the transcendental, see Carr 1974, 27–33; Carr 2000, 146; Carr 2003, 184; Moran 2003.

32. Hua VI, 114, 116. See also Hua I, 118.

33. In the words of David Carr: "It could be argued that the two transcendental philosophies are only formally similar in grounding the objectivity of the world in something called 'the transcendental,' whereas what is actually understood by this term is in each case totally different. That which ultimately renders possible the objectivity of the world-as-meant is, for Kant, a set of pure concepts, principles, or rules, not acts of consciousness" (Carr 1974, 32).

34. Carr 1999, 116–17; Depraz 1999, 464–65.

35. Hua VI, 181; Hua I, 86; Hua II, 47; Hua VI, 159, 173, 181; Husserl 2006, 1; Ms. A V 17, 10a; see also Fink 1933, 370. For an analysis of the relationship between facticity and transcendental philosophy, see Crowell 2003.

36. Hua I, 65.

37. Hua VI, 170, 114–15.

38. Concerning Husserl's relation to Kant, see Kern 1964; Kockelmans 1977; Crowell 2001, 23–36.

39. Hua VI, 271–72. See also Hua I, 118.

40. Hua I, 119.

41. Hua VI, 74–84, 116–18.

42. Ibid., 181–82.

43. Merleau-Ponty 1945, xii/xix.

44. Hua XXIX, 85. See also Hua XXIX, 64; Merleau-Ponty 1945, 388/393.

45. Hua XXIX, 332. See also Hua VI, 182–190; Hua XXXIX, 664–66.

46. Merleau-Ponty 1945, 75/71–72. In this sense, Lanei Rodemeyer's interpretation, for instance, is too Kantian: she claims that the absolute ego is not a singular, but "is all egos" (see Rodemeyer 2003, 147).

47. In his manuscripts, Husserl discusses the transcendental ego also as an "absolute fact," as "absolute self-temporalization" (e.g., Hua XV, 669, 667; Hua XVII, 243–44; see also Held 1966, 146–50). He also speaks of the "fact of my transcendental subjectivity," investigates the "transcendental factical genesis" of subjectivity (Hua XV, 489), and analyzes the constituting ego in its "primal facticity" (*Urfaktizität*): "Ich bin das Urfaktum" (Ms. E III 9, 51a-b). See also Hua XV, 54; and Husserl 2006, 386. See also Landgrebe 1974, 482; Theunissen 1977; Landgrebe 1982, 45–47, 15–26; Bernet 1999, 204–5.

48. Hua IX, 208. See also Hua I, 100. On the notions of ego in Husserl and Kant, see Carr 1977.

49. Hua I, 100–115; Hua XV, 388; Hua XXXIV, 198–201, 451–53; and Ms. E III 4, 61. In the 1930s, Husserl often discusses transcendental intersubjectivity as a community of persons (*transzendentalen Intersubjektivität als Gemeinschaft von Personalitäten*) (Ms. E III 9, 55a–55b). In addition, the *Husserliana* is full of characterizations of transcendental subjectivity in its personal-individual concretion (e.g., Hua IV, 101, 103, 214, 222, 273, 299–300, 359; Hua VI, 188; Hua XIII, 446). See also Merleau-Ponty's discussion on the style of constituting subjectivity (Merleau-Ponty 1945, 317–18/319–20). See also Diemer 1956, 375–76; Stack 1974, 269; Luft 2005.

50. See Bernet, Marbach, and Kern 1993, 196–98.

51. See, for example, Hua XXIX, 426. Sometimes Husserl also states that the static analysis enables the genetic one (Hua XXXV, 408). See also Larrabee 1976, 171–72. The development of Husserl's work should be considered as a constant deepening of the insights that remain implicit in the earlier texts. That is to say, instead of revising and abandoning his earlier ideas, Husserl instead always seeks to radicalize his own views—he always seeks for a more comprehensive view. In this sense, it is understandable that the early static analyses are not simply left behind when Husserl engages in genetic investigations, and neither are the genetic investigations when Husserl moves toward "generative" investigations (see, e.g., Bernet, Marbach, and Kern 1993, 195–204; Zahavi 2003a, 3–4). For a detailed account of the development of Husserl's thought and an explication of the internal coherence of his methodology, see Sokolowski 1964; Sokolowski 1970; De Boer 1978; Bernet, Marbach, and Kern 1993; Steinbock 1995a; Steinbock 1995c; Biemel 2000; Moran 2000, 60–191; Welton 2000b; Steinbock 2001; Zahavi 2003a; Welton 2003; Moran 2005; Römmp 2005.

52. See, for example, Hua XI, 336–45; Hua XIV, 34–42; Hua XVII, 257, 316–17; Hua XXXV, 405; Ms. D 12 I, 6b. See also Ms. D 13 I, 73a: "Die 'Konstitution'—darunter können wir verstehen den genetischen Prozess, in dem stufenweise die Apperzeptionen und, genauer besehen, ein unendliches apperzeptives System als Habitus wird. Als Habitus: denn eine faktische Apperzeption setzt eine entsprechenden Habitus voraus, der nicht auf diese Apperzeption speziell bezogen ist, sondern als Habitus für den ganzen apperzeptiven Typus begründet, genetisch entwickelt worden ist."

53. See Steinbock 2003. For a challenging account of Husserl's complex methodology, and a concise elaboration of generative phenomenology, see Steinbock 1995a.

54. See Hua XXXIX, 477.

55. The word *Leib* has an etymological root in the German verb *leben* (to live). I will throughout use the term "lived-body," and not, for example, "living body," as a translation of the German term. This expression is favored in order to emphasize the first-person dimension of the body, and the expression is unified with a hyphen in order to enhance readability in expressions such as "lived-bodily interiority" (*Innenleiblichkeit*). This term will be clarified in detail later on.

56. The best-known posthumously published texts dealing with embodiment are *Thing and Space* (1907) and the second book of *Ideas Pertaining to a Pure Phenomenology and to a Phenomenological Philosophy* (1912–25), but also the manuscripts concerning the problems of intersubjectivity (1905–35) and lifeworld (1916–37) provide detailed analyses of embodiment. Husserl's late manuscripts on spatiality, the D-manuscripts, currently still unpublished, also provide rich and insightful formulations on the topic.

57. For instance, since Husserl's published writings focus mainly on problems of intentionality, it soon became the received view that Husserl conceived the problems of intersubjectivity and self-awareness as particular intentional relations. The manuscripts have proven this to be a complete misunderstanding: to be sure, intentionality was always for Husserl a grand theme of phenomenol-

ogy, but he also dedicated thousands of pages to the problem of intersubjectivity, arguing that our relation to others is neither fundamentally nor most of the time an intentional relation (see, e.g., Zahavi 2005, 163–68).

58. See Hua IV, 282.

59. Martin Dillon, for instance, renders Husserl as an advocate of the "intellectualism" that Merleau-Ponty criticizes in his *Phenomenology of Perception*, and thus identifies Husserl's phenomenology with Kant's transcendental philosophy (Dillon 1997, 26–34). Likewise, in their introduction to the *Cambridge Companion to Husserl*, Barry Smith and David Woodruff Smith introduce Husserlian philosophy as intellectualistic (see Smith and Smith 1995, 10). Following Hubert Dreyfus, Sean Kelly likewise labels Husserl a "cognitivist" (see Dreyfus 1982b, 8–9; Kelly 2005, 77). Other commentators even claim that Husserl "can only conceive the body as a physical thing that possesses the sensations" (Hansen 2005, 247), or that in "Husserl's transcendental analysis, the body is reduced to a perceived object and appears to have no role in the production of perceptual experience" (Gallagher 1995, 233). Gallagher also claims that "Husserl attempts to isolate consciousness and explore its intentional structure. . . . As a result of the phenomenological reduction, analysis is limited to a description of the body as it is presented in consciousness. . . . Due to the limitations of Husserl's model of intentionality, [the latter therefore] appears *ex nihilo*, a pure spontaneity that begins at the noetic act of consciousness and moves in the direction of the noema. Everything of importance happens . . . 'out in front' of the noetic act" (Gallagher 1995, 231–32; see also Fuchs 2000, 43). These scholars and many others maintain that the body is for Husserl merely something constituted, an intentional object that has no constitutive relevance (e.g., Philipse 1995, 256; Goto 2004, 78), and hence they argue for a "sharp and irreconcilable difference" between Husserl and Merleau-Ponty (see, e.g., Carman and Hansen 2005b, 9).

60. It should perhaps be further noted that Merleau-Ponty was familiar not only with Husserl's published works, but also with the unpublished manuscripts: in the late 1930s, after Husserl's death and before writing his early works, Merleau-Ponty visited the Husserl Archives in Leuven several times. For Merleau-Ponty's reading of Husserl, see, for example, Behnke 2002; Bruzina 2002; Heinämaa 2002; and Zahavi 2002c.

61. See, for example, Smith and McIntyre 1982; Spiegelberg 1982; Miller 1984; Bell 1990; Kockelmans 1994; Moran 2005; Farber 2006; Smith 2007. See also Mensch 2001.

62. See for example, Schütz 1932; Straus 1966; Minkowski 1970; Leder 1990; Waldenfels 1997; Zahavi 1999; Zahavi 2002b; Heinämaa 2003; Fuchs 2008; Gallagher and Zahavi 2008.

63. For instance, Ulrich Claesges and Elmar Holenstein discuss the constitution of space in relation to the lived-body; Alphonso Lingis and Anthony Steinbock elaborate certain corporeal dimensions of intentionality; Donn Welton has focused on the relation between the lived-body and the physical body; Christian Lotz and Dan Zahavi have written on the relation between bodily self-affectivity and selfhood; and Steven Crowell has studied the normative aspects of

the lived-body (Claesges 1964; Holenstein 1999; Lingis 1971; Steinbock 1995a; Steinbock 1999; Welton 1999; Welton 2000a; Zahavi 1999; Lotz 2005, 2007; Crowell 1995, 1996).

64. See Ricoeur 1967, 35–81; Zahavi 1994; Behnke 1996; Dodd 1997.

One

1. The phenomenological concept of consciousness remarkably deviates from the psychoanalytic concept: in the conceptual framework of the latter, it makes good sense to speak of unconscious mental processes, and even unconscious affects and emotions, since in this framework the concept of consciousness is limited to what phenomenologists would term focal consciousness. Hence to declare that "unconscious experiences" *in the phenomenological sense* are countersensical does not imply that there could not be unconscious mental processes *in the psychoanalytic sense*. As Merleau-Ponty nicely puts it: "The lived is certainly lived by me, nor am I ignorant of the feelings which I repress, and in this sense there is no unconscious" (Merleau-Ponty 1945, 343/345). On the relationship between the phenomenological and the psychoanalytic concept of unconscious, see Bernet 2002b.

2. See Hua III/1, 251.

3. Hua X, 126.

4. Hua IX, 8; see also Hua X, 127. Self-awareness has a *modal* aspect as well as a *factical* one. Here I am not yet discussing the former, the mode or "manner of being conscious" (Hua XIX/1, 395–96), but rather the facticity of consciousness, the constant non-intentional experience of undergoing an experience.

5. See Hua X, 89.

6. Hua XXXIII, 188.

7. Sartre 1943, 19/13.

8. Sartre 1943, 20/14.

9. Hua X, 129.

10. See Zahavi 1999, 14–37; Zahavi 2007.

11. Hua XIX/2, 669; Sartre 1943, 19/12; Levinas 1969, 111; Merleau-Ponty 1964, 36/19.

12. See Hua IV, 101–2; Hua XV, 15; Hua XXXIII, 48, 103.

13. Sartre 1943, 20/14.

14. Ibid., 21/15. See also Merleau-Ponty 1945, 433/439.

15. Sartre 1943, 19/13.

16. Hua III/1, 164; cf. 95.

17. See Ricoeur 1994, 3ff.

18. See Hua XV, 9, 15. As Zahavi puts it: "Nothing can be present *to me* unless I am *self*-aware" (Zahavi 1999, 72).

19. Zahavi 2001c, 341. See also Gallagher 2004.

20. Hua XV, 194. See also Hua XIV, 257; Hua XV, 9; and Ms. D 12 I, 6b.

21. Hua X, 129.

22. Hua XV, 65.
23. On Husserl's philosophy of time-consciousness, see Kortooms 2002; Zahavi 2003b; Rodemeyer 2006.
24. Hua X, 100; Hua X, 25.
25. Carr 1986, 29.
26. Husserl 1948, 76; see also Hua XI, 128. The last sentence of the quoted text is curiously missing from the Churchill-Ameriks translation; the original runs as follows: "Dauerndes immanentes Datum ist nur dauerndes als Datum seines Inhaltes." Elsewhere Husserl states: "We now understand the inner truth of the Kantian claim, *time is the form of sensibility*, and therefore it is the form of any world of objective experience" (Hua XXXIII, 352).
27. Hua XV, 66.
28. As David Carr puts it, "my experience of time is a function of the events that I live through" (Carr 2004, 9).
29. Hua X, 68. See also Hua XXXIX, 180–81; Husserl 2006, 82–83. See also Hua III/1, 183; Hua XVI, 273. Compare Merleau-Ponty's discussion about "the flesh of time" (*chair du temps*) (Merleau-Ponty 1964, 148/111).
30. Hua X, 103–4.
31. Hua IV, 336; Hua X, 67.
32. Hua X, 126, 127. See also Waldenfels 2000, 275: "Sensing means that I am related to myself, that I sense myself."
33. See, for example, Henry 1973, 461ff.; Henry 1975, 77–107, 140–44.
34. Husserl employs the term "affective" (*affektiv*) in many different ways. He sometimes distinguishes "affective acts" (*affektiven Akte*) from practical and theoretical acts (e.g., Hua IV, 212), thus connecting affectivity with sensibility (perception is an affective act par excellence), and giving sensibility the foundational status (see Hua IV, 213). Husserl also associates affectivity with experiences that involve emotional aspects (e.g., Hua IV, 122) or primal valuing (e.g., feelings of pleasing or displeasing) (e.g., Hua IV, 8, 247–48). Accordingly, Husserl's notion of self-affectivity covers both sensuous self-awareness and primal self-valuing of experiences. However, self-valuing is constitutionally *built upon* self-sensing (although it might be the case that sensation does not *temporally precede* valuing), and in this sense the basic meaning of Husserl's notion of affectivity lies in sensibility. In my use of the term, I refer with "self-affectivity" to *immediate material self-awareness*: "*Sensing* is nothing but the living-through of the content in question" (*Empfinden ist nichts weiter als das Erleben der bezüglichen Inhalte*) (Hua XXXVIII, 138). We can here leave open the question whether all self-sensing necessarily involves a primal valuing (see Lotz 2007). On Husserl's notions of affectivity, sensibility, and pre-predicative constitution, see Hart 1996, 108–12; Zahavi 1998b; Kühn and Staudigl 2003; Steinbock 2004. On the relation of the phenomenological notion of affectivity to the psychoanalytical notion, see Welton 1998.
35. Hua IX, 8. See also Husserl 2006, 35.
36. See Hua X, 88–89.
37. Hua X, 107; see also Hua XXXIX, 471, 474. See also Lohmar 2008, 67, 85–102.
38. Hua IV, 153; Hua XXXIX, 484. Husserl therefore also talks of "belief-

sensations," for example, distinguishing them from judging (Hua X, 103): when we *have* a belief that X, there is something *it is like* to believe that X.

39. Hua X, 126–27.
40. Hua V, 11. For a more detailed explication of the phenomenological notion of materiality and sensibility, see Landgrebe 1963, 111–23; and Landgrebe 1968, 135–47.
41. Hua X, 90.
42. Hua XIX/1, 525; Hua XIX/1, 382.
43. See Held 1966, 111ff.
44. Husserl argues that "every 'consciousness' has either the character of sensation or phantasma" (Hua X, 103), and explains that phantasma are modifications of sensations—namely, they are imaginary sensations.
45. Zahavi 1999, 126.
46. Hua X, 96. More generally, as Husserl argues in his manuscripts: "Auch ideale Gegenstände weisen in ihrem Sein auf die Existenz von Subjekten notwendig zurück"; "Ein idealer Gegenstand ist nicht denkbar ohne die ideale Möglichkeit seiner Erkenntnis als ursprünglicher Gegebenheit, also ohne die ideale Möglichkeit eines Ich solcher Erkenntnis" (Ms. D 4, 25, 27). Elsewhere Husserl argues further that even though *ideal* objectivities are not given sensuously, their givenness "arises" from the sensous sphere: "Die Idee ist als solche nicht sinnlich. . . . Aber freilich, sie stammt aus dem sinnlichen" (Ms. D 13 I, 163a).
47. Hua X, 107. See also Depraz 1998 and 2000.
48. Hua IV, 57. See alsoHua XVI, 181; Hua XXXIX, 616–17.
49. Hua XIX/1, 387.
50. See Hua X, 107; see also Hua XV, 130.
51. Hua XI, 17. This is also the reason why Husserl makes a distinction between "sensations" (*Empfindungen*) and "sensings" (*Empfindnisse*) (see, e.g., Hua IV, 144–47; see also Welton 1999, 45–46; Waldenfels 2008, 130). In short, "sensings" are sensations in their self-manifestation.
52. Husserl 2006, 86. See also Hua IV, 214; Hua X, 233; Hua XV, 128; Hua XXXIX, 472; Zahavi 1998a, 26–29; Zahavi 1999, 115–27; Taguchi 2006, 222–26. Here we should make a brief interpretative clarification. As Lotz argues, Husserl does not always, for instance in *Ideas I*, treat sensations as something we affectively *undergo* (see Lotz 2007, 87; Hua III/1, 263.). This incoherence has to do with Husserl's lack of clarity regarding the internality/externality of sensations (see Zahavi 1999, 246 n. 59). Sometimes Husserl identifies color-sensations, for instance, with the *appearances* of the colorful thing—and in this regard, "sensations" are not something we consciously *undergo*, but something that we sense *in the object*, and moreover something that pertain to our sensuous-perceptive experiences alone. However, elsewhere, and increasingly in his later work, Husserl takes "sensations" in the broader sense that we have here been employing and will employ: namely, as the affective feature of immediate and pre-reflective undergoing. Considered in their self-affectivity, sensations are "sensings" (*Empfindnisse*) (see Hua IV, 146).
53. Gallagher 1986, 142.
54. Hua XI, 137–38.

55. Hua XIX/2, 610. However, hyletic sensing is not as yet proper intentional awareness, but only the basis of the latter. As Husserl puts it, appearances are hyletic before they are objective (Hua XV, 661). See also Hua XXXIX, 229; and Hua XI, 185.

56. It should be mentioned here that Husserl does not throughout coherently subscribe to this view. In the first book of *Ideas*, Husserl still holds on to the distinction between "formless content" and "contentless form," and thus he claims that *"the sensuous . . . has in itself nothing pertaining to intentionality"* (Hua III/1, 192, 75). The basic insight of Husserl's later "genetic phenomenology" instead is that the "content" is already full of meaning: "Was not my original conception of the immanent sphere . . . a remnant of old psychology and its sensualistic empiricism? . . . After all, sense data without conception cannot be given. Being-conceived, being-a-'representation' is indigenous" (Hua XXXIX, 229). For a more detailed elaboration of this issue, see Rabanaque 2003.

57. Hua IV, 158; Hua XI, 298; see also Merleau-Ponty 1945, 286/288; Merleau-Ponty 1960, 221/175. Husserl also argues that should the pure ego not be embodied, it could have no awareness of a "Here" (Hua XIII, 248).

58. Hua XVI, 161. In the D-manuscripts Husserl notes similarly: "Es gibt ein subjektives Ich-bewege, das im physischen Leib Bewegung zur forge hat: Es ist keine physische Kraft, sie steht 'ausserhalb der Natur,' sofern sie ausserhalb des in sich geschlossenen Kräfte- bzw. Gesetzsystems der 'Natur für sich' . . . absehen" (Ms. D 13 I [1923], 132b). Accordingly, Husserl distinguishes between two kinds of egoic activities (*Ichtätigkeiten*): subjective acting (perceiving, thinking; i.e., all activities pertaining to the constitutional theory of nature, to the correlation between nature and experience), and the "objective" doing (*das 'objektive' Machen*) (Ms. D 13 I [1923], 134a–b). See also Hua VI, 164.

59. Hua XVI, 161. See also Hua IV, 57.

60. Hua XVI, 160. See also Ms. D 2, 6. This is why Merleau-Ponty insists that one should avoid saying "that our body is *in* space or *in* time," but rather use expressions such as "our body *inhabits* space and time" (Merleau-Ponty 1945, 162/161). As Lilian Alweiss puts it in the same connection, instead of being *in* space, our lived-body is "the absolute stability of the world" (Alweiss 2003, 164). See also Sheets-Johnstone 1999, 139ff.

61. Hua XVI, 298.

62. As Sheets-Johnstone puts it, originary self-movement is characterized by the peculiarity that "what is created and what is constituted are one and the same" (Sheets-Johnstone 1999, 153).

63. Husserl also states this in the following manner: "Transcendency in every form is an immanent existential characteristic, constituted within the ego" (Hua I, 117).

64. Henry 1973, 246ff., 268.

65. Hua XVI, 170.

66. Hua XI, 14.

67. Hua XVI, 187–88. In this passage Husserl discusses *visual* perception, and therefore he uses the term "i[mage]-component." I have substituted this

term with "presenting component" since the latter is apt only for visual perception. See also Husserl 1940b, 30–31.

68. Hua XVI, 177 (my emphasis). See also Hua IV, 42; and Ms. D 12 I, 12a: "Nicht ein blosses Koexistieren der entsprechenden Phasen, ein wechselseitig gleiches Miteinandersein, sondern ein kausales, einseitiges Miteinander; das jeweilige Sein des *k* bedingt das Mitdasein der zugehörigen Erscheinung *e*; das *k* motiviert das *e*."

69. Hua XVI, 183, 177–78; Merleau-Ponty 1945, 358/361.

70. Hua XI, 107.

71. Hua XVI, 183.

72. Hua XVI, 187. This early view is still operative in the later Husserl, who speaks of the "regular cooperation" (*regelmässiges Miteinander*) of "the egoic kinestheses and the *hyle* that runs with it" (*Die ichliche Kinästhese und das mit ihr Verlaufen des Hyletischen*) (Ms. D 10 I, 20).

73. Ms. D 10 I, 24: "Die Konstitution von schlechthin Seiendem vollzieht sich mittels der kinästhetischen Vermöglichkeit als Abhängiges in einer schwindelnd reichen Mittelbarkeit von Stufen."

74. Hua XVI, 181.

75. Ibid., 170; compare 178.

76. See Ms. D 12 I, 15b: "Die Teilung in Organe, wie die Rede von Gesamtorgan, hat Beziehung auf Kinästhesen: jedes Organ hat sein 'kinästhetisches System', jedes mit anderen zusammen fungierend konstituiert sozusagen ein kinästhetisches Organ höherer Stufe und so das All der Organe ein Organ gemäss einer Totalkinästhese als Synthesis aller, nämlich aller miteinander fungierenden oder möglicherweise fungierenden Organe."

77. Hua XVI, 179–80.

78. Ibid., 170.

79. Ibid., 171.

80. Ibid., 177.

81. Hua XVI, 161. On the other hand, there are reported pathological cases of kinesthetic deficiency, where a patient can learn to hold her posture by externally observing her own body parts—and thus to move her body in a controlled manner with the help of the visual sense (see Cole 1991, 128). However, even in such cases, we cannot say that vision *substitutes* kinesthesia—no more than we can say that, for blind people, the sense of hearing can *substitute* for their loss of vision. Hearing is unable to restore visual qualities, and likewise the visual sense is unable to restore, and thus substitute or serve vicariously for, kinesthetic self-awareness.

82. Hua XI, 15.

83. Hua X, 91; Husserl 2006, 199.

84. Merleau-Ponty 1945, 344/347.

85. See Ms. D 10 I, 22: "Das System der Kinästhesen ist aber nicht im voraus konstituiert, sondern seine Konstitution erfolgt in eins mit der Konstitution hyletischer Objekte." See also Hua XXXV, 408; Hua XXXIX, 472. See also Ströker 1987, 140: "*Corporeality and spatiality . . .* require one another for their

meaning.... One does not precede the other—neither ontically-genetically nor ontologically. Corporeity was not 'before' spatiality, since to be corporeal, i.e., the foundation, is to assume spatiality; the latter, in turn, was not 'before' corporeity, since corporeity determines spatiality of corporeal movement."

86. See Zahavi 1999, 124.
87. Hua XIV, 244.
88. Sartre 1943, 345/405; Henry 1975, 71–72, 32.

Two

1. On the equiprimordial distinctness and unity of the senses, see Merleau-Ponty 1945, 255–58/256–59, 270/271.
2. See Zahavi 1999, 119.
3. Hua XXXIX, 35.
4. Husserl 2006, 81. See also 76.
5. This claim is not contested even by pathological cases of *synesthesia*. There is, for instance, a study of a musician who experiences different tastes in response to hearing different musical tone intervals (Beeli, Esslen, and Jäncke 2005, 38). Yet, even in this case, taste-sensations do not *stand out over against* tone-sensations, even if they are *motivated* by the latter. And regardless of whether they are motivated by tone-sensations or not, experiences of particular taste-sensations can arise only against the background provided by other taste-sensations.
6. See Hua XI, 138. See also Hua XXXIX, 403.
7. See, for example, Hua XI, 162ff.; Husserl 2006, 81.
8. Hua XI, 138.
9. See Hua VI, 160.
10. See Merleau-Ponty 1945, 260/262.
11. Hua XI, 415.
12. Ibid., 415.
13. Fischer 1929, 558–59; see also Merleau-Ponty 1945, 326/329.
14. Hua XI, 138.
15. Hua XV, 275; see also Merleau-Ponty 1945, 271/272; Merleau-Ponty 1964, 175/134.
16. See also Ricoeur who distinguishes between "instincts," "reflexes," and "preformed skills" in detail (Ricoeur 2007, 231–50).
17. To follow the wording of José Luis Bermúdez, the sting and the hand stung are not experienced as being located in an objective system of coordinates but in a "body-relative space" (Bermúdez 2005, 301).
18. See Merleau-Ponty 1945, 91–92/89, 99/96.
19. See Hua IV, 160, 286.
20. Hua IV, 146; Hua XXXIX, 616–17.
21. Hua IV, 146; Hua XV, 296; Hua XXXIX, 630.
22. Hua XIII, 115; Hua IV, 150.

23. Hua XV, 293.
24. See also Merleau-Ponty 1945, 173/171–72.
25. See Hua XIII, 239. See also Casey 1997, 219–20.
26. As Husserl also puts it, the localized body is "*quasi*-extended" (quasi *extendiert*) (Hua XV, 324), unlike the actually extended objective body (Hua XXXIX, 630).
27. Sartre 1943, 372/437.
28. Merleau-Ponty illustrates, with pathological examples, the difference between pointing and grasping (see Merleau-Ponty 1945, 120/118). In certain cases, as Merleau-Ponty reports, patients have lost their ability to pinpoint the locus of sensation, whereas they are still able to spontaneously slash at the place where a mosquito stings them. These examples serve as proof of the real distinction between localization and self-objectification. In the words of Sartre, the location of the mosquito is "not defined by pure spatial coordinates but in relation to axes of practical reference" (Sartre 1943, 361/424). Merleau-Ponty likewise writes: "Bodily space and the external space form a practical system" (Merleau-Ponty 1945, 119/117).
29. Hua XVI, 369. In the same passage Husserl also explicates that he means this in the *genetic*-phenomenological sense. See also Hua XXXIX, 14.
30. Henry 1975, 58.
31. Hua IV, 150–51.
32. Hua IV, 146; Hua XV, 260; Hua IV, 151.
33. Hua IV, 151.
34. See, for example, Husserl 2006, 157–58. Sartre formulates this claim in the following manner: "The structure of the world demands that we cannot see without being visible," "to say that . . . there is a world, or that I have a body is one and the same thing" (Sartre 1943, 357/419). Merleau-Ponty likewise argues that "he who sees cannot possess the visible unless he is possessed by it, unless he *is of it*" (Merleau-Ponty 1964, 175/134–35). Merleau-Ponty also writes: "The body is our general medium for having a world" (Merleau-Ponty 1945, 171/169); "to be a body is to be tied to a certain world" (Merleau-Ponty 1945, 173/171); "we are in the world through our body," "we perceive the world with our body" (Merleau-Ponty 1945, 239/239). In this sense, as Jan Patočka notes, "Descartes overlooked the fact that even a dreamer has a body, albeit a dream body, that the dreamer is not disembodied, that a body is necessary even in the world of dreams. . . . The dream actually is no argument against the subjective body" (Patočka 1998, 11–12; see also Hua IV, 56).
35. See Carr 1986, 38.
36. Hua XV, 644.
37. See Sartre 1943, 371/436ff.
38. Ibid., 371/436.
39. See Hua IV, 155.
40. Sartre 1943, 373/438. See also Heidegger 2001, 107. Merleau-Ponty, too, claims: "After all, we grasp the unity of our body only in that of the thing, and it is by taking things as our starting point that our hands, eyes and all our

sense-organs appear to us as so many interchangeable instruments" (Merleau-Ponty 1945, 372/375). It is the confrontation with the non-self that reveals consciousness to itself (Zahavi 1999, 124).

41. See Leder 1990, 74.

42. See Sartre 1943, 374–75/440. See also Ms. D 10 III, 24b. In a related sense, Edward Casey discusses the intimate bond between subject and place: "When places change aspect or fade in significance, I change and fade with them: *their* alteration is *my* alteration" (Casey 1993, 307; see also Weiss 1999, 81).

43. As Heidegger argues, *mood* (*Stimmung*) is not something that is added to an allegedly neutral being-in-the-world, but something that necessarily outlines or "sketches" the latter in advance: being-in-the-world is always already somehow "attuned" (*befinden*) (Heidegger 2001, 134–40). For Husserl's theory of mood, see Lee 1998.

44. Hua XVI, 161, 365–67.

45. Husserl also says that, instead of a material thing, the perceiving body rather resembles a "persisting phantom" (Ms. D 13 I, 136a).

46. Hua XI, 15; see also Hua XXXIX, 4, 12. Sartre likewise argues that "my body indicates my possibilities in the world" (Sartre 1943, 344/403). Merleau-Ponty, too, formulates this idea: "There is an immediate equivalence between the orientation of the visual field and the awareness of one's own body as the potentiality of that field" (Merleau-Ponty 1945, 238/239; see also Merleau-Ponty 1945, 358/361).

47. Hua IV, 255; Hua IV, 261. See also Hua XV, 203; Hua XXXIX, 4, note 1. See also Staudigl 2003, 137.

48. See Hua XV, 652, where Husserl writes: "Bodily mobility and the [external] resistance belong constitutively together." In a similar manner, Henry argues that "the world that is *originally* given to us is precisely this world of the body, a world whose being at its origin is nothing more than the transcendent terminus on movement" (Henry 1975, 73): accordingly, "the being of our body is truly one of an ontological knowledge because, in its own revelation to itself, the being of the world will also be manifested to it" (Henry 1975, 71–72).

49. Hua XI, 100. See also Stern 1985, 52.

50. Hua IV, 70; see also Ms. D 13 I, 177a.

51. Hua IV, 150. See also Hua XV, 248.

52. Hua XI, 100.

53. Merleau-Ponty 1945, 367–68/371.

54. Ibid., 260/262.

55. Hua XI, 100.

56. Merleau-Ponty 1945, 270/271: "the intersensory object is to the visual object what the visual object is to the monocular images of double vision."

57. Merleau-Ponty 1945, 368/371.

58. Ibid., 271/273: "With the notion of the body schema we find that not only is the unity of the body described in a new way but also, through this, the unity of the senses and of the object."

59. Merleau-Ponty 1945, 377/381.

60. Whereas "body schema" refers to our tacit awareness of the union be-

tween interoception and exteroception, "body image" refers to a *quasi-exteroception* of the body: it is the correlate of a reflective (imaginative) awareness of one's own body as an aesthetic object. Gallagher explicates the difference between these two clearly in Gallagher 1995, 226ff.; and Gallagher 2005, 24–25.

61. For example, Hua XXXIX, 17; Merleau-Ponty 1945, 158/157.

62. There are examples of pathology where a patient cannot hold his or her posture without constantly monitoring his or her own body parts (see Cole 1991, 128).

63. Merleau-Ponty 1945, 116/115. The comet's tail is a metaphor that Husserl employs when describing *retention* (see Hua XI, 317).

64. Merleau-Ponty 1945, 275/277.

65. Ibid., 237/237.

66. Ibid., xiii/xx.

67. See Henry 1975, 71–72.

68. Hua XV, 275.

69. Sartre 1943, 369/434.

70. Hua IV, 159.

71. Ibid., 145.

72. Ibid., 145.

73. See Hua IV, 155. Merleau-Ponty emphasizes that the ambiguity remains, because neither of the hands is *simultaneously* present as touching and touched (see Merleau-Ponty 1945, 109/106).

74. Hua IV, 195; Merleau-Ponty 1945, 111/109.

75. Sartre claims instead that double sensations are merely a phenomenological curiosity, without constitutive significance, and that one can rid oneself of them with a shot of morphine, for instance (Sartre 1943, 343/402). However, as I will argue, it is highly problematic to consider the lived-body as a transparent field of sensing that cannot become an object for itself.

76. Hua IV, 150.

77. See Hua IV, 150.

78. For example, Hua XV, 648ff.; Ms D 13 I, 176b. This view has been common in the history of philosophy, at least since Aristotle (e.g. *De anima*, 435a-b).

79. Hua IV, 150–51.

80. Ibid., 148.

81. Ibid.

82. Ibid.

83. Ibid., 146.

84. See Hua IV, 150.

85. See Hua XV, 283, 287. See also Merleau-Ponty 1945, 119/117: "there would be no space for me if I had no body."

86. See Sartre 1943, 343/402.

87. See Hua XV, 648ff.

88. Hua XIII, 48. See also Hua IV, 145; Hua VI, 164; Hua IX, 131; Hua XXXIX, 623, 633.

89. Hua XV, 326–27. See also Hua XV, 15.

90. Hua XIII, 263: "Also mein Leib ist in doppelter Weise vorstellbar, un-

mittelbar in der Selbstwahrnehmung und überhaupt Selbsterscheinung, und mittelbar in einer äusseren auf eine Selbsterscheinung zurückweisenden Erscheinung." See also Hua XV, 8.

91. For example, Hua XIV, 328–29, 336–37.

92. For example, Merleau-Ponty 1945, 173–75/171–73: "je suis mon corps"; Merleau-Ponty 1945, 194–95/193: "j'ai un corps"; Henry 1975, 196.

93. Here my account contrasts with that of Elizabeth Behnke, who claims that the *Innenleib* is "one's own lived body as a peculiar inner 'object'" (Behnke 2008, 148).

94. Sartre 1943, 357–58/419–420.

95. Ibid., 365/429.

96. See Leder 1990, 15–35.

97. Henry 1975, 73. See also Melle 1983, 114ff.; Taipale 2013b.

98. Merleau-Ponty 1945, 365/369. In the words of Edith Wyschogrod: "Touch never lets me forget that I am my body" (Wyschogrod 1981, 41).

99. See Merleau-Ponty 1945, 383/387: "if I am at all times and everywhere, then I am at no time and nowhere." See also Patočka 1998, 33.

100. As Husserl notes in a manuscript from 1932: "What I touch, e.g., the floor with the feet, or the table with the hands—I am already by it" (*Was ich berühre, z.B. den Fussboden mit den Füssen oder mit den Händen den Tisch etc., als Schrank oder Tisch—bei dem bin ich schon*) (Ms. D 10 I, 30).

101. See Hua IV, 160, 286.

102. Hua XIII, 263.

103. Hua XIV, 327.

104. Ibid., 284; see also 14.

105. Hua XIV, 327, 328, 331, 337; see also Hua XV, 83.

106. Heidegger, too, claims: "We do not 'have' a body; rather, we 'are' bodily" (Heidegger 1961, 99). Most of what Heidegger says about the lived-body, can be found in his *Zollikon Seminars* (see Heidegger 1987, 97–129).

Three

1. Hua IV, 253.

2. Ms. D 12 I, 15a: "kinästhetische Ruhe ist der Stand der Passivität, des Null hinsichtlich des Strebens." See also Hua XXXIX, 397ff.

3. Husserl argues that immobility (*Ruhe*), too, is experienced kinesthetically (Hua VI, 108; Hua XV, 269; Hua XXXIX, 398; Ms. D 12 I, 10a–b and 15a), not to mention that, while holding still, we are kinesthetically aware of intrabodily movements such as heartbeat and breathing. Moreover, the *standard or normal positions* of our bodily organs are defined by Husserl in terms of kinesthetic passivity: "So hat jedes Organ bzw. hat jede Organkinästhese ihre eigene Null-Lage, die aber relativ ist auf die totale Null-Lage der Gesamtkinästhese bzw. Gesamtkörpers als 'Leibes in seiner jeweiligen Ruhe'" (Ms. D 12 I, 16b). While standing up, for instance, the standard position of the hand is to "hang" at the side of our body, in the sense that this position of the hand is the starting point

NOTES TO PAGES 57-63

for our movements, a position "starting from which" (*von denen aus*) we move ourselves: we *raise* our hand, we *reach* for something, but we do not actively *hold* our hand at our side in the null position (see Ms. D 12 I, 19a; see also Hua XXXIX, 397-99; see also Ms. D 12 I, 16a-21b).

4. Lewis Thomas hilariously writes that he would much sooner be told in a 747 above the clouds that he would have to take control over the plane, than to be told that he would have to take control over the functioning of his *liver:* "at least I would have the hope of bailing out, if I could find a parachute and discover quickly how to open a door. Nothing would save me and my liver if I were in charge. For I am, to face the facts squarely, considerably less intelligent than my liver" (Thomas 1980, 66). See also Leder 1990, 48; Leder 1998, 123.

5. Noë 2004, 1.

6. See Hua IV, 213; Hua XXXI, 3-4. Merleau-Ponty argues that our body comprises two layers, that of "the habit body" and that of "the body at this moment," and he claims that the former serves as a "guarantee" for the latter (Merleau-Ponty 1945, 97-98/95).

7. See Sass 1994, 91; Sass 2000; Sass 2001, 267ff.; Sass and Parnas 2001, 352; Parnas and Sass 2001, 107; Parnas 2003; Sass 2003.

8. See Hua XV, 290.

9. Hua IV, 151, 310.

10. See, for example, Hua XXXIX, 616. Instead, Sartre, for instance, discusses the body as an "instrument" (Sartre 1943, 359/422ff.). On the differing conceptions of Husserl, Heidegger, Sartre, and Merleau-Ponty concerning the relation between body and tools, see Heinämaa 2003, 61ff.

11. Hua XXXIX, 616.

12. See Bernet 2000, 47.

13. Hua XV, 663.

14. Hua XV, 274. See also Hua XV, 273.

15. Hua XV, 274.

16. Merleau-Ponty 1945, 167-68/165-66.

17. Hua XVI, 283-84; Hua XV, 276, 299.

18. See Hua XV, 274.

19. Merleau-Ponty 1945, 166/164, 168/166.

20. Hua XV, 299.

21. Merleau-Ponty 1945, 177/175-76.

22. Hua XV, 299.

23. It would be interesting to develop the Husserlian idea of incorporation further by comparing it with Heidegger's famous argument that tools are constituted as conspicuous and obtrusive things when they do not fill their practical purpose (e.g., when they break down) (Heidegger 2001, 74-75). This, however, would exceed the purposes of this book.

24. Henry 1975, 73.

25. See Hua XV, 28, 287, 657. As Sokolowski puts it, reversibility shows that my transcendental ego is "partitioned out into a body"; "Our felt corporeality sets up a place within which the transcendental ego exercises all its intentionalities" (Sokolowski 2000, 125).

26. Merleau-Ponty 1969, 158/112.
27. Hua XV, 283, 644. See also Hua IV, 212–13.
28. Hua XV, 283; Husserl 2006, 380. Husserl also writes: "My lived-body is over and against me—as body but not as lived-body" (Hua IV, 317). See also Sokolowski 2000, 119, 124, 154.
29. Hua VI, 110; Hua XIV, 331; Hua XVI, 161; Hua XXXIX, 623; see also Hua IV, 92–93; Hua XXXIX, 181.
30. See Hua XXXIX, 632–34. See also Hua XV, 19.
31. Hua XV, 645; Ms. D 12 I, 4b; Hua XXXIX, 617. See also Overgaard 2004, 152–58.
32. Hua XV, 645.
33. See Hua XXIX, 183.
34. See Henry 1975, 191.
35. Hua XXXIX, 633, 624.
36. See Hua XV, 8, 326–27.
37. Henry 1973, 464.
38. Merleau-Ponty 1945, 108–9/105–6.
39. See Merleau-Ponty 1960, 134/107.
40. Accordingly, one should not take Merleau-Ponty literally when he states that the lived-body is originally *neither* an object *nor* a subject, but instead something like "a third genre of being" (Merleau-Ponty 1945, 402/408).

Four

1. There are two basic tendencies prevalent in Husserl's writings on intersubjectivity (see Zahavi 2001a; 155ff.; Zahavi 2001b, 52ff.; Merleau-Ponty 2001, 41/44–45). On the one hand, starting from an abstract layer of intersubjective experiences (the so-called *sphere of ownness* or *Eigenheitssphäre*), Husserl attempts to clarify how the ego comes to experience others by way of *empathy*. This approach is explicated in Husserl's "Fifth Cartesian Meditation"—which, for a long time, was Husserl's only published text concerning the problem of intersubjectivity. However, on the other hand, the less well-known approach employed by Husserl starts from the horizontal structure of experience, and discloses it as an intersubjective dimension. In this latter approach, as will be clarified, empathy "discloses" transcendental intersubjectivity that was already operative before any actual experience of others.
2. See, for example, Zahavi 2005, 165. Moreover, phenomenologists argue that to constitute oneself as "the only one," or as being alone, already *presupposes* concrete experiences of others (e.g., Hua I, 125, 157; Hua IV, 81; Heidegger 2001, 120; Merleau-Ponty 1945, 412/418; Merleau-Ponty 1960, 221/175).
3. See Hua I, 82.
4. Hua VI, 167; see also Hua XI, 3.
5. Merleau-Ponty 1945, 84/80, 254/255, 415/421. See also Hua I, 82–83.
6. Merleau-Ponty 1945, 269/271.
7. Hua XVI, 124.

NOTES TO PAGES 71-73

8. See Hua I, 139; Hua XV, 26-27, 84, 87, 124; Hua XXXIX, 138, 403ff.
9. See Zahavi 1999, 65.
10. Hua III/1, 184-85.
11. See Gallagher 2008, 172: "The object is perceived at any given moment as possessing a plurality of *co-existing* profiles."
12. Merleau-Ponty 1945, 413/419; see also 411/417.
13. Hua VI, 160.
14. Merleau-Ponty 1945, 84/81.
15. Merleau-Ponty 1945, 83/79. See also Merleau-Ponty 1964, 232/180, where Merleau-Ponty renders things as "variants of successful *Einfühlung*."
16. Hua XIII, 377-378. Husserl states that even God would have to perceive things through appearances, and thus "imperfectly" (see Hua III/1, 351).
17. "A priori intersubjectivity," as I call it, has been discussed by Zahavi under the heading "open intersubjectivity" (see, e.g., Zahavi 2001b, 33-61; see also Hua XIV, 51, 289). As I see it, in addition to a *primordial structural reference to possible co-perceivers*, the concept of "open intersubjectivity" also covers transcendental intersubjectivity in its concrete, historically sedimented form: that is, "open intersubjectivity" covers *both* "a priori intersubjectivity" *and* what Husserl terms "generative intersubjectivity." As will be shown in what follows, however, it is important to distinguish between these two facets of transcendental intersubjectivity. In generative intersubjectivity, the co-posited others are co-constituting "homecomrades," and they are hence posited as sharing our *intersubjective normality*, whereas in "a priori intersubjectivity," the co-posited others are anonymous co-perceivers and they are—as I will argue later—posited as sharing our *primordial normality*. This distinction will prove fruitful in my treatment of normality and world-constitution in the last part of this work.
18. Husserl 2006, 394. See also Hua XXXIX, 404.
19. Zahavi 2001b, 56; Kojima 2000, 6. Instead of "intersubjectivity," Kojima prefers to employ the terms "potential plurality of the transcendental ego" and "interintentionality" (Kojima 2000, 7ff.). See also Held's discussion concerning the "self-communalization" of the ego (Held 1966, 164ff.; Held 1972, 46).
20. Hua I, 123, 124; see also Hua XIV, 122; Hua XV, 12, 17, 110; Hua XXXIX, 606, 625; Sartre 1943, 272/316; Kern 1973, xxxiii.
21. See Hua XXXVI, 157, where Husserl discusses the nature of "*a priori* possible subjects."
22. Hua VI, 262; see also Hua VI, 275; Hua XV, 74-75, 191, 192. In an unpublished manuscript (from 1932) Husserl explicitly specifies that the constitution of the *world for anybody* does not presuppose concrete experiences of others (*das Sein des Mitmenschen geht hier nicht voraus*) (Ms. A VII 11, 12a). For similar passages, see also Hua XV, 194, 200, 203-4; Hua XXIX, 332.
23. Hua VI, 162-63, 257, 259; Hua XV, 46; Hua XXXIX, 474.
24. Hua XI, 162; Hua XV, 350, 604; Hua XXXV, 391.
25. Hua IV, 222; see also Hua XI, 323; Hua XV, 598; Hua XXXIII, 276.
26. See Merleau-Ponty 1945, 401/6; see also 249/250. See also Marbach 1974, 77, 90; Zahavi 1999, 153; Zahavi 2000, 63.
27. See Hua XV, 350; Hua VI, 114-16; Hua IX, 147; Hua XIV, 429; Hua

XXXIII, 278; Ms. A VII 14, 21b; Merleau-Ponty 1945, 99/97, 408/414. Merleau-Ponty also explicitly refers to Husserl when discussing anonymity (see Merleau-Ponty 1945, 496/504). On the relationship between the notions of "anonymous" and "unconscious" (*unbewusst*), see Hua XXXIX, 24–27.

28. See Hua VI, 188; see also Hua IV, 253.

29. Merleau-Ponty 1945, 249/250. See also Merleau-Ponty 1945, 277/279; Merleau-Ponty 1960, 221/175; Merleau-Ponty 1964, 115/84; Merleau-Ponty 1994, 103/71.

30. See Merleau-Ponty 1945, 250/250–51; Hua IV, 193. See also Zahavi 2002a; Zahavi 2005, 52ff.

31. See Hua IV, 81; Hua XV, 6.

32. See, for example, Merleau-Ponty 1964, 162/123, where Merleau-Ponty speaks of "visibility older than my operations or my acts." See also Barbaras 2005, 226.

33. Merleau-Ponty 1945, 250/250–51.

34. See Merleau-Ponty 1969, 29/20.

35. Waldenfels 2004, 238. See also Sokolowski's discussion of the transcendental ego as the "dative of manifestation" (Sokolowski 2000, 113, 118, 121).

36. Merleau-Ponty 1945, 191/189–90. Merleau-Ponty also argues that the "relations of sentient to sensible are comparable with those of the sleeper with its slumber" (Merleau-Ponty 1945, 245/245).

37. See Hua I, 158–59. Elsewhere Husserl writes: "Therefore everything object-like that stands before my eyes in experience and primarily in perception has an apperceptive horizon of possible experiences, my own and those of others. Ontologically speaking, every appearance that I have is from the very beginning a part of an open endless, although not explicitly realized totality of possible appearances of the same, *and the subjectivity of these appearances is the open intersubjectivity*" (Hua XIV, 289). Husserl also specifies that in this sense intersubjectivity pertains already to primordial experience (Hua XXXIX, 498).

38. Hua XIV, 69. See also Kojima's discussion on the relation between Merleau-Ponty's "one" and Heidegger's *Das Man* (Kojima 2000, 137–43).

39. Hua XXXIX, 635. See also Hua XV, 157. Husserl also writes: "To be sure, the world is beforehand not [experienced as] my, the fictively isolated ego's, world, but as the objective world, a world for anyone" (Hua XXXIX, 606).

40. See Hua IV, 297.

41. See, for example, Merleau-Ponty 1960, 212–13/168, 218/173.

42. See Waldenfels 1998, 79; Waldenfels 2004, 246; Hua VI, 258–59; Hua XV, 200; Hua I, 150–51. See also Carr 1973, 29ff.

43. See Hua XV, 116; see also Hua IV, 297.

44. Merleau-Ponty 1964, 185/142.

45. See Husserl 2006, 436. See also Hua I, 168; Hua XV, 14, 108.

46. I have studied this theme more comprehensively, also taking into account the more recent takes on the problem, elsewhere (see Taipale 2013a).

47. Merleau-Ponty 1997, 179/119. See also Gallagher and Meltzoff 1996; Soffer 1999, 152; Stawarska 2004; Zahavi 2002a.

48. Merleau-Ponty 1997, 179/119. A few years later, Margaret Mahler, a

psychoanalyst and a pioneer of the symbiosis theory, captures the classical psychoanalytic theory in the following manner: "Normal autism and normal symbiosis are the two earliest stages of nondifferentiation—the former is objectless, the latter, preobjectal. The two stages occur before differentiation of the undifferentiated or nondifferentiated matrix; that is, before separation and individuation and the emergence of the rudimentary ego as a functional structure" (Mahler et al. 1975: 48; see also Spitz 1965: 16).

49. Merleau-Ponty 1997, 180/120.

50. Ibid., 183/122.

51. Hua XV, 605; Husserl 2006, 437, 604. I have developed these lines of thought further in separate articles (see Taipale 2013a and Taipale 2013b).

52. Merleau-Ponty 1997, 183/121.

53. Ibid., 183/122.

54. Ibid.

55. Ibid., 186/124.

56. See Husserl's discussion in Hua XV, 511, 582, 604–5; and Ms. A V 25, 6b.

57. Hua XXXIX, 615. This view is supported by several studies, especially since the 1980s. See, for example, Stern 1985. For an attempt at reconciling the two views, see Taipale 2013a.

58. Hua XXXIX, 624. See also Hua XIV, 7.

59. Merleau-Ponty 1997, 180/119.

60. Elsewhere Merleau-Ponty argues that adult merger-like experiences also necessarily involve self-awareness. For example, in falling in love, a person might feel herself to be "one" with the other, but this is not to lack primordial self-awareness, but rather to be aware *of oneself* in a particularly modified manner (see Merleau-Ponty 1945, 410/416).

61. See Merleau-Ponty 1945, 250/250–51; Hua IV, 193; Zahavi 2002a; and Zahavi 2005, 52ff. My account contrasts with that of James Hart, for instance, who claims that there is a phase in which the infant's experiential life is "not yet self-reflexive" (Hart 1992, 193).

62. Stern 1985, 69–70; see also Gallagher and Meltzoff 1996, 229; Taipale 2013a.

63. See, for example, Hua IV, 168; Hua XIII, 415; Hua XIV, 7, 336–38; Hua XV, 159, 660, 643; Husserl 2006, 439; Merleau-Ponty 1945, 405/410, 427–28/434, 511/520; Merleau-Ponty 1960, 212/168; Hua XIII, 333.

64. Merleau-Ponty 1997, 181/121.

65. Stern 1985, 45; Stern 1985, 7; see also 37–68. Husserl, too, argues that children are already temporally self-aware before they have an organized experience of the world (Hua XIV, 334).

66. Hua I, 112; Hua XIV, 333; see also Ms. D 10 II, 20b; Merleau-Ponty 1945, 179/177; Sokolowski 1974, 108–9.

67. Merleau-Ponty 1997, 185/123.

68. Ibid., 184/122.

69. Ibid., 185/123.

70. Ibid.

71. Merleau-Ponty 1997, 187/125. See also Hua XIV, 328–329.

72. See Waldenfels, 2004, 244; Waldenfels 2007, 82.
73. Hua I, 139. See also Hua XV, 12.
74. Hua XIV, 336; see also Hua XIV, 9–10; Hua XV, 85.
75. Hua XIV, 4. See also Hua XIV, 284–86.
76. Hua VI, 303.
77. Merleau-Ponty also argues that "reasoning by analogy already presupposes what it is called on to explain" (see Merleau-Ponty 1945, 404/410).
78. See, for example, Hua I, 168; Hua XV, 14.
79. See Hua XXXIX, 629.
80. Hua I, 144; see also Hua II, 80.
81. Hua IV, 164; Hua XV, 182; Hua XXXIX, 617, 629.
82. For example, Hua XV, 29, 31, 38. See also Steinbock 1995a, 57–60.
83. Hua I, 141. On the historical context of the Husserlian concept of empathy, see Moran 2004 and Zahavi 2010.
84. See Hua XV, 255; Hua I, 142. Hua XIII, 338–39.
85. Hua XXXIX, 617.
86. On the threshold of the discovery of a priori intersubjectivity, Husserl ponders: "When empathy enters the picture, is there already community, an intersubjectivity: is empathy therefore a merely disclosing achievement?" (Husserl 2006, 436; see also Hua I, 168; Hua XV, 14, 108).
87. See Hua IV, 166.
88. Hua XV, 190; see also 192.
89. Hua IV, 297.
90. Hua XIV, 336, 547; see also Hua IV, 85, 150–51; Hua XV, 158; Hua XXXIX, 616; Ms. D 13 I, 136a.
91. Hua XIV, 7. See also Hua IV, 168; Hua XIII, 415; Hua XIV, 285; Hua XV, 660; Husserl 2006, 439; Merleau-Ponty 1945, 511/520. See also Hua XIII, 333, where Husserl explicates that this precedence is not only static but genetic.
92. Merleau-Ponty 1945, 427–28/434. See also Merleau-Ponty 1945, 405/410, 511/520; Hua XIV, 336–38; Hua XV, 643, 159.
93. Merleau-Ponty 1960, 212/168.
94. Zahavi 2001b, 160–61. Husserl also writes: "that I . . . can become aware of someone else . . . , presupposes that not all my own modes of consciousness are modes of my self-consciousness" (Hua I, 135; see also Hua XV, 634). Or, as Merleau-Ponty puts it: "as an embodied subject, I am exposed to the other person" (Merleau-Ponty 1969, 28/18); "other people are no more closed systems than I am myself" (Merleau-Ponty 1945, 389/393).
95. Merleau-Ponty 1945, 403/409.
96. Ibid., 407/413.
97. See Hua XIV, 332; Merleau-Ponty 1960, 215/170.
98. Hua XV, 18.
99. Hua XV, 138: "Being confronted with [others] is but one form of being with [others]." See also Hua I, 124; Hua XXXIX, 636; Zahavi 2005, 163–68.
100. See Hua XV, 116. See also Kojima 2000, 5–6: "Anonymous other egos already function in the primordial sphere of my ego"; "The back [of an object] is nothing other than the front confronted by another ego."

101. See Brand 1979, 115; Zahavi 2001b, 56.
102. Merleau-Ponty 1945, 407/413.
103. See, for example, Hua XV, 69, 73, 76, 228.
104. Husserl distinguishes between "psychological empathy" and *"transcendental* 'empathy'" (transzendentale *"Einfühlung"*). He argues that although psychological empathy has remarkable constitutive effects, it is itself made possible by "transcendental empathy," which is an essential "structure of constitution," and refers to appresentation (Hua XV, 116).
105. Waldenfels 2004, 247.
106. Merleau-Ponty 1964, 231/180. See also Hua VI, 258–59.
107. See Hua I, 137; Hua VI, 189, 199; Hua XV, 16, 111, 190; Hua XXXIX, 485–86. See also Merleau-Ponty 1964, 224/172, where Merleau-Ponty refers to the "pure others" of Husserl's *Cartesian Meditations*.

Five

1. Hua XIV, 8; Hua VIII, 495.
2. Hua XV, 19.
3. See Hua IX, 511. On the relationship between Husserl and Levinas, see Bernet 2002a; Overgaard 2003; Overgaard 2007.
4. See Hua XIV, 133. In this sense, sociality is a matter of a "second-person perspective." That is to say, in sociality the other appears, not as a *He* or *She* or *It*, but as *a You*—moreover, as a You for whom I likewise appear as a singular being. For an interesting developmental-psychological account of the second-person perspective, see Reddy 2008.
5. Husserl defines social acts as those that involve an I and a Thou (*Ich–Duakten*) in, for example, Hua I, 159; Hua IV, 205; Hua VI, 175; Hua XV, 19, 205, 208.
6. See Hua I, 35; see also Hua I, 159; Hua IX, 539.
7. Hua XIV, 328, 331, 337.
8. Hua XIV, 327. See also Hua XXXIX, 346. Husserl also discusses the differences between bodily expressions and linguistic expressions. (See Hua XV, 89ff. See also Heinämaa 2003, 32ff.)
9. Hua I, 151.
10. See Merleau-Ponty 1945, 215/214.
11. As Edith Stein puts it, a "feeling in its pure essence is not something complete in itself . . . , it is loaded with an energy which must be unloaded. . . . By nature, . . . [feelings, etc.] must always be expressed" (Stein 1917, 57). In a very similar manner, Merleau-Ponty argues further that feelings or thoughts can be *repressed* only insofar as they originally tend to be expressed: "thought *tends* towards expression as towards its completion" (Merleau-Ponty 1945, 206/206; see also 211/211).
12. See, for example, Stern 1985, 128–33; Zahavi 1999, 174–80.
13. Zahavi 1999, 177.
14. In a manuscript Husserl argues that mutual understanding already presupposes the constitution of a common world (Ms. D 13 I, 78b).

15. Hua XIII, 65. See also Hua VI, 369; Hua XV, 83.
16. Hua IV, 297. See also Hua XIII, 368–69.
17. Carr 1987, 270.
18. Hua I, 126.
19. The idea of horizontal otherness can perhaps be developed in an interdisciplinary manner by relating it to the fact that in some cases of schizophrenia, one feels that one is being watched: this could be understood as involving the thematization of the horizontal otherness that accompanies all our perceptions, but normally remains implicit.
20. See Hua XV, 141.
21. It should be emphasized that we are here explicating the structures of constitution: even if terms such as "exclusion" are employed, one must keep in mind that this does not mean any form of political or ethical exclusion, racism, or discrimination.
22. Hua XIV, 206. See also Holenstein's critique of the Husserlian view (Holenstein 1999, 80–88).
23. Hua XIV, 404; Hua XV, 56.
24. See Hua I, 160; Hua IV, 182, 195; Hua XIII, 106–7; Hua XIV, 201, 205; Hua XV, 56, 58; Hua XXIX, 58, 198. See also Carr 1987, 267; Melle 1996, 28ff.
25. Hua XIV, 206; Hua XXXIX, 181.
26. See Hua XV, 154.
27. Ibid., 67.
28. Hua VI, 175; see also Hua VI, 172.
29. Hua IX, 484–85; 511. Husserl also argues that, unlike what Leibniz stated, monads do have "windows" (Hua XIII, 473; Hua XIV, 295)—"drafty" windows, as John Brough specifies (Brough 1996, 7)—and by windows Husserl refers to empathy (*die Fenster sind die Einfühlungen*) (Hua XIV, 260). In the *Crisis*, Husserl writes: "All souls make up a single unity of intentionality with the reciprocal implications of these life-fluxes of the individual subjects" (Hua VI, 260). Regarding this issue, see also Overgaard's article on the affinities between Husserl and Levinas (Overgaard 2003).
30. Husserl 2006, 437.
31. See Hua XV, 66.
32. This also allows for the possibility of decentralization. The subject can be temporally decentered in regard to socially established time without being excluded from it. If we are late for a meeting with our friends with the common plan of seeing a movie together, we can feel a non-synchronicity of our temporal horizons, and if we are late enough, and others leave without us, we no longer experience a shared future of seeing the movie together. Yet, we share time in a deeper sense. Similarly, in relation to a common endeavour, one can be temporally *ahead* or *behind* in relation to the project as a whole—despite one's subjective goals. Similarly, a scientific genius can be ahead of her times, that is, ahead of the time socially established by the scientific community in which she is situated.
33. Hua IV, 190.
34. On Husserl's notion of a priori, and its differences in comparison to

the Kantian notion, see Lohmar 2008, pp. 25ff; Lohmar 2003, 106. See also Dufrenne 1966.

35. Our pertinence to communities can be, to some extent, a kind of harmonious sedimentation and coincidence—like that of geometrical circles included in larger ones without intersection of the lines—but communities in which the subject participates can also partly cross (*kreuzen*) (Hua XIII, 107), and therefore also *intra*subjective conflicts are possible (see Carr 1986, 160; Steinbock 1998, 15ff.).

36. See Hua I, 159; Hua IV, 78ff.; Merleau-Ponty 1945, 406/412.

37. Hua VI, 256. See also, for example, Hua I, 125; Hua IV, 78, 81; Hua VI, 186; Hua XVII, 210; Zahavi 2001b, 162; and Carr 1986, 144.

38. Hua IV, 288; Hua VI, 270.

39. Hua XIV, 170–71. See also Hua I, 144; Hua XIV, 175; Hua XV, 137.

40. Hua XIV, 175. See also Hua XIV, 163; Hua XV, 19.

41. Hua XV, 193. See also Hua I, 166; Hua VI, 175; Hua XXXIX, 606, 613.

42. In the analytical tradition, the problem of personal identity arises as a partial problem within a more general metaphysical discussion concerning the identity of any *existing object* whatsoever. Different accounts can be roughly divided into two main categories. First of all, there are those that endorse a *psychological approach*, and hence argue that personal identity resides in psychological continuity of "person-phases," "person-stages," or "soul-phases" (see Shoemaker 1984, 75; Shoemaker 1996, 158; Perry 1975, 11; Schechtman 1996, 7–25; Quinton 1973, 89, 103; Chisholm 1999; see also Quinton 1962, 402). On the other hand, some commentators opt for the *physical* or *somatic approach*, arguing that personal identity consists in bodily continuity (see Ayer 1936, 194, 197–98; Williams 1957; see also Parfit 1999, 376, 369; Johnston 1999, 397). What the psychological and the somatic approaches have in common is that, in both, the theme of inquiry is understood and described in *objectifying terms*. In the psychological approach, subjective experiences are discussed from a third-person perspective, as mental states (see Strawson 2005, 136; see also Shoemaker 1996, 157–58), whereas in the somatic approach, the body is understood as a material thing, ultimately as a collection of cells, organs, nervous systems, that are all included in empirical objective space (see, e.g., Shoemaker 1969, 120–21). Some commentators even go so far as to claim that personhood is something that can be objectively measured—David Lewis, for example, considers the possibility that someone could be a person only to the degree, say, of 0.02 percent (see Lewis 1969). All these accounts treat personhood as an *empirical issue*, whereas phenomenology, instead, discusses the *transcendental* dimensions of personhood.

43. Hua IV, 124.

44. Ibid., 326.

45. For example, Hua IV, 241, 349; see also Merleau-Ponty 1945, 99/96, 135/133, 154/153–54, 186/185, 201/199, 217/217, 247/248.

46. Hua IV, 270.

47. Merleau-Ponty 1945, 378/382. See also Heinämaa 2003, 66–70.

48. Hua IV, 204; see also 244, 352; Hua XIII, 70.

49. Hua IV, 235. See also Hua XIII, 76.

50. Merleau-Ponty 1945, 140/138; compare Merleau-Ponty 1945, 67/64: "the human body as the outward manifestation of a certain manner of being-in-the-world. See also Merleau-Ponty 1945, 482/489.

51. This "power of placing in abeyance" (*pouvoir suspensif*) ensures, according to Merleau-Ponty, the freedom of the person from determinism (Merleau-Ponty 1945, 453/460; 500/509).

52. Hua IV, 271.

53. Hua VI, 272.

54. Hua IX, 215. See also Hua XV, 620.

55. Hua IV, 270. See also Hua IV, 254, 272. In the *Cartesian Meditations* Husserl writes similarly: "Though convictions are, in general, only relatively abiding and have their forms of alteration . . . , the Ego shows, in such alterations, an abiding style, a 'personal character'" (Hua I, 101).

56. Hua IV, 349.

57. Ibid., 277. See also Hua IV, 270, 297, 326, 379; Husserl 2006, 386.

58. Hua IV, 271. See also Hua IV, 326, 278.

59. Merleau-Ponty 1945, 409/415, 410/417; Hua IV, 270, 278.

60. As Husserl puts it, each ego has its own "absolute singularity regardless of the general form, general essence, through which the ego is precisely an ego" (Husserl 2006, 386). Heidegger, too, stresses: "Authentic Being-one's-Self does not rest upon an exceptional condition of the subject, a condition that has been detached from the 'they'; it is rather an existentiell modification of the 'they'— of the 'they' as an essential existentiale" (Heidegger 2001, 130; translation by Macquarrie and Robinson).

61. Ms. D 11, 3b; Merleau-Ponty 1945, 186/185. Heinämaa has argued that sexuality can be seen phenomenologically as an individual modification of the masculine and feminine styles of relating to the world, to others, and to oneself (see Heinämaa 2003).

62. See Hua XV, 154–155.

Six

1. For example, Hua I, 138; Hua XIV, 122; Hua XV, 176.

2. In phenomenology, "normality" has a special meaning, as it refers to a mode of constitution. By "intersubjectively 'normal' manner of experiencing," I am accordingly referring to a manner of experiencing that is familiar in the sense that within an intersubjective community a subject is expected to experience the environment in this manner in optimal circumstances. I will distinguish different phenomenological notions of normality and study them in detail in part 3.

3. Husserl also calls the sphere of intersubjective familiarity the "intersubjective sphere of ownness" (Hua I, 137). Just as the primordial environment is the correlate of a sphere of ownness, "homeworld" is the correlate of an intersubjective sphere of familiarity. Moreover, in the C-manuscripts, Husserl distinguishes between two types of empathy: empathy toward others within a home-

world and empathy toward alien others (Husserl 2006, 372–73; see also Held 1991, 308; Zahavi 2001b, 229n7).

4. Hua XV, 225; see also 67, 174, 221; Hua XXXIX, 58, 341. Husserl also specifies that a world can be familiar, even if not all particular realities in it are familiar (Hua XV, 631).

5. Hua XV, 20; see also 624; Hua XXXIX, 177–78. See also Steinbock 1995a, 220–22.

6. See Hua XV, 169, 216, 430, 631. See also Hua I, 144.
7. See Hua XV, 633.
8. For example, Hua XV, 199.
9. Schües 2000, 111.
10. See Hua XV, 139; see also Hua XV, 195.
11. Carr 1986, 160.

12. See Hua XV, 20, 463; Husserl 2006, 436. See also Steinbock 1995a, 196. Also etymologically, "appropriation" is a suitable term for the process of "own-making": the word "appropriate" is derived from the Latin "appropriare," which means "to make one's own" ("ad," "to" + "propriare," "to take as one's own"; "proprius," "one's own").

13. Steinbock 1995a, 180.
14. Hua XV, 154; Hua XXXIX, 158.

15. See Hua XV, 38ff. To be sure, as Husserl clarifies, in the "nexus of generative life, we find no cultureless world," but it is nevertheless the case that "in the life of each individual," the "pregiven world as a cultural world refers genetically back to a yet *cultureless* . . . world" (Hua XXXIX, 28–29). That is, "in their manner of givenness, cultural determinations refer back to their genesis in me" (Hua XXXIX, 30; see also 32–34). Accordingly, as Husserl puts it in another passage, even if in the generative-intersubjective sense my parents must have existed *before* I did, in the genetic sense, my parents have come into being for me and gained their sense for me in the course of my life (Hua XXXIX, 225). In this sense, the generative necessarily has a genetic constitution.

16. See, for example, Hua XV, 57, 222; Hua XXXIX, 154. As to genetic constitution, Husserl considers the mother as the "first other" (Husserl 2006, 604): "the bond with the mother is the most original of all bonds" (Hua XV, 511).

17. Hua XV, 622.
18. See Hua XV, 169–70. See also Landgrebe 1940, 48ff.

19. Hua XV, 198. See also Hua XXXIX, 435; Husserl 2006, 159–60; and Ms. D 10 II, 20b. Moreover, in this sense, the temporal unity of a homeworld is analogical to the temporal unity of a person: "the manners of alteration [of the homeworld] pertain to the general type of the being of the homeworld" (Hua XV, 222). In this sense, like the identity of an individual person, the identity of a community is not an unchangeable unity, but a unitary way of changing.

20. Husserl claims: "The primarily existing world, I have (in my genesis beginning in childhood) as the concordantly experienced homeworld of local inhabitants" (Hua XV, 233).

21. See Hua XV, 411; Hua XV, 67, 139, 618. As Husserl also puts it: "My world, the one that I always speak about, and will speak about, is for me at all

times meant as being 'our' world, the world for *us humans*" (Hua XV, 163). It must be noted that Husserl is referring to what he elsewhere calls "transcendental humanity" (e.g., Ms. A VII 11, 8b). Namely, Husserl distinguishes between "mundane historicity" (*weltliche Historizität*) and "transcendental historicity" (*transzendentalen Historizität*) (Ms. A VII 11, 11a). Therefore, as he treats "the Absolute as absolute 'human' monadic community" (*das Absolute als absolutes "menschliches" Monadenall*) (Hua XV, 669), he does not give up transcendental phenomenology. See also Hua XV, 219; Ms. E III 11, 3b.

22. Hua XV, 142.
23. Hua XXXIX, 669.
24. For example, Hua XV, 624, 629. I adopt this translation from Steinbock (see Steinbock 1995a, 187).
25. See Ms. A VII 11, 26b, where Husserl speaks of the relativity of subjective autonomy, and discusses "autonomy within the tradition, autonomy in the limits of the Kathekon."
26. Hua XV, 177–78. See also Hua XV, 219. Husserl also identifies generativity with "descendence" (*Deszendenz*), although in quotation marks (see Hua XV, 179).
27. Husserl even considers the possibility that even our "inborn character" stems from our generative context (Hua XXIX, 88). And he argues elsewhere that "with the awakening of a new monad, the parental habituality is awakened or pre-awakened" (Husserl 2006, 436; see also 439).
28. Hua XV, 143–44. See also Hua XV, 154.
29. Hua XV, 144; see also Hua XXXIX, 158.
30. See Hua XV, 633.
31. According to Husserl, in the process of appropriation, imitation (*Nachahmung*) plays an important role: "Already when one empathically, coinciding with others, performs their valuings, efforts and achievements with them (without modalization), thereby one already learns from them, one acquires a corresponding habituality to act similarly" (Hua XV, 630). See also Hua XV, 145–46.
32. Hua XV, 142; Hua VI, 381.
33. Hua XV, 20; see also 69.
34. Hua XV, 17. See also Aguirre 1970, 159.
35. Hua XV, 139.
36. Hua VI, 370–71; Hua XV, 225. Elsewhere Husserl even argues that we are not quite humans before we participate in cultural life: "But actual human life is, essentially, cultural life, and insofar as it is not [yet] cultural, the human being is still [an] animal" (Hua XXVII, 99).
37. Hua VI, 369–70. See also Hua XV, 205.
38. Hua XIV, 133. See also Hua XV, 176.
39. Hua VI, 307.
40. Ibid., 307–8.
41. Ibid.
42. Hua XV, 220.
43. Ibid., 225.

44. Hua VI, 369.
45. Ibid., 371.
46. Hua VI, 371; see also Hua VI, 368.
47. See Hua XV, 47, 57, 61; see also Merleau-Ponty 1960, 121/96.
48. Hua VI, 372. See also Dodd 2004, 130–33. See also Heidegger's analysis of "idle talk" (*Gerede*) (Heidegger 2001, 167–170).
49. Hua VI, 369.
50. Ibid., 52.
51. See Hua XV, 223–24.
52. Hua VI, 371.
53. In the *Crisis*, Husserl argues that the cultural world "exists through tradition" (Hua VI, 366): "The whole of the cultural present, understood as a totality, 'implies' the whole of the cultural past in an undetermined but structurally determinable generality" (379); "History is from the start nothing other than the vital movement of the coexistence and the interweaving of original formations and sedimentations of meaning" (380).
54. Husserl specifies: "What is privileged in consciousness as the horizon of civilization and as linguistic community is mature normal civilization (taking away the anomalous and the world of children)" (Hua VI, 369).
55. See Hua VI, 368; see also Hua XXXIX, 175.
56. Hua XV, 139, 214, 225–26. See also Hua XV, 61; Hua XXXIX, 171.
57. Hua VI, 371. See also Ms. D 4, 8: "Die Worte haben den Stempel des 'Jedermann' und 'ich wie jedermann' drückt sich so aus, jedermann spricht sich so aus, jedermann kann so reden und verstehen."
58. See Hua XV, 138; Steinbock 1995a, 192.
59. Hua XXXIX, 669.
60. Hua I, 137. See also Ms. A VII 11, 8b; Hua XV, 150; Ms. D 17, 13a: Husserl 1940a, 318; Hua XXXIV, 246.
61. See Hua XV, 37.
62. Ibid.,154–55; see also Hua XV, 168.
63. Hua XV, 619; Hua VI, 310; Hua VI, 256; Husserl 1940a, 323; Ms. D 17, 19a; Hua XV, 17.
64. Hua XV, 140. See also Carr 1986, 178; Schapp 2004, 148.
65. Hua XV, 463.
66. Husserl 2006, 439; see also Hua XXXIX, 155.
67. Hua VI, 378.
68. Ibid., 175. See also Hua I, 166.
69. Hua VI, 13.
70. For example, Hua I, 125; Hua IV, 81; Hua XV, 169.
71. Hua XXIX, 198. See also Hua XXXIX, 151; Hua XV, 154; and Hua XV, 77: "Transcendental intersubjectivity is something *for me*, my life is sedimented, and the basic layer is the first 'concretion,' the 'coherent' life in '*immediate*' intentionality, the level of primordiality."
72. Hua XV, 426. See also Hua XV, 212.
73. Carr 1986, 120; see also Carr 1987, 276.

74. Carr 1986, 150.
75. Zahavi 2001b, 99. As Husserl puts it, "transcendental *egology*" is necessarily the "first phenomenology" (Hua XV, 109–10; see also Hua I, 67–69).
76. See Hua VI, 272, where Husserl discusses the "inseparable correlation between individual persons and communities." See also Hua XXXIX, 651. As Hart proclaims: "Only someone who can properly say 'I' can properly say 'we'" (Hart 1989, 127).
77. Hua VI, 188.
78. Ibid., 190.
79. See Hua XV, 614; see also Hua XXIX, 332.
80. See Hua XV, 138. Husserl also formulates this view by claiming that the subjects of historicity are nothing else than "the persons who create cultural formations" (Hua VI, 381).
81. Hua VI, 381; Hua XV, 631.
82. Hua VI, 382. See also Hua VI, 256; Hua XV, 38, 667.
83. Hua XV, 61. See also Hua XV, 219, 640, 667.
84. Hua XV, 634; Hua XXXIX, 628.
85. Hua VI, 256.
86. Hua XV, 17, 168, 195; Hua XXIX, 332.
87. See Heidegger 2001, 237–41.
88. Hua XXIX, 332.
89. Ibid., 334.
90. Hua IV, 103; Husserl 2006, 438.
91. Merleau-Ponty 1945, 249/250.
92. Husserl 2006, 438.
93. Hua XXIX, 332.
94. Hua XV, 209.
95. See Hua XXIX, 332–38.
96. See, for example, Husserl's discussion of the primordial world-horizon as the correlate of "lived-bodily capability" (*leibliche Vermöglichkeit*) in Hua XXXIX, 498. See also Hua XXIX, 332.
97. Heidegger 2001, 262. Cf. Heidegger 2001, 250; Levinas 1987, 68–73.
98. See Hua XV, 433–36; Held 1991, 321–22. I leave here unexamined the phenomenon of *aging*: to some extent, aging involves the narrowing down of possibilities, but it is not something one can be "cured of."
99. Merleau-Ponty 1945, 418/424. See also Merleau-Ponty 1945, 250/250.
100. Hua XXXIX, 226.
101. Hua XXIX, 334.
102. Hua XXXIX, 610.
103. See ibid., 608–14.
104. Hua IV, 255; Ricoeur 2007, 233–50. See also Hua XXXIX, 475–77.
105. Hua XXXIX, 611. Husserl discusses birth and death as "limit cases" (*Grenzfällen*) (Husserl 2006, 435ff.), as "limiting forms" (*Limesgestalten*), and as limiting cases (*Limesfälle*) (Husserl 2006, 154ff.), arguing that in concrete life, and from within (*von inner her*), birth appears as "limit of aging" (*als Limes der Altern*) (Husserl 2006, 158). He further characterizes newborn subjects as still

"mentally poor" (*armselig*), discusses the "limit of beginning of the ego" (*Anfangslimes des Ich*) as the "awaking ego" (*erwachende Ich*), discusses the relationship between inborn character, instincts, and affectivity, and also explicitly distinguishes this *genetic* understanding of birth from *generative* analyses: "Of course, the beginning of an 'awaking' ego and the beginning of a wakeful life does not signify birth in the generative sense" (Husserl 2006, 155; see also Hua XXXIX, 465–77). Husserl also emphasizes that, paradoxically, the comprehensive "I cannot" cannot be experienced: "Only a limit [*Limes*] of the progressing decomposition is prefigured, with the end: not being capable of experiencing any longer" (Husserl 2006, 157).

106. Husserl compares birth with waking up from a dreamless sleep (Husserl 2006, 437; see also Hua XV, 50; Hua XXIX, 335), and he stresses that the analogy only applies to a *dreamless* sleep, because he considers dreaming as a mode of *waking* life (see, e.g., Hua XXIX, 336; Hua XXXIX, 472). On the other hand, Husserl argues that dying is not analogous to falling asleep (see, e.g., Husserl 2006, 158ff.)—although, to be sure, our experience of *other's* (peaceful) death can be compared to an empathic experience of watching another person falling asleep (Hua XXIX, 337–38).

107. Hua XXIX, 334; Hua XV, 169. In a manuscript Husserl writes that "my life is arranged between 'beginning and end' as a temporal stretch" (Husserl 2006, 166; see also Ms. E III, 11). See also Carr 1998, 127ff. See also Merleau-Ponty 1945, 249–50/250; and Heidegger 2001, 374.

108. Hua XXIX, 338; see also Hua IV, 161.

109. Steinbock 1995a, 190; see also Hua VI, 191–92. As Steinbock suggests, Husserl's statements concerning death must be understood against Husserl's methodological development: it was not until the early 1930s that Husserl was able to formulate a satisfactory account of generativity and historicity (Steinbock 1995a, 46ff.; Steinbock 2008). Likewise, Husserl's earlier claim that the death of the transcendental ego is unthinkable (Hua XI, 377–81; Hua XXIX, 334) is not to be understood as a claim concerning the immortality of human beings: within the genetic-phenomenological framework, from the point of view of an individual subjectivity, one's own birth and death are not among possible occurrences, not something we are capable of in the sense of "I can," and in this sense, as already explained, we *cannot* be born and we *cannot* die.

110. Hua XV, 138, 169. Husserl also claims that "in the order of constitution . . . the first human being is the other, and it is initially from there that I gain the meaning 'human being'" (Hua XV, 19). Elsewhere he likewise argues that we come to grasp our mortality in the proper sense by grasping the mortality of others (Hua XV, 153, 209): when someone close to us passes away, our normal familiar course of life is altered and our futural horizon becomes modified (Hua XV, 210–11). Husserl also argues that analogically a community can become aware of its finitude when familiarity breaks down in a "borderline situation" (*Grenzsituation*) (see Hua V, 213). As intersubjective events, birth and death have an essential significance for world-constitution. To realize that past and futural others also share the world with us, transforms the "openness" of transcendental intersubjectivity: the world becomes the historical world, the world given over in

a tradition. Without birth and death, there could be no families, kins, no traditions whatsoever—and correlatively no historical lifeworld. In this sense, birth and death are indeed empirical and mundane events, but at the same time also constitutive or transcendental occurrences (*transzendentale Vorkommnisse*) (Husserl 2006, 439; Hua XV, 171).

111. Hua XXIX, 333. See also Hua XV, 38ff.
112. Hua XV, 66.
113. Hua XXIX, 332. See also Hua XXXIX, 228.
114. Hua XV, 37–38.
115. Husserl 2006, 438; Hua XXXIX, 609. This is why mortality can be properly revealed only within a community—as Minkowski puts it: "The solitary man would cease to live, perhaps, but he would not die" (Minkowski 1970, 136).
116. Husserl writes: "Thus the 'We' lives on . . . while the individual 'dies,' that is, the individual can no longer be 'remembered' empathically by others, but 'lives' only in historical memory whereby the memory-subject can be substituted for the individual who 'dies'" (Husserl 1940a, 325; Ms. D 17, 20b; see also Hua XXXIX, 384).
117. Hua XV, 195.
118. See Hua IV, 191.
119. See Hua XV, 169, 171. See also Hua XIV, 132.
120. See Zahavi 2001b, 58.
121. See Steinbock 1995a, 190.

Seven

1. For example, Ms. D 13 I, 213a; Hua XXXIX, 669.
2. See Hua XV, 34; Merleau-Ponty 1964, 110/80; de Folter 1983, 178. Merleau-Ponty also writes: "the thing perceived by the other is doubled: there is *the one he perceives*, God knows where, and there is the one I see, outside his body, and which I call the true thing—just as he calls true thing the table *he sees* and consigns to the category of appearances the one I see" (Merleau-Ponty 1964, 25/9–10).
3. *Oxford Encyclopedia of Philosophy*, 626.
4. Hua XV, 143. Husserl also argues: "Human normality does not only signify a mere externally describable style, but an inner unity, a unity of a person in his life, a unity of the respective humankind as analogon of a person" (Hua XV, 154).
5. Ms. D 13 I, 183a; see also de Folter 1983, 167; Canguilhem 1991, 226; Barbaras 2005, 215.
6. Hua XIV, 68; Hua XIV, 123, 154; Hua XV, 35.
7. See, for example, Durkheim 1982, 91: "those facts which appear in the most common form we shall call normal and the rest morbid or pathological."
8. Canguilhem 1991, 161.
9. For different approaches to the phenomenology of normality, see de Folter 1983; Römmp 1992, 89–91; Steinbock 1995a and 1995b; and Zahavi 2001b,

86–97. The distinctions of different commentators overlap in manners that are too complex to be elaborated here in detail. See also Taipale 2010; Taipale 2012.

10. Hua XIII, 364. See also Hua VI, 165; Hua XIII, 366; Hua XXIII, 490; Hua XXV, 83.

11. Hua IV, 66, 72, 74; Hua XIII, 366; Hua XV, 52, 156; Hua XXXIX, 639, 667. In a related discussion, Crowell has argued that Husserl's analyses of passive synthesis provide a way of understanding how mental content can be norm-governed independently of conceptual capacities (Crowell 2012). See also Dahlstrom 2007; Crowell 2008b.

12. See, for example, Ms. D 13 I, 174a; Hua XXXVIII, 212–13; Hua XXXIX, 639–40. The example of a burned hand originally comes from Locke's *Essay Concerning Human Understanding* (book 2, chapter 8; see Locke 1975).

13. As Canguilhem puts it, anomaly "can shade into disease but does not in itself constitute one" (Canguilhem 1991, 137, 140, 144). Etymology likewise suggests that "anomaly" and "abnormality" should be distinguished: whereas "normal" and "abnormal" come from the Latin *norma*, and the Greek *nomos*, the word "anomalous" is derived from the Greek word *anomalia*, which is a subjectivated negation of *homalos*, meaning "uniform" or "homogeneous." As Steinbock further points out, unlike "abnormality," "anomaly" is a purely *descriptive* and not a *normative* concept (Steinbock 1995a, 132–33; see also Hua XV, 158).

14. Hua XV, 34, 166; Hua XXXIX, 315, 642. See also Hua XXXIX, 405, 648. On the other hand, Husserl stresses: "For the individual subject, normality is originally (in the genetic sense) not conscious" (Hua XXXIX, 656; and Ms. D 13 I, 183a), and he explains that it is the experience of anomaly that first reveals the underlying normality *as such:* "Aber normal heisst das erst durch Kontrast mit Anomalitäten, die von diesem ersten, notwendig zuerst konstituierten System der Einstimmigkeit abweichen" (Ms. D 13 I, 232a; see also Ms. D 13 I, 183a; Hua XXXIX, 656). As Husserl also formulates, insofar as experience proceeds without discordance, normality remains "in the dark" (*im "Dunkel"*) (Ms. D 11, 3b).

15. Hua XXXIX, 657.

16. "Each kind of anomaly designates first a type of disturbance of the concordance of experience, a disappointment of the experiential anticipation (expectation) that lies in experience and initially evidently validates it" (Hua XXXIX, 646).

17. Hua XXXIX, 651. See also Hua XV, 157; Hua XXXIX, 657; and Ms. D 13 I, 175a; Ms. D 13 I, 78b.

18. Hua XXXIX, 646.

19. Hua XIII, 366–67.

20. Hua XXXIX, 646; Ms. D 13 I, 215b; see also Steinbock 1995a, 135.

21. Hua XIII, 646; Hua XIV, 121, 123, 134.

22. Hua XIII, 379; Hua XXXVIII, 53, 55. Husserl further distinguishes between subjective and objective circumstances (Ms. D 13 I, 180a). Concerning the former, I have already discussed "kinesthetic circumstances" in detail. Objective circumstances, again, include lighting, perceptual medium, and so on. Husserl is referring to these circumstances when he argues that perception involves "a certain mediatedness" (Hua XXXIX, 637). Sokolowski exemplifies: "There is

an interesting difference between air and water as mediums of sound; water allows the transmission of something like vowels but not consonants, whereas air permits both" (Sokolowski 2008, 201).

23. Hua XIII, 370, 379; Ms. D 13 I, 184a.

24. Husserl stresses, moreover, that despite the fact that he illustrates optimality mainly in respect to sense perception, he thinks that the reference to optimum pertains to all other types of experience as well: "Zur Konstitution gehört in allem Stufen die Beziehung auf Optima und optimale Erfahrungsumstände (als die zugehörigen Normen, Normalitäten)" (Ms. D 13 II, 63a).

25. Ms. D 13 II, 63a: "Die normale Leiblichkeit bedeutet dann diejenige, die einen Kreis von Optima herstellt oder ermöglicht. Mit verbrannten Finger betaste ich 'schlecht,' mit myopischen Augen sehe ich die Ferne schlecht usw."

26. Hua IV, 77; Ms. D 13 I, 80a: "Das Optimale bezeichnet das Wahre, das wolle Optimum, das Reale selbst, das 'wie es ist.'" Similar formulations can be found at least in Ms. D 10 I, 24; Ms. D 13 I, 81a; and Ms. D 13 I, 175a.

27. Hua IV, 69; see also Hua XI, 30–34; Hua XXXIX, 659–60.

28. Husserl speaks of "optimalization" (*Optimalisierung*) at least in Ms. D 13 I, 65b, and he exemplifies it in Hua XIV, 121. Husserl also connects this discussion with an analysis of the development of technological innovations (Hua XXXIX, 660–62).

29. Hua XXXIX, 638.

30. Hua XXXVIII, 209.

31. Hua XIII, 370.

32. Merleau-Ponty 1945, 349/352; Merleau-Ponty 2010, 437; Merleau-Ponty 1964, 59/37.

33. Hua VI, 160; see also Ms. D 13 I, 182a: "das Ding wird in einer gewissen Entfernung gesehen, ästhetisch beurteilt, und die dafür massgebende Erscheinungsweise ist hinsichtlich der Farbe, die ästhethetisch wesentlich bestimmend ist, die normgebende."

34. Hua XV, 155. See also Hua XV, 213; Ms. D 13 I, 216a.

35. Hua XIV, 121; see also Hua XV, 230–31.

36. Steinbock 1995a, 158–59. See also Hua VI, 281; Hua XXXIX, 658.

37. Steinbock 1995a, 159.

38. See Hua XV, 622.

39. Ibid., 142.

40. Hua VI, 312. See also Hua XV, 143–44, 611; Hua XXXVII, 41; Hua XXXIX, 661. The interpolation ("bestimmen") is made by the editor of *Husserliana VI*, Walter Biemel.

41. Hua XV, 144, 231; Hua XIII, 106, 107; Hua XXIX, 42. As Heidegger puts it, averageness (*Durchschnittlichkeit*) is an existential characteristic of *Das Man* (Heidegger 2001, 127).

42. Hua XIV, 133–34; Hua XV, 631, 231. In a manuscript, Husserl subscribes to the view that, *objectively speaking*, normality is species-specific (Ms. D 13 I, 160b).

43. Hua XV, 154; Hua XXXIX, 649; Ms. D 13 I, 78b.

44. Hua XIII, 389; Hua XV, 66. See also Hua XIII, 361, 388. Consequently,

a phenomenology of primordial experience is possible only within intersubjectivity (see, e.g., Hua XIII, 361; Hua XV, 131).

45. For example, Hua XV, 219; Hua XXXIX, 498; Ms. D 10 I, 27; Ms. A VII 11, 50b.

46. Hua XV, 53; Hua IV, 77. For examples of this with respect to the perception of colors, see Ms. D 13 I, 179a–179b and Ms. D 13 I, 180a.

47. As Husserl illustrates: "Das Aberdrot 'ergiesst' über alles in ihrer roten Schein, aber sie sind nicht rot. Die Nacht taucht alles in ihre schwarzen Tinten, aber es ist nicht alles schwärzlich" (Ms. D 13 I, 180b).

48. See Hua IV, 82. This "general denominator" (*Generalnenner*), which is posited as identical in all alterations of the color at the moment (*momentane Farbe*), is the color itself, the color as it would appear in optimal circumstances (Ms. D 13 I, 179b–180a). In this connection, it should also be emphasized that the thing itself, the optimum, is not a second entity in addition to "the thing as it appears in certain circumstances." For example, the appearance of a tree in twilight does not intentionally refer to another tree, but precisely to this particular tree as it would appear in optimal perceptual circumstances; or, to use another example, a coin is intended as round, even if it may seem oval when viewed from an angle (see Hua XV, 157; Hua XIV, 132; Ms. D 10 I, 18). In the language of Husserl's *Ideas I*, the object, or the "noematic core" (i.e., the perceived thing *itself*) is not a second entity in addition to the "noema" (i.e., the perceived thing as it appears in the current circumstances) (see Hua III/1, 203–8).

49. Hua XXXVIII, 147. See also Hua XIII, 370.

50. As we already saw Merleau-Ponty formulating, the house itself is not the house seen from nowhere, but the house "seen from everywhere" (Merleau-Ponty 1945, 83/79). See also Kelly 2005.

51. Hua XXXIX, 637–38; Ms. D 12 II 26a; Ms. D 11, 3a; Ms. D 13 I, 182a.

52. Hua IV, 60 (*my italics*). See also Hua XVI, 194. In one of his manuscripts, Husserl exemplifies that what is touched with the foot, for instance, or with the elbow, intentionally refers to a possible touching with hands and to an optimal touching with fingers (Ms. D 10 I, 31).

53. Hua IV, 59–60. See also Ms. D 13 I, 179a; Ms. D 13 I, 186a.

54. Hua XXXVIII, 53.

55. Merleau-Ponty 1945, 367–68/371.

56. See, for example, Merleau-Ponty 1945, 348–49/352; Carman 2005, 70; Kelly 2005, 85, 106, 107.

57. See Hua XV, 262.

58. See Soffer 1999, 161–62.

59. Hua XXXIX, 649. This "solitary normality" is not systematically elaborated by Husserl, and it is hardly visible in the published works, but in the manuscripts the theme surfaces relatively often. The theme figures especially in the D-manuscripts: "Jedes solitäre Subjekt kann in der solitären Einstellung sich als nicht normal bezeichnen und vorfinden" (Ms. D 13 I, 216a); "Denken wir uns nun ein solipsistisches Ich mit orthoaesthetischer und logischer Normalität" (Ms. D 13 I, 174a); "'Zuerst' hat das solipsistische Ich seine Welt, es konstituiert sie als normale Welt" (Ms. D 13 I, 214a); "Genetisch muss eine harmonische

Urkonstitution vollzogen sein und muss also zur Norm werden" (Ms. D 13 I, 232b). Somewhat similar formulations can be found at least in Hua XIV, 131; Hua XV, 37, 158, 236; Ms. D 13 I, 212a; Ms. D 13 I, 78b; Ms. D 13 I, 166b; and Hua XIV, 132: "A system of normality must be originally constituted; the question is merely whether it is necessary that such a system must throughout remain the frame of reference." Husserl's closest assistants, who studied and transcribed his manuscripts, were familiar with the idea of primordial normality—Edith Stein, for instance, makes explicit notes to Husserl's manuscripts relating to this topic (see marginal notes, e.g., in Ms. D 13 I, 178a and 185a). See also Taipale 2012.

60. Hua XIV, 132; Hua XXXII, 74. See also Held 1991, 319–20. This "expectation" of similarity, Husserl argues, precedes actual comparison (Hua XIV, 143).

61. Hua XV, 229–30; Hua IV, 168. See also Ms. D 4, 12: "Was ich solipsistisch gegeben habe und ohne jeden Gedanken an einen Genossen vor mir habe, gegeben als Ding dort im Raume, ist dasselbe, was der Andere ebenso solipsistisch gegeben hat (nur gegeben in anderer Erscheinungsweise, in anderen Perspektiven)."

62. See Hua XV, 29; Hua IV, 185, 168–69; see also Steinbock 1995a, 289.

63. Hua XV, 48. Elsewhere Husserl writes the following: "The normal thing is the norm to which all deviating appearances must be referring. For the *solus ipse* it is the true thing" (Hua XIV, 132).

64. Hua I, 154, 157. See also Hua XVII, 243–44, 248.

65. Hua XV, 135–36. See also Hua XV, 37.

66. Hua XXXIX, 669; see also Hua XV, 38, 86, 165; Hua XXXIX, 54, 486; de Folter 1983, 171. Because of its constitutive primacy, one's own lived-body cannot primordially appear as pathological throughout (Hua XIII, 368; Hua XXXIX, 649).

67. Hua XIV, 126. See also Hua XIII, 57; Hua XIV, 131, 483; Hua XV, 29, 183, 572, 639; Hua XXXIX, 46; Husserl 1940a, 323 (Ms. D 17, 19a); Merleau-Ponty 1994, 108/75.

68. I have developed this line of thinking also in Taipale 2012.

69. Hua XXXIX, 649. See also Hua XIII, 381.

70. Hua XV, 34–35. In a manuscript Husserl even states that in this sense the intersubjective is secondary in respect to the subjective (Ms. D 13 I, 166b). See also Hua XV, 6, 13, 14–15, 22, 29, 39, 135; Hua XXXIX, 29, 33–34.

71. Hua XIII, 378.

72. Hua XXXIX, 649.

73. See Hua IV, 202; Hua XIV, 385; Hua IX, 324; Hua XV, 382; Zahavi 2001b, 103.

74. Hua XIII, 289, 377–78; Hua XV, 19; Hua I, 138. The similarity of the perceiving bodies also includes the similarity of the primal generative (*urgenerativen*) structures: that is, bodily needs related to eating, drinking, sleeping, etc. (see Hua XV, 433; Held 1991, 321ff.; Lohmar 1998, 215).

75. Hua XIII, 117, 376–77, 379; Hua XV, 156–57; see also de Folter 1983, 168ff.

76. Hua XV, 251; Hua XIII, 379; Hua IV, 86; Hua XV, 47.
77. Crowell 1996, 100.
78. Hua IV, 86; see also Hua XXXIX, 44.
79. See Hua XIII, 397; Hua IV, 73–74.
80. Hua IV, 87, 83; Hua XIII, 385. See also Crowell 1996, 100–101. In Ms. D 13 I, 165a, Husserl argues that an "objective system of places" cannot be perceived sensuously. Consequently, even the constitution of "naturalistic nature," the nature of physics, arises from the basis of a certain normality: "Die physikalische Wahrheit hat die Objektivität einer Idee, sie ist bezogen auf die Idee einer Normalwelt, einer Welt von Normalphänomenen" (Ms. D 13 I, 212a).
81. Hua XXXIX, 649.
82. Ibid. Husserl also stresses in particular that a shared concordance is the presupposition for communication (Hua XIII, 368, 369).
83. See Hua XV, 154–55, 176–77.
84. Hua XXXIX, 660.
85. Ibid., 640; Hua VI, 270.
86. See Hua XXXIX, 646, 656.
87. See Hua XV, 47, 165, 168–69, 230, 251.
88. Cf. Hua II, 38. As Merleau-Ponty argues, the blind person's world differs from that of the seeing person not only quantitatively, in respect to the amount of material at his disposal, but also qualitatively, in respect to the structure of the whole (Merleau-Ponty 1945, 259/261). See also Noë 2004, 3–4.
89. See also Hua I, 137.
90. See Hua XV, 262; de Folter 1983, 161.
91. See Steinbock 1995a, 264.
92. Hua XV, 251. See also Hua XV, 165, 168–69, and Zahavi 2001b, 103.
93. See Hua XV, 53.
94. Hua XV, 155. See also Hua XV, 35, 37, 137, 173ff., 212–13; Hua XXXIX, 660, 668.
95. Hua XIII, 106; Hua XV, 422.
96. Hua XIII, 106–7. In a related context, Crowell argues that "conscience is Dasein's opening to the normative as such" (Crowell 2008a, 266).
97. See McKenna 2003.
98. Hua XIV, 111. See also Hua XV, 146–47; Hua IV, 131. As Husserl also puts it, the broadest thinkable intersubjectivity is that which comprises "each possible subject that potentially enters into the community of mutual understanding," and only as the correlate of this broadest thinkable intersubjectivity is objectivity "absolute" (Ms. D 4, 21).
99. Ms. D 4, 5.
100. Hua XV, 142, 165; Hua XXXIX, 669. See also Hua XV, 179; Hua XXXIX, 385ff.
101. Hua XXXIX, 669. See also Hua I, 124; Hua XV, 171n.
102. See Hua I, 137, 161–62. See also Hua XV, 61, 170, 215.
103. William McKenna even writes that the comportment of a person from an alien culture initially appears not only as foreign, but simply as the "wrong"

way to comport oneself (McKenna 2004, 117). Brand likewise argues that in this sense the alienworld always stands in an open or latent conflict with the homeworld (Brand 1971, 490).

104. See Canguilhem 1991, 183.

105. As Steinbock phrases it, a "liminal experience" motivates the "co-generation" of homeworld and alienworld (see Steinbock 1995a, 178-85; Steinbock 1996, 76).

106. See Hua XV, 233, 179; Hua I, 161. In this connection, Steinbock argues for an "axiological asymmetry" between homeworld and alienworld (Steinbock 1995a, 248; see also Carr 1986, 110ff.; Lohmar 1998). Husserl likewise suggests that also within the homeworld the higher and more general levels (e.g., nation) are constitutively founded on the more elementary and "restricted" ones (e.g., family, sphere of the close ones, circle of acquaintances)—both in the genetic and in the static sense (Hua XXXIX, 154–55). As Husserl illustrates in a manuscript: "Europa ist für mich Europa von 'mir als Deutschem' aus konstituiert" (Ms. E III 11, 3b). In another related passage, Husserl argues that even natural science is ultimately related to a world which is initially outlined by normal embodiment (Hua XXXIX, 642–43).

107. Hua XV, 214.

108. Ibid., 233. See also Hua XV, 59–60, 176n, 214–15; Hua XXXIX, 661.

109. Steinbock 1995a, 182.

110. Hua XV, 215; see also Hua XV, 19–20.

111. Hua XV, 411; Hua XV, 216.

112. Hua I, 162. See also Hua XV, 206–7.

113. Hua XV, 632. See also Hua VI, 383; Hua XV, 227. See Held 1998. Cf. Mohanty 1986, 63–66; Lohmar 1996, 24ff.

114. Hua XV, 53, 215, 216.

115. See Hua XV, 216–17.

116. Hua XV, 632; see also Hua XV, 67. See also Hua XV, 226, where Husserl speaks of the "terrestrial and celestial" world, referring to the fact that all particular homeworlds are situated under the same sky and upon the same earth.

117. Hua XV, 216.

118. Hua XV, 216. See also Hua XV, 169, 205–6.

119. Hua XV, 214, 232.

120. Ibid., 232–33.

121. Hua I, 161; Hua VI, 361.

122. Hua XV, 139–40. See also Hua I, 161–62; Hua XV, 158, 206, 219, 226; Hua XXXIX, 28, 177.

123. Hua I, 167.

124. Hua XV, 162; see also Hua XV, 446, 492.

125. Hua XV, 235.

126. See ibid., 215.

127. See Gail Soffer's critique of relativism in Soffer 1991, 171–91.

128. Hua XV, 231; see also Hua XV, 47, 230, 231. Husserl argues that, in this minimal sense, human beings live in a loose community (see Hua I, 160).

129. See, for example, Hua XIV, 124; Hua XXXIX, 666.

130. See Hua XIV, 111.

131. In Hua XV, 178, Husserl argues that maturity designates the fulfillment of the type "person." Similar claims can be found at least in Hua XXXIX, 15n1; and Hua XXXIX, 230. As to animals, Husserl explicitly denies that he would consider them as kinds of machines; at times he even considers animals as personal beings (e.g., Hua XV, 61).

132. Hua XV, 162. See also Hua XV, 207–8; Zahavi 2003c, 244. In Hua XXXIX, 486 Husserl is even more frank: "We have excluded animals, 'savages,' infants, and the insane from world-constitution. They do not constitute and have not constituted the world with us."

133. Hua XIII, 382.

134. To be sure, these cases represent remarkably different kinds of abnormality. However, as my general task here is to illustrate the manner in which the constitution of the objective world has a normative structure, and to clarify how this normativity relates to primordial bodily self-constitution, I will therefore not elaborate the differences between these cases any further.

135. Hua XIV, 133–34.

136. Hua XV, 37, 53.

137. For example, ibid., 121, 219.

138. See also Ms. D 13 I, 213a; Hua XIV, 132; Ms. D 4, 20. Again, this is to be understood in the sense of constitution. For example, all extended things have a visual form, and we give universal validity to such claims regardless of our knowledge of there being persons who have been born blind. The "exclusion" of blind persons from the constitution of the visual world is neither a matter of opinion nor that of discrimination: it is inherent in the structure of our experience.

Eight

1. For example, Hua XIII, 57; Hua XV, 572.

2. Hua VI, 361.

3. Hua XXIX, 85. Elsewhere Husserl likewise explicitly claims that in eidetic variation we are bound to the limits of our factical possibilities (Ms. E III 9, 51b). See also Hua III/1, 101; Hua XXIX, 64; Hua XXXIX, 653; Merleau-Ponty 1945, 388/393.

4. Hua IV, 56; Hua VIII, 116. See also Hua XXXVI, 161–62.

5. Hua XV, 35. See also Hua XV, 39, 151. In a related discussion, Husserl argues that transcendental philosophy is "necessarily related to me, and from me, to ... my humanity" (Hua XXIX, 332).

6. Heidegger likewise speaks of "transposing oneself" (*Sichversetzen*) and "going along with" (*Mitgehen*), arguing that with respect to animals it is a question of "transposition" that allows no "going along with" (Heidegger 2004, 309).

7. See Hua XV, 218, where Husserl identifies "relative environment" with "situation."

8. Hua XV, 258; Hua XIII, 338–39. See also Zahavi 2010.

9. Hua XV, 250–51.
10. See Hua XV, 252.
11. Hua XV, 258; see also Hua XV, 19, 156.
12. Hua XV, 31. See also Hua IV, 168; Hua XV, 39, 114.
13. Hua XV, 29; Hua I, 151–52. See also Hua XV, 33, 87, 156. For the compatibility of the phenomenological notion of empathy with the theory of mirror neurons, see, for example, Lohmar 2006 and Gallese 2008.
14. Hua IV, 162; Hua XV, 29, 39, 96; Hua I, 125.
15. Hua XV, 252. See also Hua XV, 27, 29, 42, 182.
16. Hua XV, 36.
17. Hua XXXIX, 650. Husserl also stresses this point in the following manner: "It is implicit in the sense of my successful apperception of others that their world, the world belonging to their appearance-systems, must be experienced forthwith as the same as the world belonging to my appearance-systems; and this involves an identity of our appearance-systems" (Hua I, 154). In this sense, "it is essential for a continuously self-affirming [i.e., successful] empathy that we, the involved parties, are together related to *the same world*" (Hua XV, 234). In this connection, Husserl also explicitly reinterprets the so-called preestablished harmony of monads, proposed by Leibniz (see Hua XIII, 376–78). See also Hua IV, 168–69; Hua VI, 86, 307–8; Hua XV, 47; Hua XXXIX, 666.
18. Hua I, 150–51. See also Hua XV, 65.
19. Hua XV, 191. See also Hua XV, 162; Ms. D 4, 13: "Ich kenne Intersubjektives, also Objektives, nur durch Einfühlung."
20. Hua XV, 240.
21. Ibid., 29. See also Ms. D 4, 12: "Durch Einfühlung erkenne ich erfahrend den Anderen, durch Appräsentation seine Subjektivität mit allem Subjektiven, seine solipsistische Gegebenheit seines Leibes, seine solipsistischen in den und den Gegebenheitsweisen von ihm erfahrenen Gegenstände jeder Art."
22. For example, Hua VI, 183; Hua XXXIV, 246. See also Hua XIV, 136; Hua XV, 163–64, 219; Hua XXXIX, 664–66; and Ms. A VII 11, 8b.
23. Hua XIV, 132. Elsewhere Husserl specifies that the world of animals is "not a world in the proper sense" (Hua XV, 155), and that animals "do not have a generative, historical world, and thereby no real world either, and hence, in the proper sense, no time, no space, no universe of reality with an ontical structure; these are not constituted for them, but for us" (Hua XV, 160; see also Hua XV, 180, 627; Ms. D 13 I, 213b). On the other hand, Husserl states that although animals can have "something like an ego-structure" (Hua XV, 177), they are nevertheless not persons (Hua XV, 180), they are not "our kind" (*meinesgleichen, unseresgleichen*) (Hua XV, 169). Husserl also stresses that the difference between humans and animals is not like the difference between higher and lower animals, and not a gradation in this sense (Hua XV, 180; see also 627). Heidegger likewise emphasizes that the claim that animals experience "poorly" is not a *quantitative* assessment (Heidegger 2004, 288).
24. Hua XV, 155. See also Hua XV, 173; Hua XXXIX, 478, 485–87; Lotz 2006, 198–200.

25. Hua XIV, 133–35; Hua XV, 231; Ms. D 13 I, 160b. That is to say, animals are not anomalous in themselves (see Hua XV, 155).
26. Heidegger 2004, 291.
27. See Hua XV, 225.
28. See Nagel 1974. Merleau-Ponty exemplifies, moreover, that the sexual behavior of a dog, cockchafer, or a praying mantis can be scientifically studied, but it cannot be experientially grasped or empathically "understood," no more than a child can understand the sexual intercourse of adults that she happens to witness (Merleau-Ponty 1945, 215/214).
29. This is discussed in detain in Crowell 1996. See also Hua XV, 216.
30. Ms. E III 9, 51b: "Mein faktisches Sein kann ich nicht überschreiten."
31. Hua I, 162. As Husserl also explicates, the environing world is the "homelike" (*heimisch*) world in the broadest sense, the world in which the human being consciously lives (*bewusst hineinlebt*), and thus, for us, "the true environment is the one that we call the cultural world" (Hua XXXIX, 154; Ms. D 13 I, 147a).
32. In the words of Husserl: "One can say only this much: in the human environment, and in the human being as the subject of the latter, there is a stratum that perhaps can be distinguished in abstraction as . . . that which is common with the animal" (Hua XV, 180).
33. Hua XXXIX, 662. See also Hua XV, 174.
34. Hua XXXIX, 663.
35. Hua XIV, 133.
36. Hua XV, 166.
37. See, for example, Hua XV, 205, 227; Hua XXXIX, 636; Heidegger 2004, 296; and Lohmar 2007.
38. Hua XV, 182, 184. Husserl goes on to argue that animal psychology is bound to remain purely constructive, something built on human psychology (Hua XV, 185).
39. Husserl 1940a, 323 (Ms. D 17, 19b); Hua XXXIX, 663. See also Hua XXIX, 157.
40. Hua I, 154. See also Hua XV, 135, 155, 157, 159, 173; Hua VI, 191. Merleau-Ponty captures the Husserlian view in a provocative manner: "For human beings, there can be only human beings: animals, Husserl says, are no more than variants of humanity" (Merleau-Ponty 1994, 111/77).
41. Hua XXXIX, 664. See also Hua XIV, 136. As Husserl also puts it: "Explication of the normality of nature that is constituted through normal human sensibility . . . , that would be an ontological explication of the normal thing as essential form and normal nature in general" (Hua XV, 156; see also Hua XV, 666–67).
42. Merleau-Ponty 1964, 232/180.
43. Hua XV, 166. Husserl argues elsewhere that the distinction between home and alien necessarily occurs "within a historical humanity," and that humanity in this transcendental sense has no further community next to it (*neben sich*); humanity is the total community of subjects, or intersubjectivity in "full universality" (*vollen Universalität*) (Ms. A V 25, 9a). In this sense, according to

Husserl, all particular environments—whether human or animal—must be embedded in the human world.

44. Hua XV, 167.
45. See ibid., 162.
46. See ibid., 622; Hua XXXIX, 172.
47. Hua XV, 166. As Merleau-Ponty emphasizes, even if we quite well "know," from the basis of scientific inquiries, that a fly visually perceives the environment in a remarkably different manner, the visual characteristics that flies allegedly perceive are not transferred to what we ourselves take to be the thing itself (see Merleau-Ponty 1945, 367/371).
48. Hua XV, 166; Hua XXXIX, 641; Hua VI, 183. See also Hua XIV, 136; Hua XV, 35, 53, 163–64, 219; Hua XXXIX, 246, 655, 664–66; and Ms. A VII 11, 8b.
49. Hua XXXIX, 650, 662. Consequently, Husserl argues, a different organization of human bodies would imply a "transformation" (*Änderung*) of the whole experiential nature and thereby a transformation of the whole experiential world (Hua XXXIX, 667). See also Hua XIV, 136; Hua XV, 639.
50. See Hua XXXIX, 655, 648.

Nine

1. Hua XV, 14.
2. See Ms. D 13 I, 165a: "Jedes Subjekt hat seinen 'Orientierungsraum,' sein Hier und seine möglichen Dort."
3. See Ms. D 17, 4b: Husserl 1940a, 309.
4. Husserl also states that the sky (*Himmel*) is not a thing (*Ding*) (Ms. D 13 I, 179a; see also Hua XXXIX, 185–89).
5. Accordingly, as Manfred Sommer observes, unlike particular things and objects, the ground cannot originally present itself as something "standing in our way" (Sommer 1998, 135; see also Kersten 1981, 217).
6. See Steinbock 2007, 7–12.
7. It is important to stress that, even though Husserl argues that the ground *as the ground* cannot be constituted as moving (if it was, it would have to be experienced as moving in relation to the ground, in which case it could not itself be the ground), he is not thereby claiming that the Copernican theory of the universe is mistaken. In other words, Husserl is not criticizing this *natural scientific model* as such, but the absolutization of this model as a *world-view*. It is worth noticing that even the original title of the manuscript runs as "'Umsturz' der kopernikanischen Lehre *in der gewöhnlichen weltanschaulichen Interpretation*" (Ms. D 17, 1a: Husserl 1940a, 307). In the same manuscript Husserl even hints that to declare without further elaboration that the Earth does not move would be as misguiding as to claim that our lived-body cannot move (see Ms. D 17, 9b–10a: Husserl 1940a, 314–15). Of course, *as the zero-point of spatial orientation*, our lived-body apparently cannot be grasped as a moving thing in the subjective space that spreads *around* it; and analogically the Earth-ground *as* the ultimate point of reference for all experienced movement cannot be said to be a moving entity

in the space for which it serves as the point of reference. However, to be sure, like the lived-body, the Earth can be presentified and objectified and, *as such*, it can well be treated as a particular moving entity among others (see Ms. D 17, 15a; Husserl 1940a, 320; see also Hua XXXIX, 184–89). Husserl's point is not to argue that this kind of objectification is not possible or justified, but rather to clarify how the objectivation of the Earth presupposes an experience of an immobile ground, that gives meaning to "movement" and "rest," and to which all our experiences and theories of (planetary) movement hence remain generatively bound. For a different interpretation of Husserl's ideas, see Himanka 2000 and Himanka 2005.

8. Steinbock distinguishes three types of "vertical" experience: (1) *religious experience* pertaining to the "vertical" experience of the Holy; (2) *moral experience* pertaining to the "vertical givenness" of the other person; and (3) *ecological experience* pertaining to the "vertical" givenness of Earth as an aesthetic ground (Steinbock 2007, 15). Here I am interested in the last of these dimensions, and I will argue that in world-constitution, the tradition is given in a manner analogical to the manner in which the ground is given in perceptual experience.

9. See Straus 1952, 531ff.

10. See Husserl 1940a, 318; Ms. D 17, 12a. Sommer formulates: "Ground and body are so closely interrelated that the ground can be looked upon as a sort of prolongation and expansion of the body and correspondingly, the body can be seen as a sort of contraction and detaching of ground thus rendered movable" (Sommer 1998, 135).

11. See Ms. D 17, 11a: Husserl 1940a, 316.

12. Hua IV, 75.

13. Merleau-Ponty 1994, 108/75 (*my emphasis*); see also Merleau-Ponty 1945, 287/289; Merleau-Ponty 2010, 437.

14. Hua XV, 220. See also Hua IV, 159; and Hua XXXIX, 54, 151–53, 181–83. See also the discussion of the relativity of orientation in Holenstein 1999, 80–84.

15. See Crowell 1996, 102.

16. For example, Hua VI, 182ff.; Hua XXXIX, 613; Ms. A VII 11, 38a.

17. Hua XV, 143.

18. Hua XXXIV, 248.

19. The structural similarities in the manner of givenness of the Earth-ground and the manner of givenness of the tradition are not accidental. The tradition is ultimately the tradition of humanity, and humanity is generatively bound to the Earth. Particular cultures are oriented according to their particular homeplace or "territory" (Hua XXXIX, 154–55; Hua XV, 205–6), but what constitutes the ultimate homeplace for all cultures and traditions—and, thus, for humanity—is the Earth. As Merleau-Ponty formulates: "Earth is the root of our history" (Merleau-Ponty 1994, 111/77). The experience of the ground unites humanity (see Hua XV, 139), and as such the "earthly horizon" serves as the ultimate spatial "form of access" to alien lifeworlds, and hence to alien traditions (see Hua XV, 206).

20. Hua IV, 153. See also Hua XXXIX, 11–12.

21. Hua XIV, 128.
22. Hua VIII, 112.
23. Hua XXXIX, 662.
24. Hua XV, 657. See also Ms. A VII 14, 29b: "Die Struktur eines einheitlichen Wahrnehmungfeldes und der Welt als reiner Wahrnehmungswelt. Das ist eine Urform aller Erfahrung."
25. See Hua XV, 254.
26. Hua I, 161–62.
27. See Hua XXXIX, 670–71.
28. See Hua II, 38.
29. Husserl's example here is color blindness. He argues that in the primordial sense, a color-blind person does not see "wrongly," whereas in the intersubjective sense she does (Hua XV, 47–48, 137).
30. Therefore, *in the intersubjective sense*, as Husserl argues, subjectivity can constitute itself as anomalous throughout (see Hua XV, 154).
31. Hua XXIX, 328; Hua XV, 111. See also Hua XV, 38–39, 61; Hua VI, 154; Hua I, 130.
32. Hua VI, 260. Husserl also phrases: "But, considered more closely, I . . . precede this 'We' and the being of the world; the world is for us, only through the fact that the 'We' is my 'We'" (Hua XXXIX, 613). In other words: "The world is continually there for us, but in the first place it is there for me" (Hua XVII, 249). See also Hua IV, 87; Hua XIII, 407; Hua XXXIX, 625.
33. Hua XXXIX, 628. As Husserl also puts it: "My primordial being, to which also all my empathic lived experiences belong as original givennesses of my pure being (as lived-experiences of it), is the basis of validity for the being of others" (Hua XXXIX, 627); "All brutes, all living beings, all beings whatever, only have being-sense by virtue of my constitutive genesis" (Husserl 1940a, 324; Ms. D 17, 19b).
34. Hua VI, 262, 191; Hua XXXIX, 658. See also Ms. D 17, 19a; Husserl 1940a, 323.
35. Hua XV, 114; Hua XXXIX, 486.
36. See Hua XXIX, 333.
37. Whereas our own bodily abilities outline primordially what counts for us as the "natural thing 'itself'" (*Naturding "selbst"*), the cultural thing itself is outlined intersubjectively (Hua XV, 48). Yet, of course, by becoming defined in its cultural meaning, the thing does not lose its naturality.
38. See, for example, Carr 1999; Rinofner-Kreidl 2003, 183–205; Dodd 2004, 197–208.
39. Hua VI, 265. See also Hua VI, 182ff.; Hua XXXIX, 22, 613.
40. Even though subjectivity eventually constitutes itself as normal or anomalous in relation to an intersubjective normality, or "by virtue of a normal community" (Hua XV, 142; see also Hua XXXIX, 669), it must nevertheless first *become* a member of the respective community and *gain* or *appropriate* intersubjective normality (Hua XV, 154–55, 20).
41. See Hua VI, 266; Hua XXXIX, 613.
42. See Hua XV, 158.

43. See Schapp 2004, 1, 146ff.
44. Hua XXXIX, 610.
45. Carr 1970, 262; see Hua VI, 266.
46. Hua XV, 293. In another manuscript Husserl writes: "Subjekte [werden] zu Objekten (Menschen) durch Verleiblichung in der physischen Welt" (Ms. D 4, 22).
47. Husserl 2006, 50; see also Held 1966, 114.
48. Hua XV, 326; Hua XIII, 263. See also Hua XV, 8, 327; Hua XXXIX, 617–18, 651; and Ms. D 13 I, 183a: "Was wir normal funktionierenden Leib nennen, das ist sinnlich eine Erscheinungseinheit, die selbst wieder auf normal funktionierende Leiblichkeit bezogen ist. Das ist kein schädlicher Zirkel, weil der Leib zugleich Organ und Objekt sein kann, und das, weil er ein System aufeinander in der Funktion bezogener Organe ist, wobei das funktionierende Organ bezogen ist auf andere Organe als Objekte der Funktion."
49. Hua IV, 56; see also Hua XI, 297; Hua XV, 40, 61, 667; Hua XXXIII, 300.

Concluding Remarks

1. Hua IV, 297.
2. Hua XIV, 8. See also Hua VIII, 495.

Bibliography

Works by Edmund Husserl

Husserliana Gesammelte Werke (Hua)

Hua I: *Cartesianische Meditationen und Pariser Vorträge*. Edited by Stephan Strasser. The Hague: Martinus Nijhoff, 1950.
Hua II: *Die Idee der Phänomenologie: Fünf Vorlesungen*. Edited by Walter Biemel. The Hague: Martinus Nijhoff, 1950.
Hua III/1: *Ideen zu einer reinen Phänomenologie und phänomenologische Philosophie. Erstes Buch: Allgemeine Einführung in die reine Phänomenologie*. Edited by Karl Schuhmann. The Hague: Martinus Nijhoff, 1950.
Hua IV: *Ideen zu einer reinen Phänomenologie und phänomenologische Philosophie. Zweiter Buch: Phänomenologische Untersuchungen zur Konstitution*. Edited by Marly Biemel. The Hague: Martinus Nijhoff, 1952.
Hua V: *Ideen zu einer reinen Phänomenologie und phänomenologische Philosophie. Drittes Buch: Die Phänomenologie und die Fundamente der Wissenschaften*. Edited by Marly Biemel. The Hague: Martinus Nijhoff. 1952.
Hua VI: *Krisis der europäischen Wissenschaften und die transzendentale Phänomenologie: Eine Einleitung in die Phänomenologische Philosophie*. Edited by Walter Biemel. The Hague: Martinus Nijhoff, 1954.
Hua VIII: *Erste Philosophie. Zweiter Teil: Theorie der phänomenologischen Reduktion*. Edited by Rudolf Boehm. The Hague: Martinus Nijhoff, 1959.
Hua IX: *Phänomenologische Psychologie: Vorlesungen Sommersemester 1925*. Edited by Walter Biemel. The Hague: Martinus Nijhoff, 1962.
Hua X: *Zur Phänomenologie des inneren Zeitbewusstseins (1893–1917)*. Edited by Rudolf Boehm. The Hague: Martinus Nijhoff, 1966.
Hua XI: *Analysen zur passiven Synthesis: Aus Vorlesungs- und Forschungsmanuskripten, 1918–1926*. Edited by Margot Fleischer. The Hague: Martinus Nijhoff, 1966.
Hua XIII: *Zur Phänomenologie der Intersubjektivität. Texte aus dem Nachlass. Erster Teil: 1905–1920*. Edited by Iso Kern. The Hague: Martinus Nijhoff, 1973.
Hua XIV: *Zur Phänomenologie der Intersubjektivität. Texte aus dem Nachlass. Zweiter Teil: 1921–28*. Edited by Iso Kern. The Hague: Martinus Nijhoff, 1973.
Hua XV: *Zur Phänomenologie der Intersubjektivität. Texte aus dem Nachlass. Dritter Teil: 1929–35*. Edited by Iso Kern. The Hague: Martinus Nijhoff, 1973.

Hua XVI: *Ding und Raum. Vorlesungen 1907*. Edited by Ulrich Claesges. The Hague: Martinus Nijhoff, 1973.

Hua XVII: *Formale and transzendentale Logik: Versuch einer Kritik der logischen Vernunft*. Edited by Paul Janssen. The Hague: Martinus Nijhoff, 1974.

Hua XIX/1–2: *Logische Untersuchungen. Zweiter Teil. Untersuchungen zur Phänomenologie und Theorie der Erkenntnis. In zwei Bänden*. Edited by Ursula Panzer. The Hague: Martinus Nijhoff, 1984.

Hua XXIII: *Phantasie, Bildbewusstsein, Erinnerung: Zur Phänomenologie der anschaulichen Vergegenwärtigungen. Texte aus dem Nachlass (1898–1925)*. Edited by Eduard Marbach. The Hague: Martinus Nijhoff, 1980.

Hua XXIV: *Einleitung in die Logik und Erkenntnistheorie: Vorlesungen 1906/07*. Edited by Ullrich Melle. The Hague: Martinus Nijhoff, 1985.

Hua XXV: *Aufsätze und Vorträge: 1911–1921*. Edited by Thomas Nenon and Hans Rainer Sepp. The Hague: Martinus Nijhoff, 1986.

Hua XXVII: *Aufsätze und Vorträge: 1922–1937*. Edited by Thomas Nenon and H. R. Sepp. The Hague: Kluwer Academic Publishers, 1989.

Hua XXIX: *Die Krisis der europäischen Wissenschaften und die transzendentale Phänomenologie. Ergänzungsband. Texte aus dem Nachlass 1934–1937*. Edited by Reinhold N. Smid. Dordrecht: Kluwer Academic Publishers, 1993.

Hua XXXI: *Aktive Synthesen: Aus der Vorlesung "Transzendentale Logik." 1920/21. Ergänzungsband zu "Analysen zur passiven Synthesis."* Edited by Roland Breeur. The Hague: Kluwer Academic Publishers, 2000.

Hua XXXII: *Natur und Geist: Vorlesungen Sommersemester 1927*. Edited by Michael Weiler. Dordrecht: Kluwer Academic Publishers, 2001.

Hua XXXIII: *Die "Bernauer Manuskripte" über das Zeitbewußtsein (1917/18)*. Edited by Rudolf Bernet and Dieter Lohmar. Dordrecht: Kluwer Academic Publishers, 2001.

Hua XXXIV: *Zur phänomenologischen Reduktion: Texte aus dem Nachlass (1926–1935)*. Edited by Sebastian Luft. Dordrecht: Kluwer Academic Publishers, 2002.

Hua XXXV: *Einleitung in die Philosophie: Vorlesungen 1922/23*. Edited by Berndt Goossens. Dordrecht: Kluwer Academic Publishers, 2002.

Hua XXXVI: *Transzendentaler Idealismus: Texte aus dem Nachlass (1908–1921)*. Edited by Robin D. Rollinger and Rochus Sowa. Dordrecht: Kluwer Academic Publishers, 2003.

Hua XXXVII: *Einleitung in die Ethik: Vorlesungen Sommersemester 1920 und 1924*. Edited by Henning Peucker. Dordrecht: Kluwer Academic Publishers, 2004.

Hua XXXVIII: *Wahrnehmung und Aufmerksamkeit: Texte aus dem Nachlass (1893–1912)*. Edited by Thomas Vongehr and Regula Giuliani. Dordrecht: Springer, 2004.

Hua XXXIX: *Die Lebenswelt: Auslegungen der vorgegebenen Welt und ihrer Konstitution. Texte aus dem Nachlass (1916–1937)*. Edited by Rochus Sowa. Dordrecht: Springer, 2008.

BIBLIOGRAPHY

Unpublished manuscripts (Ms.)

Ms. A V 17 (1927)
Ms. A V 25 (1932)
Ms. A VII 11 (1925–1932)
Ms. A VII 14 (1920 and 1926)
Ms. D 2 (1933)
Ms. D 4 (1921)
Ms. D 10 I (1932)
Ms. D 10 II (1932)
Ms. D 10 III (1932)
Ms. D 11 (1931)
Ms. D 12 I (1931)
Ms. D 12 II (1931)
Ms. D 13 I [I–XIV] (1917–1926)
Ms. D 13 II [XV–XXII] (1907–1921)
Ms. D 17 (1934)
Ms. E III 4 (1930)
Ms. E III 9 (1931–1933)
Ms. E III 11 (1934)

Other Published Works by Husserl

Husserl, Edmund. 1940a. "Grundlegende Untersuchungen zum phänomenologischen Ursprung der Räumlichkeit der Natur." In *Philosophical Essays in Memory of Edmund Husserl*, ed. Marvin Farber. Cambridge, Mass.: Harvard University Press.
———. 1940b. "Notizen zur Raumkonstitution." Edited by Alfred Schütz. *Philosophy and Phenomenological Research* 1, no. 1: 21–37.
———. 1948. *Erfahrung und Urteil: Untersuchungen zur Genealogie der Logik*. Edited by Ludwig Landgrebe. Hamburg: Claassen Verlag.
———. 2006. *Husserliana Materialen, Vol. VIII, Späte Texte über Zeitkonstitution (1929–1934). Die C-Manuskripte*. Edited by Dieter Lohmar. Dordrecht: Springer.

Other Works

Aguirre, Antonio. 1970. *Genetische Phänomenologie und Reduktion. Zur Letztbegründung der Wissenschaft aus der radikalen Skepsis im Denken E. Husserls*. The Hague: Martinus Nijhoff.
Alanen, Lilli. 2003. *Descartes's Concept of Mind*. Cambridge, Mass.: Harvard University Press.
Alweiss, Lilian. 2003. *The World Unclaimed. A Challenge to Heidegger's Critique of Husserl*. Ohio: Ohio University Press.

Aristotle. 1986. *De anima (On the Soul)*. Translated by Hugh Lawson-Tancred. London: Penguin Books.
Ayer, Alfred J. 1936. *Language, Truth and Logic*. London: Victor Gollancz.
Barbaras, Renaud. 2005. "A Phenomenology of Life." In *Cambridge Companion to Merleau-Ponty*, ed. Taylor Carman and Mark Hansen. Cambridge, Eng.: Cambridge University Press.
Beeli, Gian, Michaela Esslen, and Lutz Jäncke. 2005. "Synaesthesia: When Coloured Sounds Taste Sweet." *Nature* 434, no. 3: 38.
Behnke, Elizabeth. 1996. "Edmund Husserl's Contribution to Phenomenology of the Body in *Ideas II*." In *Issues in Husserl's Ideas II*, ed. Thomas Nenon and Lester Embree. Dordrecht: Kluwer.
———. 2002. "Merleau-Ponty's Ontological Reading of Constitution in *Phénoménologie de la perception*." In *Merleau-Ponty's Reading of Husserl*, ed. Ted Toadvine and Lester Embree. Dordrecht: Kluwer.
———. 2008. "Interkinaesthetic Affectivity: A Phenomenological Approach." *Continental Philosophy Review* 41: 143–61.
Bell, David. 1990. *Husserl*. London: Routledge.
Bermúdez, José Luis. 2005. "The Phenomenology of Bodily Awareness." In *Phenomenology and Philosophy of Mind*, ed. David Woodruff Smith and Amie Thomasson. Oxford: Clarendon.
Bernet, Rudolf. 1999. "Husserl." In *A Companion to Continental Philosophy*, ed. S. Critchley and W. Schroeder. Oxford: Blackwell.
———. 2000. "The Encounter with the Stranger: Two Interpretations of the Vulnerability of the Skin." In *The Face of the Other and the Trace of God: Essays on the Philosophy of Emmanuel Levinas*, ed. Jeffrey Bloechl. New York: Fordham University Press.
———. 2002a. "Levinas's Critique of Husserl." In *Cambridge Companion to Levinas*, ed. Simon Critchley and Robert Bernasconi. Cambridge, Eng.: Cambridge University Press.
———. 2002b. "Unconscious Consciousness in Husserl and Freud." *Phenomenology and the Cognitive Sciences* 1: 327–51.
Bernet, Rudolf, Eduard Marbach, and Iso Kern. 1993. *Introduction to Husserlian Phenomenology*. Evanston, Ill.: Northwestern University Press.
Biemel, Walter. 2000. "The Decisive Phases in the Development of Husserl's Phenomenology." Translated by R. O. Elveton. In *The Phenomenology of Husserl: Selected Critical Readings*, ed. R. O. Elveton. 2nd edition. Seattle: Noesis.
Brand, Gerd. 1971. *Die Lebenswelt: Eine Philosophie des konkreten Apriori*. Berlin: Walter de Gruyter.
———. 1979. "Die Normalität des und der Anderen und die Anomalität einer Erfahrungsgemeinschaft bei Edmund Husserl." In *Alfred Schütz und die Idee des Alltags in den Sozialwissenschaften*. Stuttgart: Ferdinand Enke.
Brough, John B. 1996. "Presence and Absence in Husserl's Phenomenology of Time-Consciousness." In *Phenomenology, Interpretation, and Community*, ed. Lenore Langsdorf, Stephen Watson, and Marya Bower. Albany: State University of New York Press.

Bruzina, Ronald. 2002. "Eugen Fink and Maurice Merleau-Ponty: The Philosophical Lineage in Phenomenology." In *Merleau-Ponty's Reading of Husserl*, ed. Ted Toadvine and Lester Embree. Dordrecht: Kluwer.
Canguilhem, Georges. 1991. *The Normal and the Pathological*. Translated by Carolyn R. Fawcett and Robert S. Cohen. New York: Zone Books.
Carman, Taylor. 2005. "Sensation, Judgment, and the Phenomenal Field." In *Cambridge Companion to Merleau-Ponty*, ed. Taylor Carman and Mark Hansen. Cambridge, Eng.: Cambridge University Press.
Carman, Taylor, and Mark Hansen, eds. 2005a. *Cambridge Companion to Merleau-Ponty*. Cambridge, Eng.: Cambridge University Press.
———. 2005b. "Introduction." In *Cambridge Companion to Merleau-Ponty*, ed. Taylor Carman and Mark Hansen. Cambridge, Eng.: Cambridge University Press.
Carr, David. 1970. "Translator's Introduction" and translator's footnotes in Husserl, *The Crisis of European Sciences and Transcendental Phenomenology. An Introduction to Phenomenological Philosophy*. Evanston, Ill.: Northwestern University Press.
———. 1973. "The 'Fifth Meditation' and Husserl's Cartesianism." In *Philosophy and Phenomenological Research* 34: 14–35.
———. 1974. *Phenomenology and the Problem of History. A Study of Husserl's Transcendental Philosophy*. Evanston, Ill.: Northwestern University Press.
———. 1977. "Kant, Husserl, and the Nonempirical Ego." *Journal of Philosophy* 74: 682–90.
———. 1986. *Time, Narrative, and History*. Bloomington: Indiana University Press.
———. 1987. *Interpreting Husserl: Critical and Comparative Studies*. Dordrecht: Kluwer.
———. 1998. "Phenomenology and Historical Knowledge." In *Phenomenology of Interculturality and Life-World*, ed. Ernst Orth and Chan-Fai Cheung. Munich: Karl Alber.
———. 1999. *The Paradox of Subjectivity: The Self in the Transcendental Tradition*. New York: Oxford University Press.
———. 2000. "Heidegger and Transcendental Philosophy." In *The Empirical and the Transcendental: A Fusion of Horizons*, ed. Gupta. Lanham, Md.: Rowman and Littlefield.
———. 2002. "Husserl's Paradox: On the Ontological Status of the Transcendental Subject." In *Subjektivität—Verantwortung—Wahrheit*, ed. David Carr and Christian Lotz, 23–36. Frankfurt am Main: Peter Lang.
———. 2003. "Transcendental and Empirical Subjectivity: The Self in the Transcendental Tradition." In *The New Husserl*, ed. Donn Welton. Bloomington: Indiana University Press.
———. 2004. "Time Zones: Phenomenological Reflections on Cultural Time." In *Space, Time, and Culture*, ed. David Carr and Chan-Fai Cheung. Dordrecht: Kluwer.
Casey, Edward S. 1993. *Getting Back Into Place: Toward a Renewed Understanding of the Place-World*. Bloomington: Indiana University Press.

———. 1997. *The Fate of Place: A Philosophical History*. Berkeley: University of California Press.
Chisholm, Roderick. 1999. "The Persistence of Persons." In *Metaphysics: An Anthology*, ed. Jaegwon Kim, Daniel Korman, and Ernest Sosa. Oxford: Blackwell.
Claesges, Ulrich. 1964. *Edmund Husserls Theorie Der Raumkonstitution*. The Hague: Martinus Nijhoff.
Cole, Jonathan. 1991. *Pride and a Daily Marathon*. Cambridge, Mass.: MIT Press.
Cottingham, John. 1986. *Descartes*. Oxford: Basil Blackwell.
Crowell, Steven Galt. 1995. "Solipsism (Modalities of the Strange)." In *The Prism of the Self*, ed. Crowell. Dordrecht: Kluwer.
———. 1996. "The Mythical and the Meaningless." In *Issues in Husserl's Ideas II*, ed. Thomas Nenon and Lester Embree. Dordrecht: Kluwer.
———. 2001. *Husserl, Heidegger, and the Space of Meaning: Paths toward Transcendental Phenomenology*. Evanston, Ill.: Northwestern University Press.
———. 2003. "Facticity and Transcendental Philosophy." In *From Kant to Davidson: Philosophy and the Idea of the Transcendental*, ed. Jeff Malpas. London: Routledge.
———. 2008a. "Measure-Taking: Meaning and Normativity in Heidegger's Philosophy." *Continental Philosophy Review* 41: 261–76.
———. 2008b. "Phenomenological Immanence, Normativity, and Semantic Externalism." In *Synthese*, vol. 160/3: 335–354.
———. 2012. "The Normative in Perception." In *Contemporary Kantian Metaphysics: New Essays on Space and Time*, ed. Roxana Baiasu, Graham Bird, and A. W. Moore, 81–106. Houndsmills, Eng.: Palgrave Macmillan.
Dahlstrom, Daniel. 2007. "The Intentionality of Passive Experience: Husserl and a Contemporary Debate." In *The New Yearbook for Phenomenology and Phenomenological Philosophy*, vol. 7, ed. Steven Crowell and Burt Hopkins. Durham: Acumen.
De Boer, Theodore. 1978. *The Development of Husserl's Thought*. Translated by Theodore Plantinga. The Hague: Martinus Nijhoff.
Depraz, Natalie. 1998. "Can I Anticipate Myself? Self-Affection and Temporality." In *Self-Awareness, Temporality, and Alterity: Central Topics in Phenomenology*, ed. Dan Zahavi. Dordrecht: Kluwer.
———. 1999. "When Transcendental Genesis Encounters the Naturalization Project." In *Naturalizing Phenomenology: Issues in Contemporary Phenomenology and Cognitive Science*, ed. Jean Petitot, Francisco J. Varela, Bernard Pachoud, and Jean-Michel Roy. Stanford, Calif.: Stanford University Press.
———. 2000. "Hyletic and Kinetic Facticity of the Absolute Flow and World Creation." In *The Many Faces of Time*, ed. John Brough and Lester Embree. Dordrecht: Kluwer.
Descartes, René. 1967. *The Philosophical Works of Descartes*. Vol 1. Translated by Elizabeth S. Haldane and G. R. T. Ross. Cambridge, Eng.: Cambridge University Press.
———. 1970. *Philosophical Letters*. Translated by Anthony Kenny. Oxford: Clarendon.

BIBLIOGRAPHY

———. 1984. *The Philosophical Writings of Descartes. Volume II*. Translated by John Cottingham, Robert Stoothoff, and Dugald Murdoch. Cambridge, Eng.: Cambridge University Press.

———. 1988. *Selected Philosophical Writings*. Translated by John Cottingham, Robert Stoothoff, and Dugald Murdoch. Cambridge, Eng.: Cambridge University Press.

Diemer, Alwin. 1956. *Edmund Husserl: Versuch einer systematischen Darstellung seiner Phänomenologie*. Meisenheim am Glan: Verlag Anton Hain.

Dillon, Martin C. 1997. *Merleau-Ponty's Ontology*. 2nd edition. Evanston, Ill.: Northwestern University Press.

Dodd, James. 1997. *Idealism and Corporeity: An Essay on the Problem of the Body in Husserl's Phenomenology*. Dordrecht: Springer.

———. 2004. *Crisis and Reflection: An Essay on Husserl's Crisis of the European Sciences*. Dordrecht: Kluwer.

Dreyfus, Hubert. 1982a. "Husserl's Perceptual Noema." In *Husserl, Intentionality and Cognitive Science*, ed. Dreyfus. Cambridge, Mass.: MIT Press.

———. 1982b. "Introduction." In *Husserl, Intentionality and Cognitive Science*, ed. Dreyfus. Cambridge, Mass.: MIT Press.

Dufrenne, Mikel. 1966. *The Notion of Apriori*. Translated by Edward Casey. Evanston, Ill.: Northwestern University Press.

Durkheim, Émile. 1982. *The Rules of Sociological Method*. Translated by W. D. Halls. New York: Free.

Farber, Marvin. 2006. *The Foundation of Phenomenology: Edmund Husserl and the Quest for a Rigorous Science of Philosophy*. New Jersey: Ontos Verlag.

Fink, Eugen. 1933. "Die phänomenologische Philosophie Edmund Husserls in der gegenwärtigen Kritik." *Kant-Studien*, vol. 38: 319–83.

———. 1988. *VI. Cartesianische Meditation. Teil 1: Die Idee einer transzendentalen Methodenlehre*. Husserliana Dokumente Bd. II/1. Edited by Hans Ebeling, Jann Holl, and Guy van Kerckhoven. Dordrecht: Kluwer Academic Publishers.

Fischer, Franz. 1929. "Zeitstruktur und Schizophrenie." In *Zeitschrift für die gesamte Neurologie und Psychiatrie*, 121: 544–74.

Føllesdal, Dagfinn. 1982a. "Brentano and Husserl on Intentional Objects and Perception." In *Husserl, Intentionality and Cognitive Science*, ed. Hubert Dreyfus. Cambridge, Mass.: MIT Press.

———. 1982b. "Husserl's Notion of *Noema*." In *Husserl, Intentionality and Cognitive Science*, ed. Hubert Dreyfus. Cambridge, Mass.: MIT Press.

———. 1982c. "Husserl's Theory of Perception." In *Husserl, Intentionality and Cognitive Science*, ed. Hubert Dreyfus. Cambridge, Mass.: MIT Press.

Folter, Rolf J. de. 1983. "Reziprozität der Perspektiven und Normalität bei Husserl und Schütz." In *Soziatität und Intersubjektivität: Phänomenologische Perspektiven der Sozialwissenschaften im Umkreis von Aron Gurwitsch und Alfred Schütz*. Munich: Wilhelm Fink.

Fuchs, Thomas. 2000. *Leib, Raum, Person: Entwurf einer phänomenologischen Anthropologie*. Stuttgart: Klett-Cotta.

———. 2008. *Leib und Lebenswelt: Neue philosophisch-psychiatrische Essays*. Kusterdingen: Die Graue Edition.

Gallagher, Shaun. 1986. "Hyletic Experience and the Lived Body." *Husserl Studies* 3: 131–66.
———. 1995. "Body Schema and Intentionality." In *Body and Self*, ed. José Luis Bermúdez, Anthony Marcel, and Naomi Eilan. Cambridge, Mass.: MIT Press.
———. 2004. "Agency, Ownership, and Alien Control in Schizophrenia." In *The Structure and Development of Self-Consciousness: Interdisciplinary Perspectives*, ed. Dan Zahavi, Thor Grünbaum, and Josef Parnas. Amsterdam and Philadelphia: John Benjamins.
———. 2005. *How the Body Shapes the Mind*. Oxford: Clarendon.
———. 2008. "Intersubjectivity in Perception." *Continental Philosophy Review* 41: 163–78.
Gallagher, Shaun, and Andrew N. Meltzoff. 1996. "The Earliest Sense of Self and Others: Merleau-Ponty and Recent Developmental Studies." *Philosophical Psychology* 9: 211–33.
Gallagher, Shaun, and Dan Zahavi. 2008. *The Phenomenological Mind: An Introduction to Philosophy of Mind and Cognitive Science*. New York: Routledge.
Gallese, Vittorio. 2008. "Empathy, Embodied Simulation, and the Brain: Commentary on Aragno and Zepf/Hartmann." *Journal of the American Psychoanalytic Association* 56: 769–81.
Goto, Hiroshi. 2004. *Der Begriff der Person in der Phänomenologie Edmund Husserls: Ein Interpretationsversuch der Husserlschen Phänomenologie als Ethik im Hinblick auf den Begriff der Habitualität*. Wurzburg: Königshausen & Neumann.
Hansen, Mark. 2005. "The Embryology of the (In)visible." In *Cambridge Companion to Merleau-Ponty*, ed. Taylor Carman and Mark Hansen. Cambridge, Eng.: Cambridge University Press.
Hart, James G. 1989. "I, We, and God: Ingredients of Husserl's Theory of Community." *Husserl-Ausgabe und Husserl-Forschung*, ed. Samuel Ijsseling. Dordrecht: Kluwer Academic Publishers.
———. 1992. *The Person and the Common Life: Studies in a Husserlian Social Ethics*. Dordrecht: Kluwer Academic Publishers.
———. 1996. "Agent Intellect and Primal Sensibility." In *Issues in Husserl's Ideas II*, ed. Thomas Nenon and Lester Embree. Dordrecht: Kluwer Academic Publishers.
Heidegger, Martin. 1961. *Nietzsche. Erster Band*. Stuttgart: Verlag Günther Neske.
———. 1987. *Zollikoner Seminare: Protokolle—Gespräche—Briefe*. Edited by Menard Boss. Frankfurt am Main: Vittorio Klostermann.
———. 2001. *Sein und Zeit*. Tübingen: Max Niemeyer Verlag.
———. 2004. *Die Grundbegriffe der Metaphysik: Welt—Endlichkeit—Einsamkeit*. Frankfurt am Main: Vittorio Klostermann.
Heinämaa, Sara. 2002. "From Decisions to Passions: Merleau-Ponty's Interpretation of Husserl's Reduction." In *Merleau-Ponty's Reading of Husserl*, ed. Ted Toadvine and Lester Embree. Dordrecht: Kluwer.
———. 2003. *Toward a Phenomenology of Sexual Difference: Husserl, Merleau-Ponty, Beauvoir*. Lanham, Md.: Rowman and Littlefield.

BIBLIOGRAPHY

Held, Klaus. 1966. *Lebendige Gegenwart. Die Frage nach der Seinsweise der transzendentalen Ich bei Edmund Husserl, entwickelt am Leitfaden der Zeitproblematik.* The Hague: Martinus Nijhoff.
———. 1972. "Das Problem der Intersubjektivität und die Idee einer phänomenologischen Transzendentalphilosophie." In *Perspektiven transzendentalphänomenologischer Forschung*, ed. Ulrich Klaesges and Klaus Held. The Hague: Martinus Nijhoff.
———. 1991. "Heimwelt, Fremdwelt, die eine Welt." In *Perspektiven und Probleme der Husserlschen Phänomenologie*. Munich: Karl Alber.
———. 1998. "Sky and Earth as Invariants of the Natural Life-World." In *Phenomenology of Interculturality and Life-World*, ed. Ernst Orth and Chan-Fai Cheung. Munich: Karl Alber.
———. 2000. "Generative Experience of Time." In *The Many Faces of Time*, ed. John Brough and Lester Embree. Dordrecht: Kluwer.
Henry, Michel. 1973. *Essence of Manifestation*. Translated by Girard J. Etzkorn. The Hague: Martinus Nijhoff.
———. 1975. *Philosophy and Phenomenology of the Body*. Translated by Girard J. Etzkorn. The Hague: Martinus Nijhoff.
Himanka, Juha. 2000. "Does the Earth Move? A Search for a Dialogue Between Two Traditions of Contemporary Philosophy." *Philosophical Forum* 31: 57–83.
———. 2005. "Husserl's Argumentation for the Pre-Copernican View of the Earth." *Review of Metaphysics* 58: 621–44.
Holenstein, Elmar. 1999. "The Zero-Point of Orientation: The Placement of the I in Perceived Space." Translated by Lanei Rodemeyer and Sebastian Luft. In *The Body: Classic and Contemporary Readings*, ed. Donn Welton. Oxford: Blackwell.
Johnston, Mark. 1999. "Human Beings." In *Metaphysics: An Anthology*, ed. Jaegwon Kim, Daniel Korman, and Ernest Sosa. Oxford: Blackwell.
Kant, Immanuel. 1954. *Träume eines Geistersehers*. Edited by Friedrich Bassenge. Berlin: Aufbau-Verlag.
———. 1998. *Kritik der reinen Vernunft*. Edited by Jens Timmerman. Hamburg: Felix Meiner.
Kelly, Sean Dorrance. 2005. "Seeing Things in Merleau-Ponty." In *Cambridge Companion to Merleau-Ponty*, ed. Taylor Carman and Mark Hansen. Cambridge, Eng.: Cambridge University Press.
Kern, Iso. 1964. *Husserl und Kant: Eine Untersuchung über Husserls Verhältnis zu Kant und zum Neukantianismus*. The Hague: Martinus Nijhoff.
———. 1973. "Einleitung des Herausgebers." In *Zur Phänomenologie der Intersubjektivität: Texte aus dem Nachlass. Dritter Teil: 1929–35*, by Edmund Husserl, edited by Iso Kern. The Hague: Martinus Nijhoff.
———. 1977. "The Three Ways to the Transcendental Phenomenological Reduction in the Philosophy of Edmund Husserl." Translated by Frederick Elliston and Peter McCormick. In *Husserl: Expositions and Appraisals*, ed. Frederick Ellison and Peter McCormick. Notre Dame: University of Notre Dame Press.

Kersten, Fred. 1981. "Introduction." In *Husserl: Shorter Works*, ed. Frederick McCormick and Peter Elliston. Notre Dame: University of Notre Dame Press.

Kockelmans, Joseph J. 1977. "Husserl and Kant on the Pure Ego." In *Husserl: Expositions and Appraisals*, ed. Frederick Elliston and Peter McCormick. Notre Dame: University of Notre Dame Press.

———. 1994. *Edmund Husserl's Phenomenology*. West Lafayette, Ind.: Purdue University Press.

Kojima, Hiroshi. 2000. *Monad and Thou: Phenomenological Ontology of Human Being*. Athens, Ohio: Ohio University Press.

Kortooms, Toine. 2002. *Phenomenology of Time: Edmund Husserl's Analysis of Time-Consciousness*. Dordrecht: Kluwer Academic Publishers.

Kühn, Rolf, and Michael Staudigl. 2003. "Passivity as Pre-Predicative Constitution in Husserl: Structure and Discussion." In *Phenomenology World Wide: Foundations—Expanding Dynamics—Life Engagements: A Guide for Research and Study*, ed. Anna-Teresa Tymieniecka. Dordrecht: Kluwer Academic Publishers.

Landgrebe, Ludwig. 1940. "The World as a Phenomenological Problem." Translated by Dorion Cairns. *Philosophy and Phenomenological Research* 1: 38–58.

———. 1963. *Der Weg der Phänomenologie: Das Problem einer ursprünglichen Erfahrung*. Gütersloh: Gerd Mohn.

———. 1968. *Phänomenologie und Geschichte*. Gütersloh: Gerd Mohn.

———. 1974. "Reflexionen zu Husserls Konstitutionlehre." *Tijdschrift voor Filosofie* 36, no. 3.

———. 1982. *Faktizität und Individuation. Studien zu den Grundfragen der Phänomenologie*. Hamburg: Felix Meiner Verlag.

Langsdorf, Lenore, Stephen Watson, and Marya Bower, eds. 1996. *Phenomenology, Interpretation, and Community*. Albany: State University of New York Press.

Larrabee, Mary Jeanne. 1976. "Husserl's Static and Genetic Phenomenology." *Man and World* 9, no. 2: 163–74.

Leder, Drew. 1990. *The Absent Body*. Chicago: University of Chicago Press.

———. 1998. "A Tale of Two Bodies: The Cartesian Corpse and the Lived Body." In *Body and Flesh: A Philosophical Reader*, ed. Donn Welton. Oxford: Blackwell.

———. 1999. "Flesh and Blood: A Proposed Supplement to Merleau-Ponty." In *The Body: Classic and Contemporary Readings*, ed. Donn Welton. Oxford: Blackwell.

Lee, Nam-In. 1998. "Edmund Husserl's Phenomenology of Mood." In *Alterity and Facticity: New Perspectives on Husserl*, ed. Natalie Depraz and Dan Zahavi. Berlin: Springer.

Lenkowski, William Jon. 1978. "What Is Husserl's *Epoché*? The Problem of the Beginning of Philosophy in a Husserlian Context." *Man and World* 3, no. 4: 299–323.

Levinas, Emmanuel. 1969. *Totality and Infinity: An Essay on Exteriority*. Translated by Alphonso Lingis. Pittsburgh: Duquesne University Press.

———. 1987. *Time and the Other*. Translated by Richard Cohen. Pittsburgh: Duquesne University Press.

BIBLIOGRAPHY

Lewis, David. 1969. "Survival and Identity." In *The Identities of Persons*, ed. Amélie Rorty. Berkeley: University of California Press.
Lingis, Alphonso. 1971. "Intentionality and Corporeity." *Analecta Husserliana* 1: 75–90.
Locke, John. 1975. *An Essay Concerning Human Understanding*. Edited by Peter Nidditch. Oxford: Clarendon.
Lohmar, Dieter. 1996. "The Role of Life-World in Husserl's Critique of Idealizations." In *Phenomenology, Interpretation, and Community*, ed. Lenore Langsdorf, Stephen Watson, and Marya Bower. Albany: State University of New York Press.
———. 1998. "The Foreignness of a Foreign Culture." In *Self-Awareness, Temporality, and Alterity: Central Topics in Phenomenology*, ed. Dan Zahavi. Dordrecht: Kluwer.
———. 2003. "Husserl's Type and Kant's Schemata." Translated by Julia Jansen and Gina Zavota. In *The New Husserl*, ed. Donn Welton. Bloomington: Indiana University Press.
———. 2006. "Mirror Neurons and the Phenomenology of Intersubjectivity." *Phenomenology and the Cognitive Sciences* 5: 5–16.
———. 2007. "How Do Primates Think? Phenomenological Analyses of Non-Language Systems of Representation in Higher Primates and Humans." In *Phenomenology and the Non-Human Animal*, ed. Corinne Painter and Christian Lotz. Dordrecht: Springer.
———. 2008. *Phänomenologie der schwachen Phantasie: Untersuchungen der Psychologie, Cognitive Science, Neurologie und Phänomenologie zur Funktion der Phantasie in der Wahrnehmung*. Dordrecht: Springer.
Lotz, Christian. 2005. *Vom Leib zum Selbst. Kritische Analysen zu Husserl and Heidegger*. Freiburg: Alber Verlag.
———. 2006. "Psyche or Person. Husserl's Phenomenology of Animals." In *Interdisziplinäre Perspektiven der Phänomenologie*, ed. Dieter Lohmar and Dirk Fonfara. Dordrecht: Springer.
———. 2007. *From Affectivity to Subjectivity: Husserl's Phenomenology Revisited*. Hampshire: Palgrave Macmillan.
Luft, Sebastian. 2005. "Husserl's Concept of the 'Transcendental Person': Another Look at the Husserl–Heidegger Relationship." *International Journal of Philosophical Studies* 13, no. 2: 141–77.
Mahler, Margaret, Fred Pine, and Anni Bergman. 1975. *The Psychological Birth of the Human Infant*. New York: Basic Books.
Marbach, Eduard. 1974. *Das Problem des Ich in der Phänomenologie Husserls*. The Hague: Martinus Nijhoff.
McKenna, William. 2003. "The Constitutive Effect of the Other's Awareness of Me." *Husserl Studies* 19, no. 3: 193–203.
———. 2004. "Objectivity and Inter-Cultural Experience." In *Space, Time, and Culture*, ed. David Carr and Chan-Fai Cheung. Dordrecht: Kluwer.
Melle, Ullrich. 1983. *Das Wahrnehmungsproblem und seine Verwandlung in phänomenologischer Einstellung: Untersuchungen zu den phänomenologischen Wahrnehmungstheorien von Husserl, Gurwitsch, und Merleau-Ponty*. The Hague: Martinus Nijhoff.

―――. 1996. "Nature and Spirit." In *Issues in Husserl's Ideas II*, ed. Thomas Nenon and Lester Embree. Dordrecht: Kluwer.
Mensch, James. 2001. *Postfoundational Phenomenology: Husserlian Reflections on Presence and Embodiment*. University Park: Pennsylvania State University Press.
Merleau-Ponty, Maurice. 1945. *Phénoménologie de la perception*. Paris: Gallimard. (*Phenomenology of Perception*. Translated by Colin Smith. London: Routledge, 2002.)
―――. 1960. *Signes*. Paris: Gallimard. (*Signs*. Translated by Richard McCleary. Evanston, Ill.: Northwestern University Press, 1964.)
―――. 1964. *Le visible et l'invisible*. Edited by Claude Lefort. Paris: Gallimard. (*Visible and Invisible*. Translated by Alphonso Lingis. Evanston, Ill.: Northwestern University Press, 1968.)
―――. 1969. *La prose du monde*. Edited by Claude Lefort. Paris: Gallimard. (*The Prose of the World*. Translated by John O'Neill. Evanston, Ill.: Northwestern University Press, 1973.)
―――. 1994. *La Nature: Notes: Cours du Collège de France*. Edited by Dominique Séglard. Paris: Éditions du Seuil. (*Nature: Course Notes from the Collège de France*. Translated by Robert Vallier. Evanston, Ill.: Northwestern University Press, 2003.)
―――. 1997. "Les relations avec autrui chez l'enfant." In *Parcours 1935–1951*, by Merleau-Ponty. Paris: Verdier. ("The Child's Relations with Others." In *Primacy of Perception: And Other Essays on Phenomenological Psychology, the Philosophy of Art, History, and Politics*, ed. James Edie. Article translated by William Cobb. Evanston, Ill.: Northwestern University Press, 1964.)
―――. 2001. "La conscience et l'acquisition du langage." In *Psychologie et pédagogie de l'enfant: Cours de Sorbonne 1949–1952*, by Merleau-Ponty. Edited by Jacques Prunair. Paris: Verdier. (*Consciousness and the Acquisition of Language*. Translated by Hugh Silverman. Evanston, Ill.: Northwestern University Press, 1979.)
―――. 2010. *Child Psychology and Pedagogy. The Sorbonne Lectures 1949–1952*. Translated by Talia Welsh. Evanston, Ill.: Northwestern University Press.
Miller, Izchak. 1984. *Husserl, Perception, and Temporal Awareness*. Cambridge, Mass.: MIT Press.
Minkowski, Eugène. 1970. *Lived Time: Phenomenological and Psychopathological Studies*. Translated by Nancy Metzel. Evanston, Ill.: Northwestern University Press.
Mohanty, J. N. 1986. "On the Possibility of Transcendental Philosophy." In *The Life of the Transcendental Ego: Essays in Honor of William Earle*, ed. Edward Casey and Donald Morano. Albany: State University of New York Press.
Moran, Dermot. 2000. *Introduction to Phenomenology*. London: Routledge.
―――. 2003. "Making Sense: Husserl's Phenomenology as Transcendental Idealism." In *From Kant to Davidson: Philosophy and the Idea of the Transcendental*, ed. Jeff Malpas. London: Routledge.
―――. 2004. "The Problem of Empathy: Lipps, Scheler, Husserl and Stein." In *Amor amicitiae: On the Love That Is Friendship: Essays in Medieval Thought and*

BIBLIOGRAPHY

Beyond in Honor of the Rev. Professor James McEvoy, ed. Thomas Kelly and Philipp Rosemann. Leuven: Peeters.
———. 2005. *Husserl. Founder of Phenomenology*. Cambridge, Eng.: Polity.
Nagel, Thomas. 1974. "What Is It Like to Be a Bat?" *Philosophical Review* 83, no. 4: 435–450.
Noë, Alva. 2004. *Action in Perception*. Cambridge, Mass.: MIT Press.
Overgaard, Søren. 2003. "On Levinas' Critique of Husserl." In *Metaphysics, Facticity, Interpretation: Phenomenology in the Nordic Countries*, ed. Dan Zahavi, Sara Heinämaa, and Hans Ruin. Dordrecht: Springer.
———. 2004. *Husserl and Heidegger on Being in the World*. Dordrecht: Kluwer Academic Publishers.
———. 2007. "In Defense of Subjectivity: Husserl, Levinas, and the Problem of Solipsism." In *Subjectivity and Transcendence*, ed. Arne Grøn, Iben Damgaard, and Søren Overgaard. Tübingen: Mohr Siebeck.
Parfit, Derek. 1999. "Personal Identity." In *Metaphysics: An Anthology*, ed. Jaegwon Kim and Ernest Sosa. Oxford: Blackwell.
Parnas, Josef. 2003. "Self and Schizophrenia: A Phenomenological Perspective." In *The Self in Neuroscience and Psychiatry*, ed. Tilo Kircher and Anthony David, 217–41. Cambridge, Eng.: Cambridge University Press.
Parnas, Josef, and Louis Sass. 2001. "Self, Solipsism, and Schizophrenic Delusions." *Philosophy, Psychiatry, & Psychology* 8, nos. 2–3: 101–20.
Patočka, Jan. 1998. *Body, Community, Language, World*. Translated by Erazim Kohák, edited by James Dodd. Chicago: Open Court.
Perry, John. 1975. "The Problem of Personal Identity." In *Personal Identity*, ed. Perry. Berkeley: University of California Press.
Philipse, Herman. 1995. "Transcendental Idealism." In *Cambridge Companion to Husserl*, ed. Barry Smith and David Woodruff Smith. Cambridge, Eng.: Cambridge University Press.
Quinton, Anthony. 1962. "The Soul." *Journal of Philosophy* 59, no. 15.
———. 1973. *The Nature of Things*. London: Routledge and Kegan Paul.
Rabanaque, Luis Román. 2003. "Hyle, Genesis and Noema." *Husserl Studies* 19: 205–15.
Reddy, Vasudevi. 2008. *How Infants Know Minds*. Cambridge, Mass.: Harvard University Press.
Ricoeur, Paul. 1967. *Husserl: An Analysis of His Phenomenology*. Translated by Edward Ballard. Evanston, Ill.: Northwestern University Press.
———. 1994. *Oneself as Another*. Translated by Kathleen Blamey. Chicago: University of Chicago Press.
———. 2007. *Freedom and Nature: The Voluntary and the Involuntary*. Translated by Erazim V. Kohák. Evanston, Ill.: Northwestern University Press.
Rinofner-Kreidl, Sonja. 2003. *Mediane Phänomenologie: Subjektivität im Spannungsfeld von Naturalität und Kulturalität*. Würzburg: Königshausen & Neumann.
Rodemeyer, Lanei. 2003. "Developments in the Theory of Time-Consciousness: An Analysis of Protention." In *The New Husserl*, ed. Donn Welton. Bloomington: Indiana University Press.
———. 2006. *Intersubjective Temporality: It's About Time*. Dordrecht: Springer.

Römmp, Georg. 1992. *Husserls Phänomenologie der Intersubjektivität: Und Ihre Bedeutung für eine Theorie intersubjektiver Objektivität und die Konzeption einer phänomenologischen Philosophie.* Dordrecht: Kluwer.

———. 2005. *Husserls Phänomenologie: Eine Einführung.* Wiesbaden: Marix Verlag.

Sartre, Jean-Paul. 1943. *L'être et le néant: Essai d'ontologie phénoménologique.* Paris: Gallimard. (*Being and Nothingness: A Phenomenological Essay on Ontology.* Translated by Hazel Barnes. New York: Washington Square, 1956.)

Sass, Louis. 1994. *The Paradoxes of Delusion: Wittgenstein, Schreber, and the Schizophrenic Mind.* Ithaca, N.Y.: Cornell University Press.

———. 2000. "Schizophrenia, Self-Experience, and the So-Called 'Negative Symptoms': Reflections on Hyperreflexivity." In *Exploring the Self,* ed. Dan Zahavi. Amsterdam and Philadelphia: John Benjamins Publishing Company.

———. 2001. "Self and World in Schizophrenia: Three Classic Approaches." *Philosophy, Psychiatry, & Psychology* 8, no. 4: 251–70.

———. 2003. "Self-Disturbance in Schizophrenia: Hyperreflexivity and Diminished Self-Affection." In *The Self in Neuroscience and Psychiatry,* ed. Tilo Kircher and Anthony David, 242–71. Cambridge, Eng.: Cambridge University Press.

Sass, Louis, and Josef Parnas. 2001. "Phenomenology of Self-Disturbances in Schizophrenia: Some Research Findings and Directions." *Philosophy, Psychiatry, & Psychology* 8, no. 4: 347–56.

Schapp, Wilhelm. 2004. *In Geschichten verstrickt. Zum Sein von Mensch und Ding.* 4th edition. Frankfurt am Main: Vittorio Klostermann.

Schechtman, Marya. 1996. *The Constitution of Selves.* Ithaca, N.Y.: Cornell University Press.

Schües, Christina. 2000. "Empirical and Transcendental Subjectivity: An Enigmatic Relation?" In *The Empirical and the Transcendental: A Fusion of Horizons,* ed. Bina Gupta. Lanham, Md.: Rowman & Littlefield.

Schütz, Alfred. 1932. *Der sinnhafte Aufbau der sozialen Welt: Eine Einleitung in die verstehenden Soziologie.* Vienna: Springer.

Sheets-Johnstone, Maxine. 1999. *Primacy of Movement.* Amsterdam and Philadelphia: John Benjamins.

Shoemaker, Sydney. 1969. "Embodiment and Behavior." In *The Identities of Persons,* ed. Amélie Rorty. Berkeley: University of California Press.

———. 1984. "Personal Identity. A Dualist Theory." In *Personal Identity,* ed. Sydney Shoemaker and Richard Swinburne. Oxford: Blackwell.

———. 1996. *The First-Person Perspective and Other Essays.* Cambridge, Eng.: Cambridge University Press.

Smith, Barry, and David Woodruff Smith. 1995. "Introduction." In *Cambridge Companion to Husserl,* ed. Barry Smith and David Woodruff Smith. Cambridge, Eng.: Cambridge University Press.

Smith, David Woodruff. 2007. *Husserl.* London: Routledge.

Smith, David Woodruff, and Ronald McIntyre. 1982. *Husserl and Intentionality: A Study of Mind, Meaning, and Language.* Dordrecht: D. Reidel.

Soffer, Gail. 1991. *Husserl and the Question of Relativism.* Dordrecht: Kluwer.

———. 1999. "The Other as Alter Ego: A Genetic Approach." *Husserl Studies* 15: 151–66.
Sokolowski, Robert. 1964. *The Formation of Husserl's Concept of Constitution*. The Hague: Martinus Nijhoff.
———. 1974. *Husserlian Meditations: How Words Present Things*. Evanston, Ill.: Northwestern University Press.
———. 2000. *Introduction to Phenomenology*. Cambridge, Eng.: Cambridge University Press.
———. 2008. *Phenomenology of the Human Person*. Cambridge, Eng.: Cambridge University Press.
Sommer, Manfred. 1998. "Husserl on 'Ground' and 'Underground.'" In *Phenomenology of Interculturality and Life-World*, ed. Ernst Orth and Chan-Fai Cheung. Munich: Karl Alber.
Spiegelberg, Herbert. 1982. *The Phenomenological Movement: A Historical Introduction*. 3rd revised and enlarged edition. Dordrecht: Martinus Nijhoff.
Spitz, René. 1965. *The First Year of Life: A Psychoanalytic Study of Normal and Deviant Development of Object-Relations*. New York: International Universities.
Stack, George J. 1974. "Husserl's Concept of Persons." *Idealistic Studies* 4: 267–75.
Staudigl, Michael. 2003. *Die Grenzen der Intentionalität: Zur Kritik der Phänomenalität nach Husserl*. Würzburg: Königshausen & Neumann.
Stawarska, Beata. 2004. "Anonymity and Sociality: The Convergence of Psychological and Philosophical Currents in Merleau-Ponty's Ontological Theory of Intersubjectivity." *Chiasmi International* 5: 295–309.
Stein, Edith. 1917. *Zum Problem der Einfühlung*. (Inaugural-Dissertation.) Halle: Buchdruckerei des Waisenhauses.
Steinbock, Anthony J. 1995a: *Home and Beyond: Generative Phenomenology After Husserl*. Evanston, Ill.: Northwestern University Press.
———. 1995b: "Phenomenological Concepts of Normality and Abnormality." *Man and World* 28, no. 3: 241–60.
———. 1995c: "Generativity and Generative Phenomenology." *Husserl Studies* 12: 55–79.
———. 1996. "Homeworld/Alienworld: Toward a Generative Phenomenology of Intersubjectivity." In *Phenomenology, Interpretation, and Community*, ed. Lenore Langsdorf, Stephen Watson, and Marya Bower. Albany: State University of New York Press.
———. 1998. "Genesis, Normality, and Optimality: A Response to Wolfe Mayes." *New Ideas in Psychology* 16.
———. 1999. "Saturated Intentionality." In *The Body: Classic and Contemporary Readings*, ed. Donn Welton. Oxford: Blackwell.
———. 2001. "Translator's Introduction." In *Analyses Concerning Passive and Active Synthesis: Lectures on Transcendental Logic*, by Edmund Husserl. Dordrecht: Kluwer.
———. 2003. "Generativity and the Scope of Generative Phenomenology." In *The New Husserl*, ed. Donn Welton. Bloomington: Indiana University Press.
———. 2004. "Affection and Attention: On the Phenomenology of Becoming Aware." *Continental Philosophy Review* 37: 21–43.

———. 2007. *Phenomenology and Mysticism: The Verticality of Religious Experience.* Bloomington: Indiana University Press.
———. 2008. "From Phenomenological Immortality to Natality." In *Rethinking Facticity*, ed. François Raffoul and Eric Nelson. Albany: State University of New York Press.
Stern, Daniel. 1985. *The Interpersonal World of the Infant: A View from Psychoanalysis and Developmental Psychology.* New York: Basic Books.
Straus, Erwin. 1952. "The Upright Posture." *Psychiatric Quarterly* 26: 529–61.
———. 1966. *Phenomenological Psychology.* Translated by Erling Eng. London: Tavistock.
Strawson, Peter. 2005. "Persons." In *Self and Subjectivity*, ed. Kim Atkins. Oxford: Blackwell.
Ströker, Elisabeth. 1987. *Investigations in Philosophy of Space.* Translated by Algis Mickunas. Athens: Ohio University Press.
Taguchi, Shigeru. 2006. *Das Problem des 'Ur-Ich' bei Edmund Husserl: Die Frage nach der selbstverständlichen 'Nähe' des Selbst.* Dordrecht: Springer.
Taipale, Joona. 2010. "Normalität." In *Husserl-Lexikon*, ed. Hans-Helmuth Gander. Darmstadt: Wissenschaftliche Buchgesellschaft.
———. 2012. "Twofold Normality: Husserl and the Normative Relevance of Primordial Constitution." *Husserl-Studies* 29, 49–60.
———. 2013a. "Facts and Fantasies: Embodiment and the Early Development of Selfhood." In *Phenomenology of Embodied Subjectivity*, ed. Rasmus Jensen and Dermot Moran. Dordrecht: Springer (forthcoming).
———. 2013b. "The Feeling of Existence: Embodiment in Phenomenology and Psychoanalysis." In *Phenomenology and the Transcendental*, ed. Mirja Hartimo, Sara Heinämaa, and Timo Miettinen. London: Routledge (in press).
Theunissen, Michael. 1977. *Der Andere: Studien zur Sozialontologie der Gegenwart.* Berlin: Walter de Gryuter.
Thomas, Lewis. 1980. *Lives of a Cell: Notes of a Biology Watcher.* London: Allen Lane.
Waldenfels, Bernhard. 1997. *Topographie des Fremden—Studien zur Phänomenologie des Fremden 1.* Frankfurt am Main: Suhrkamp.
———. 1998. "Homeworld and Alienworld." In *Phenomenology of Interculturality and Life-World*, ed. Ernst Orth and Chan-Fai Cheung. Munich: Karl Alber.
———. 2000. *Das leibliche Selbst: Vorlesungen zur Phänomenologie des Leibes.* Frankfurt am Main: Suhrkamp.
———. 2004. "Bodily Experience Between Selfhood and Otherness." *Phenomenology and the Cognitive Sciences* 3: 235–48.
———. 2007. *The Question of the Other.* Hong Kong: Chinese University Press.
———. 2008. "The Role of the Lived-Body in Feeling." *Continental Philosophy Review* 41: 127–42.
Weiss, Gail. 1999. *Body Images: Embodiment as Intercorporeity.* London: Routledge.
Welton, Donn. 1998. "Affectivity, Eros and the Body." In *Body and Flesh: A Philosophical Reader*, ed. Welton. Oxford: Blackwell.
———. 1999. "Soft, Smooth Hands." In *The Body: Classic and Contemporary Readings*, ed. Welton. Oxford: Blackwell.

BIBLIOGRAPHY

———. 2000a. "Hands." In *The Empirical and the Transcendental: A Fusion of Horizons*, ed. Bina Gupta. Lanham, Md.: Rowman and Littlefield.
———. 2000b. *The Other Husserl: The Horizons of Transcendental Phenomenology*. Bloomington: Indiana University Press.
———. 2003. "The Systemacity of Husserl's Transcendental Philosophy: From Static to Genetic Phenomenology." In *The New Husserl*, ed. Welton. Bloomington: Indiana University Press.
Williams, Bernard. 1957. "Personal Identity and Individuation." In *Proceedings of the Aristotelian Society*, vol. 57. London: Harrison and Sons.
Woelert, Peter. 2007. "Kant's Hands, Spatial Orientation, and the Copernican Turn." *Continental Philosophy Review* 40: 139–50.
Wyschogrod, Edith. 1981. "Empathy and Sympathy as Tactile Encounter." *Journal of Medicine and Philosophy* 6: 25–43.
Zahavi, Dan. 1994. "Husserl's Phenomenology of the Body." *Études Phénoménologiques* 19: 63–84.
———. 1998a. "The Fracture in Self-Awareness." In *Self-Awareness, Temporality, and Alterity: Central Topics in Phenomenology*, ed. Zahavi. Dordrecht: Kluwer.
———. 1998b. "Self-Awareness and Affection." In *Alterity and Facticity: New Perspectives on Husserl*, ed. Natalie Depraz and Dan Zahavi. Berlin: Springer.
———. 1999. *Self-Awareness and Alterity: A Phenomenological Investigation*. Evanston, Ill.: Northwestern University Press.
———. 2000. "Self and Consciousness." In *Exploring the Self*, ed. Zahavi. Amsterdam and Philadelphia: John Benjamins.
———. 2001a. "Beyond Empathy: Phenomenological Approaches to Intersubjectivity." *Journal of Consciousness Studies* 8: 151–67.
———. 2001b. *Husserl and Transcendental Intersubjectivity: A Response to the Linguistic-Pragmatic Critique*. Translated by Elizabeth Behnke. Athens, Ohio: Ohio University Press.
———. 2001c. "Schizophrenia and Self-Awareness." In *Philosophy, Psychiatry, & Psychology* 8, no. 4: 339–41.
———. 2002a. "Anonymity and First-Personal Givenness: An Attempt at Reconciliation." In *Subjektivität—Verantwortung—Wahrheit*, ed. David Carr and Christian Lotz, 75–89. Frankfurt am Main: Peter Lang.
———. 2002b. "First-Person Thoughts and Embodied Self-Awareness: Some Reflections on the Relation Between Recent Analytical Philosophy and Phenomenology." *Phenomenology and the Cognitive Sciences* 1: 7–26.
———. 2002c. "Merleau-Ponty on Husserl: A Reappraisal." In *Merleau-Ponty's Reading of Husserl*, ed. Ted Toadvine and Lester Embree. Dordrecht: Kluwer.
———. 2003a. *Husserl's Phenomenology*. Stanford, Calif.: Stanford University Press.
———. 2003b. "Inner Time-Consciousness and Pre-Reflective Self-Awareness." In *The New Husserl*, ed. Donn Welton. Bloomington: Indiana University Press.
———. 2003c. "Husserl's Intersubjective Transformation of Transcendental Philosophy." In *The New Husserl*, ed. Donn Welton. Bloomington: Indiana University Press.

---. 2005. *Subjectivity and Selfhood: Investigating the First-Person Perspective*. Cambridge, Mass.: MIT Press.

---. 2007. "The Heidelberg School and the Limits of Reflection." In *Consciousness: From Perception to Reflection in the History of Philosophy*, ed. Sara Heinämaa, Vili Lähteenmäki, and Pauliina Remes. Dordrecht: Springer.

---. 2010. "Empathy, Embodiment and Interpersonal Understanding: From Lipps to Schutz." *Inquiry* 53, no. 3: 285–306.

Index

Absolute, 5–7, 28, 30, 44, 79, 91, 97, 109, 116, 117, 132, 134, 157–60, 162–68, 172, 173, 177–78, 184, 200, 202, 211
Activity, 5, 16, 26, 28, 34, 43, 45–46, 56–60, 63–64, 66, 73, 80, 85, 95, 103–6, 176, 184, 191
Adumbration, 8, 28
Affection, sensibility, 17, 21, 23–29, 31–38, 41–42, 47, 51–54, 56, 58–59, 63, 65, 78, 81, 88, 94–95, 130, 147, 158, 166, 169–70, 173, 180–83, 205, 215
Alien, Alterity, 23, 38, 48, 62, 70, 75–76, 81–85, 92, 99–100, 106, 127, 131, 132, 134, 136–45, 147, 150, 154, 157, 170, 201, 211–12, 215, 217
Animals, 15, 82, 85, 101, 141, 144, 150–56, 171, 202, 213–16
Anonymity, 15, 70, 73–75, 77, 79, 86, 90, 94, 97, 102, 115, 170–71, 193–94, 196
Anticipation, expectation, 8, 24, 44, 47, 50, 71–72, 76, 83, 92–93, 96, 101–3, 124, 129–31, 135–36, 138–39, 147, 149, 153, 171, 200, 207, 210
Appresentation, 71–72, 75–76, 81, 83–84, 86, 131–32, 149–50, 153, 170, 197
Appropriation, 11, 97–98, 101, 103, 114–15, 127, 130, 137, 161, 165, 201–2
Association, *see* Passivity
Attention, 4, 27, 41–42, 46, 58, 80, 138
Attitude, 5–7, 91, 100, 141, 176–77

Behavior, 95, 108, 123, 137–39, 215
Bernet, Rudolf, 60
Birth, 15, 61, 80, 101, 107, 110–14, 170–71, 204–6
Blindness, 61–62, 89, 122, 130–31, 134–36, 144, 162–63, 185, 211, 213, 218
Body, *see* Lived-body

Body image and body schema, 15, 28, 45–47, 61, 80, 83, 126, 188–89

Canguilhem, Georges, 123, 140
Carr, David, 8, 90, 100, 108, 165–66
Causality, 51, 83
Community, 15, 89, 91–94, 98–109, 113–17
Conscience, 137, 161, 211
Consciousness, awareness, 3–16, 21–66, 69, 73, 75, 79–80, 82, 85–86, 88, 94–95, 99, 108, 111, 121, 124, 136, 162, 167–68, 170, 173, 176, 178, 180–83, 188, 196, 203
Constitution: concept of, 7–11; generative, 117, 171; genetic, 10–11, 15, 69, 77, 79, 84, 100–102, 107–17, 122, 127, 137, 142, 147, 165–68, 170–73, 178–79, 184, 186, 187, 196, 201, 205, 207, 212, 218; self-constitution, 14–15, 31, 33, 46, 65–66, 69, 80–81, 94, 100, 109–10, 114, 116–17, 121, 127, 165–68, 170–71, 173, 213; static, 10–11, 79, 93, 179, 196, 212;
Content, *see* Form and content
Corporeality, *see* Lived-Body
Correlation, 7, 8, 10–11, 29, 33, 42–43, 45–48, 50, 53, 56, 60, 62–63, 75–76, 80, 83–84, 91, 93, 99, 102, 107, 111, 112, 115, 122, 125–26, 132, 136, 138, 140–45, 151–52, 155, 157, 164–65, 184, 189, 200, 204, 206, 211
Crowell, Steven, 132, 161
Culture, cultural, 11, 99–100, 102, 103, 105–6, 127, 137–45, 147, 150, 152, 154, 161–62, 171, 201–4, 211, 215, 217–18

Death, 107, 110–14, 170–71, 174, 180, 204–6

239

Descartes, René, 3, 9
Description, 12, 124, 148, 150, 207
Double sensation, 48–51, 54, 63–65, 167, 170, 189, 191
Dreaming, 21, 57, 187, 205

Earth-ground, 107, 141, 157–61, 172, 212, 216–17
Ego, *see* Selfhood
Eidetic variation, *see* Reduction
Embodiment, *see* Lived-body
Empathy, experience of others, 69–71, 73, 76–88, 90–94, 99–101, 103–4, 110, 115, 122, 126, 128–33, 135, 138, 144–45, 147–50, 153–54, 156, 168, 170, 192–94, 196–98, 200–202, 205–6, 214–15, 218; empathy and animals, 147–55; one-sided empathy, 87, 104, 152–54
Environment, *see* World
Epoché, *see* Reduction
Expectation, *see* Anticipation
Expressivity, 54, 59, 65, 83, 87–90, 95–97, 103–6, 110, 137, 139, 161, 167, 197

Facticity, 7–11, 88, 142, 148, 151, 155, 171, 173, 178, 181, 213
Fantasy, *see* Imagination
Finitude, *see* Birth, Death
Form and content, 24–27, 34, 47, 106, 128, 143–44, 150, 162, 182, 184, 207
Freedom, 10, 37, 40, 42, 49, 56, 148, 200
Future, *see* Past and future

Generativity, *see* Historicity
Gestures, *see* Expressivity
God, 193, 206

Habituality, 10, 41, 45, 56–59, 63–64, 94–99, 101, 126–27, 130, 137, 139, 202
Harmony, 45, 83, 93, 199, 209, 214
Henry, Michel, 25, 29, 39, 52–53, 63, 65
Historicity, 15, 98, 99, 101–3, 109–10, 113, 116–17, 163, 170, 172–74, 202, 204–5; generativity, 10–11, 15, 69, 98–117, 127, 138, 165–68, 170–73, 176–79, 193, 201–2, 205, 210, 214, 217
Horizon, *see* World
Hume, David, 8
Hyletic, 27–32, 34, 36–37, 39, 41, 49, 51–54, 56, 63–65, 80, 88, 162, 166–70, 173, 184–85

I, *see* Selfhood
"I can," 43, 45–49, 65, 84, 111–14, 151, 156, 162–63, 171, 204–5
Ideality, 71, 105–6, 112, 125, 128, 131–32, 134–36, 143, 164, 172, 183
Illusion, 70, 164
Imagination, 10, 26, 48, 148–49
Immanence, *see* Transcendence and immanence
Impression, *see* Time-consciousness
Incorporation, 59–63, 78, 191
Infants and children, 77–78, 80–82, 85, 89, 101, 107–8, 114, 116, 130, 144, 195, 201, 203, 213, 215
Infinite regress, 22, 60, 66
Instincts, 37, 103, 186, 205
Intentionality, 7–16, 21–22, 26–32, 37, 39, 42–47, 57, 63, 65, 70, 73, 82, 86, 88–90, 96, 103, 105, 114, 128–34, 137, 144, 150, 153, 157, 162, 170, 179–81, 184, 191, 193, 198, 203, 209; operative intentionality, 45–46, 57, 63
Interiority/exteriority, 7–8, 22–27, 31–32, 38–39, 51–55, 59, 63–66, 81–82, 85, 88, 109, 113, 144, 165, 167–70, 173, 175, 179
Intersubjectivity, 69–117; hierarchy between different forms of, 115–17; intercorporeity, 69, 76, 84, 89–90, 156; linguistic, 103–6; reciprocity, 69, 87–90, 94, 97, 99–100, 103–5, 107, 115, 147, 152–54, 163, 170, 198; transcendental, 10, 86, 103, 109, 114, 122, 138, 144, 154, 156, 165, 178, 192–93, 203, 205;
Intuition, 8–9, 150

Kant, Immanuel, 3, 8–10
Kinesthesia, 27–32, 36–37, 39–41, 43, 47, 50–54, 56–66, 80–81, 85, 88, 95, 144, 147, 166–70, 173, 185, 190, 207; kinesthetic effort, 40, 42, 57–59, 85; self-movement, 39–40, 50, 54, 57–58, 60, 88, 147
Kojima, Hiroshi, 73

Language, 87, 89, 98, 103–6, 138–39, 197, 203
Leder, Drew, 41, 52
Lived-body, 13, 16–17, 33–55, 59–66, 75, 79, 82–85, 88–89, 95, 110–13, 117,

INDEX

130–33, 147, 152, 155, 157–60, 162, 166–70, 172, 179–81, 184, 189–90, 192, 210, 216–17; as a complex being, 51–55; as the field of localization, 34–40, 50–54; lived-bodily interiority and exteriority, 49, 52–55, 59, 63–66, 82, 167; and the material body, 13, 52, 111–12; as the organ of free movement, 40, 42, 59, 65, 75, 83–84; as subject-object, 49, 66, 160, 167; transcendental body, 49, 53, 63–64; transparency of, 43, 49, 53–55, 189; as the zero-point of orientation, 28, 60–61, 91, 156, 158–59, 162, 216

Lived-experience, 9, 21, 23, 25, 29, 31, 42, 65, 79, 105, 162, 218

Livedness, 25, 31, 42

Living present, 10, 24, 34, 71–72, 78, 92–93, 109, 148

Localization, 13, 21, 26, 32, 34–42, 48–55, 60–65, 157, 162, 167, 170, 187

Materiality, 3, 25–27, 31, 38, 49, 51, 106, 111, 126, 144, 152, 162, 175, 182, 188, 199

Mathematics, 6, 21, 25–27, 112, 128

Meaning, meaningful, sense, 10–11, 88–89, 91, 93, 98, 99–102, 105–9, 115, 126, 138–39, 147, 151, 157, 161, 164, 177, 184, 186, 203, 205, 217–18

Melody, 7–8, 95–97

Metaphysics, 3, 7, 199

Motivation, 11, 24, 29–30, 37, 40–41, 43, 47, 51, 53, 82–84, 88, 92, 95–97, 101, 122, 129, 131, 140, 145, 149, 153, 155, 158, 168, 186, 212

Natural science, 141, 144, 212, 216

Naturalization, 3, 167, 169

Nature, 38, 76, 90, 137–56, 161–62, 164, 166–67, 169, 171, 184, 211, 215–16

Noë, Alva, 57

Noema, *see* Object

Noesis, *see* Intentionality

Norm, measure, 98, 101–2, 122–23, 125, 127, 133, 137, 140, 145, 155, 159–62, 164–65, 168, 174; abnormal, 121, 123–24, 127, 134, 136, 139–40, 145, 154, 207, 213; anomalous, 121–24, 126–27, 133–34, 136, 150, 154–55, 162–63, 203, 207, 215, 218

Normality, 121–68; concordance and discordance, 124–26, 134, 143, 207, 211; familiarity, 61, 78, 82, 91, 99–102, 104, 106, 115, 127, 137–40, 143–44, 148, 152, 161, 200–201, 205; optimality, 125–30, 133–36, 140, 150, 155, 160, 164, 200, 208–9; primordial and intersubjective normality, 121–22, 127, 131–41, 143, 145, 147, 149, 150, 156, 160–66, 171–73, 193, 210, 218; typicality, 97, 102, 125–27, 137

Normativity, 15, 101, 103, 117, 122–24, 126–27, 129, 131–36, 144–45, 147–48, 150, 152, 155–56, 158–61, 164–65, 171–74, 180, 207, 211, 213

Object: intentional/noema, 13, 16, 21, 28, 42, 44, 47, 128–31, 180; true thing, thing itself, 125, 128–29, 136, 143, 152, 208–9

Objectification, thematization, 3–4, 13, 22–23, 28, 37, 39–41, 45–49, 53–54, 60, 77, 79, 109–11, 117, 137, 173, 187, 198–99, 217

Objectivity, 44, 85, 122–23, 127, 131, 134, 136–46, 153, 155, 160, 167, 178, 211

Optimality, *see* Normality

Orientation, 12, 28–29, 40–43, 52, 60–62, 90–93, 109, 135, 141, 147–48, 156–62, 164, 172, 188, 216–17

Other, otherness, 4, 73, 74, 90, 104–5, 115, 143, 196, 198, 205, 217; contemporaneous, 69, 87–98, 103, 107, 115; homecomrades, 102, 115, 138–40, 142–43, 145, 193; horizontal, anybody, 69–86, 90, 93, 102, 115; past and future, 99–117; as a second normality, 131–32, 136, 145, 150; transcendence of, 87, 170

Pairing, *see* Passivity

Paradox of subjectivity, 70, 110, 116–17, 156–68, 172–74

Parnas, Josef, 58

Passive synthesis, 8, 22, 44, 46, 80, 83, 149, 207

Passivity, 16, 28, 34, 45–46, 56–59, 73, 80, 83, 95–96, 149, 190, 207; association, pairing, 29, 30, 39, 41, 50, 76, 82–84, 149

Past and future, 72, 92–93, 100, 102, 106–7, 109, 115, 198, 203, 205
Person: personal identity, 91, 95–97, 102, 140, 199; personalities of higher order, 26, 91–92; transcendental, 10, 95
Phantom, 45, 188
Phenomenological method, 4–11
Polanyi, Michael, 52
Positing, 5, 7, 22, 56, 72–73, 81–82, 93, 102, 123, 148, 168, 170, 172, 176, 193, 209
Presence, 27, 73–74, 85, 140, 149, 156, 158, 162, 176
Protention, see Time-consciousness
Psychoanalysis, 77, 181, 195
Psychology, 8, 10, 23, 79, 184, 197, 199, 215

Reduction, 5–7, 9–10, 21, 176–77, 180; eidetic variation, essences, 5, 10, 148, 176, 197, 200, 213; epoché, 5, 177
Reflection, 4, 21–24, 39–40, 48, 54, 59, 73, 74, 79, 112, 122, 137, 189
Reversibility, see Double sensation
Ricoeur, Paul, 113

Sartre, Jean-Paul, 22–23, 39, 41, 48, 51–53, 75
Sass, Louis, 58
Sedimentation, 11, 92–96, 99, 102, 108, 111, 113, 115, 121, 165, 171, 193, 199, 203
Self-awareness, 11, 13, 15, 17, 21–33, 42–48, 51, 53, 57–58, 60, 66, 74, 79–81, 93–94, 100–103, 108, 116, 157–59, 169–70, 174, 179, 181–83, 185, 195
Selfhood, 21–23, 27, 29, 32, 56–66, 73, 79, 169; agency, 56–59; ego, 10–11, 27, 32, 63–65, 73, 75, 77, 81, 90, 94–97, 104, 108–9, 130–31, 149–50, 163, 171, 177–78, 184–85, 191–96, 200, 204–6, 214; habitual self, 10, 56–59, 63, 94–97; ipseity, mineness, 23, 56–59, 63–64, 74, 101, 139–40, 192, 200; monad, 103, 109, 114, 130, 142, 162, 198, 202, 214; self, 21–23, 33, 36–38, 40, 56, 59, 64–66, 77, 79, 91, 93, 115, 122, 131
Self-reflexivity, see Double sensation
Sense, see Meaning
Sensibility, see Affection

Sleep, 75, 194, 205, 210
Sociality, see Intersubjectivity
Solipsism, 7, 72, 153, 209–10, 214
Space, Spatiality, 12, 17, 27, 33–51, 60, 64–65, 78, 90–91, 117, 135, 142, 156–61, 168, 173, 184, 186–87, 189, 199, 214, 216–17; intersubjective, 91, 135, 156–58; objective, 37–40, 60, 142, 199; subjective, 39, 45, 48–49, 60, 186–87, 216
Steinbock, Anthony, 101, 110, 113, 126, 157
Stern, Daniel, 79–80
Style of expression, 83, 95–97, 102–3, 130, 137–38, 200, 206
Synthesis, 8, 22, 44, 46, 49, 80, 83, 128, 141–43, 149, 162, 185, 207

Time-consciousness, 7–8, 10, 24–32, 35–36, 44, 71, 78, 82, 111, 168, 173, 189
Tradition, 69, 99, 101–3, 105, 107–8, 110, 127, 137–38, 142–43, 161–62, 165–66, 168–72, 174, 202–3, 206, 217
Transcendence and immanence, 22–24, 32, 37, 84, 87, 114, 149, 162, 169–70, 182, 184
Transcendental, 3–12, 32, 49, 53, 63–66, 69, 84, 86, 95, 97, 101, 103, 107, 109, 113–15, 122–23, 138, 143–44, 147, 149, 154, 156, 161, 163, 165, 169–70, 177–78, 180, 191–94, 197, 199, 202–6, 213, 215; historicity, 163, 201; intersubjectivity, 10, 86, 103, 109, 114, 122, 138, 144, 154, 156, 165, 178, 192–93, 203, 205; philosophy, 8, 10, 169, 178, 180, 213
Type, typicality, see Normality

Unconscious, 21, 23, 181, 194
Understanding, 51, 74, 85, 87, 95, 97, 103–9, 132, 138–39, 154, 161, 163, 165, 197, 205, 211, 215

Waldenfels, Bernhard, 75, 86
"We," 92–94, 102–3, 107–8, 114, 116, 138, 144, 161, 170
World: alienworld, 99–100, 127, 138, 141, 143–45, 154, 212; homeworld, 99–106, 127, 137–45, 147, 154, 200–201, 212; horizon, world-horizon, 6, 8, 11, 13,

INDEX

24, 29, 35, 40, 43–47, 62, 69, 70–76, 90, 92–93, 96, 99, 102, 104, 106, 108, 111–15, 121, 130–31, 136, 138–43, 147, 151, 154, 156–63, 168, 172, 192, 194, 198, 203–5, 217; lifeworld, 99, 126–27, 137–44, 147, 152, 154, 206, 217; surrounding world, environment, 12–13, 21, 28–31, 33–53, 56, 59–70, 73–76, 78, 80, 83, 86–87, 90, 93, 95–97, 99, 100, 102, 104, 115, 122, 124, 127–28, 130, 133–34, 136, 139, 141–44, 147–54, 156–57, 160, 162, 166–67, 169, 200, 213, 215–16

Zahavi, Dan, 26, 73, 85

www.ingramcontent.com/pod-product-compliance
Lightning Source LLC
Chambersburg PA
CBHW032032290426
44110CB00012B/774